COME TO YOUR
SENSES

COME TO YOUR
SENSES

CALM THE CHAOS AND TRANSFORM YOUR LIFE
THROUGH TOTAL SENSORY WELLBEING

NGAHINA RICHARDS

Copyright © Ngahina Richards 2025
First published by Hembury Books in 2025
hemburybooks.com.au
info@hemburybooks.com
Paperback ISBN 9781923517905
Ebook ISBN 9781764055291

The moral right of the author has been asserted.
All rights reserved. No portion of this book may be reproduced in any form without permission from the author and publisher, except as permitted by Australian copyright law.

Disclaimer:
The content of this book is for informational purposes only. It is not a substitute for, and should not be relied upon, for medical, health care or professional advice. The views expressed are based on personal research and experiences. Readers should consult a qualified health care provider for advice on medical conditions or health objectives.

While efforts have been made to verify the information presented, the author and publisher are not responsible for any errors, omissions or interpretations of the material. This book does not replace professional advice, and no part should be construed as providing such services. The author and publisher disclaim any liability arising directly or indirectly from the use or misuse of the information in this book. Readers are solely responsible for any decisions and actions they take based on the information provided in this book.

Credit:
This book references sensory processing concepts developed by Dr. Winnie Dunn, including the terms 'Avoider,' 'Sensor,' 'Seeker,' and 'Bystander,' as described in her book Living Sensationally. These terms are also associated with the Sensory Profile™ assessments published by Pearson Clinical. These terms are used to illustrate common patterns of sensory responsiveness and support reader reflection. Interpretations and scenarios presented are based on the author's understanding and are not intended for diagnostic or clinical use.

A catalogue record for this book is available from the National Library of Australia

For my mum and dad

You showed me that curiosity and a genuine desire to understand the differences around us can lead to a rich and fascinating, if somewhat *wabi-sabi*, life.

A special thank you to my mother, without whom I couldn't have carved out my own adventures.

Contents

Preface	ix
Introduction	xiii
Part One: Making Sense	**1**
Chapter 1. Sensory Preferences	3
Chapter 2. How We Are Wired	9
Part Two: The Senses in a Modern World	**23**
Chapter 3. Reframing the Classic Five Senses	25
Chapter 4. Aurora—Light	27
Chapter 5. Aurora—Colour	33
Chapter 6. Acoustics	43
Chapter 7. Aroma	55
Chapter 8. Appetite	69
Chapter 9. Action	83
Chapter 10. Atmosphere	101
Part Three: Shape Your Sensory Experiences	**113**
Chapter 11. Illuminate Your World	115
Chapter 12. Embrace a Colourful Life	127
Chapter 13. A Sound Mind	161
Chapter 14. Scents of Wellbeing	181
Chapter 15. Food for Thought	197
Chapter 16. Gauge the Temperature	225
Chapter 17. Scope Your Sensory Sanctuary	233
Chapter 18. Making Sense in a Wabi-sabi World	251
Part Four: Atmosphere Guides	**255**
Chapter 19. Total Sensory Wellbeing	257
Acknowledgements	271
Notes and References	273

PREFACE

Selfishly, I wrote this book because I couldn't find it. It started as a guide for myself; a way to rediscover the person I felt I had slowly lost while trekking through the corporate jungle. My days were consumed by other people's agendas, deadlines, and problems to solve, leaving me mentally drained and uninspired. I felt as though I had lost my natural enthusiasm and curiosity about the world around me. Any energy I had went on work, not living.

For years I didn't look after myself properly, which only made me feel worse. I found I was living a life in which I had become exhausted and numb. Amidst this growing sense of disconnection, I experienced a significant loss: my mother passed away. She had only just retired in her early seventies after a challenging life, yet she had managed to provide me and my brother and sister with great opportunities. Consumed by my own issues, I felt I had given her little emotional support or quality time in her later years. Perhaps through a sense of guilt as well as fear of following the same path as my mother, I went from feeling numb to frustrated, and eventually determined to transform my life. I was desperate to feel energetic and engaged again.

This wasn't about finding another job; I knew the issue was bigger than that. How different would a similar role in another company really be? This was about the quality of my everyday life and my sense of well-being. Life is short. I was done with feeling fatigued and lacklustre as the norm. I'm a realist, so I didn't aspire to frolic through sunflower fields with sunlight glinting off my long hair. For starters, I live in a city, and I have short hair. I've also come to accept that not achieving a look or a lifestyle promoted through aspirational images and 'must-dos' on social media is totally fine.

Am I settling for less? Absolutely not. It's just that I am me, and life is more complex than a social media post can communicate. Life is imperfect, or as I like to say, life is wabi-sabi. This is a Japanese philosophy that finds beauty in impermanence and imperfection. Wabi-sabi principles are often applied to old and repaired objects, but they also reflect a deeper cultural understanding of life's transience and imperfection. Put simply, wabi-sabi is the concept of being 'perfectly imperfect'. Accepting that life is wabi-sabi and I am wabi-sabi has allowed me to focus on what's right for me and my world. Don't get me wrong, aspirational imagery of perfection can be motivating, but I'm more inspired by insight and practical guidance. When I understand the 'why' and the 'how', I am enthused to try.

With this mindset, I explored practical options to improve my sense of wellbeing. The more I read, the more I realised that a core component of wellbeing is the ability to cope. Initially this seemed uninspiring, but I came to understand that coping is what allows us to navigate challenges and move towards the good stuff in life. It's about building mental fortitude and resilience; essential traits for thriving and bouncing back when things go awry. The idea of coping is not basic and boring; it is fundamental to wellbeing.

My investigation into wellbeing led me through an ironically overwhelming maze of resources and schools of thought. Over time, I discovered a common thread: our senses. Our sensory interactions with the world shape how we feel, think, and behave every moment of every day. They play a significant role in how well we can survive and thrive. Why wasn't this insight more commonly discussed? Why weren't we using sensory initiatives every day to feel our best?

Most of the information I came across focused on a single sense in a moment of time, such as the calming effect of a massage, the sense of peace from sitting quietly, or the mental reset from a walk. These are helpful, of course. But our senses don't work in isolation, and they shouldn't only be treated as remedies for fatigue or overwhelm. I wanted to understand how they work together, and how I could use them proactively to build greater resilience. This is how the concept of Total Sensory Wellbeing was born.

Now I can see how the power of sensory experiences has always resonated with me. I've lived in very different environments and fully appreciate how my surroundings have influenced my thoughts and behaviours. Growing up on a farm in New Zealand, I found peace in the quiet of nature. The open spaces ignited my imagination as I waded through creeks, built huts, and made up stories, poems, and puppet plays that I would subject my classmates to. This environment nurtured my creativity and gave me a sense of freedom and contentment.

In contrast, living in tropical settings brought intrigue and intensity. The dense jungle near my home in the Solomon Islands was both exciting and overwhelming. I'll never forget the thrill of climbing through the wreck of an old World War II plane hidden in vegetation, but also feeling a sense of unease, as though the jungle were closing in on me.

In later years, I came to appreciate how various cultures use elements like light, colour, and design to create harmonious, restorative spaces. It's been fascinating to observe how these sensory details are applied to influence the way people feel in their environments.

Urban apartment living in Vietnam was a good example of this. The noise from traffic and the hum of human activity seemed relentless. The lack of greenery and open spaces often left me feeling overstimulated and depleted. My mind couldn't breathe, and the air pollution and heat didn't help either. Sleep became elusive, and I regularly felt fatigued and irritable.

As a counterbalance to the sensory intensity of daily life, I was struck by how thoughtfully many interior spaces were designed, with elements such as plants, soft lighting, and natural materials. I began to notice how these sensory details were intentionally curated to offer relief and calm.

These spaces weren't just beautiful, they were functional sanctuaries in a city that never seemed to pause.

This environment deepened my understanding of how sensory input can shape mood and behaviour, and how even small design choices can have a profound effect on our emotional state.

Every environment I lived in shaped my emotions and energy levels differently, underscoring the powerful role of sensory input. These experiences have shown me that our surroundings aren't just backdrops to our lives; they're active influences on our senses that shape how we feel and function.

These insights, combined with years of investigating research findings, reading and learning, and talking with subject matter experts, helped me pull the threads of Total Sensory Wellbeing together. As I discussed these ideas with others, it became clear that most people were unaware of the significance of their daily sensory experiences. The phrase 'sense of wellbeing' says it all, yet we've seemingly lost touch (another sensory reference) with this concept. With that realisation, I decided to compile the information into a book to help others bolster their mental fortitude and resilience.

This book is for anyone, whether you are overwhelmed by daily demands, seeking to create a more peaceful or productive environment, or simply curious about how sensory changes can affect your mood and actions. Each chapter links research and real-world insights with practical lifestyle strategies. From the colours that shape our world to the textures we touch and the sounds that resonate around us, I aim to show how sensory awareness can enhance your wellbeing.

As you explore what follows, I invite you to take a fresh look at your sensory experiences and make mindful choices that nurture you through the imperfect beauty of your wabi-sabi life in this wabi-sabi world.

INTRODUCTION

It's morning. An alarm rudely yanks Seth out of his slumber. He opens the curtains, his eyes squinting at the contrast between darkness and the dawn light. He craves just one more hour of sleep. He hates feeling constantly worn out.

As he passes through the living room, irritation quickly sets in at the sight of dirty dishes on the coffee table. No time to deal with that now. He showers, and the water invigorates him as it runs over his neck and shoulders. He splashes his face to wake up. Seth has a meeting with his boss today, and he instinctively selects a blue shirt and black pants. They just feel right. In the kitchen, delight washes over him when the aroma of coffee hits his nostrils. It tastes so satisfying, and he needs the energy. Time to go to work!

Without him realising it, Seth's mood and energy levels have already been shaped by his senses: the jarring alarm, the natural light, the visual clutter of the dishes, the soothing flow of water, the stimulating aroma and taste of coffee, and even the colour of his clothing. These seemingly small details influence his emotions and behaviour, steering the trajectory of his day.

What about your morning? Have you ever felt like Seth, overwhelmed as well as delighted before your day even begins? The spaces we live in, the sounds we hear, the colours around us, and even the air we breathe all contribute to how we feel. Yet, many of us remain unaware of how these factors shape our energy, focus, and ability to cope.

This book introduces you to Total Sensory Wellbeing, a new way to view everyday experiences like Seth's morning. By adjusting what's right in front of your eyes, nose, ears, hands, and tastebuds, you can significantly influence your mental fortitude and resilience, because every sensory interaction informs your brain and body how to feel and behave every moment of the day.

While your preferences might differ from those of your family, friends, or colleagues, everyone exists within a framework of sensory responsiveness that evolved to help humans survive and thrive.[1] Yet our modern-day lifestyles are testing our limits. Despite incredible advancements, the way we work and live often leaves us feeling frazzled, disconnected, and overwhelmed.

Juggling professional responsibilities, family life, and personal goals can leave anyone fatigued and searching for balance. It's not surprising that a survey across eight countries found 48 per cent of workers reported fighting symptoms of burnout.[2] That's basically half of all workers in developed countries. It's a sobering reminder of how widespread and normalised chronic stress has become.

Psychologist Izabella Risteski explained that while many people describe themselves as 'burnt out', they are often experiencing a related but distinct condition: chronic stress fatigue. Burnout caused by prolonged overwhelm has been shown to literally shrink areas of the brain, particularly those involved in memory and emotional regulation. Both burnout and chronic stress fatigue can impair short-term memory and increase the long-term risk of dementia.

Risteski emphasised that these issues are often driven by sensory overload, including relentless noise, visual complexity of modern environments, and continual interruptions that overwhelm our brains' ability to regulate energy, mood, and focus.

The culprit isn't work itself; it's the way we work and live that assaults our senses on many fronts. In today's hyper-connected world, the boundaries between work and personal life have blurred. We are constantly bombarded with information, distractions, and demands like no generation before us. This perpetual state of alertness impacts our mental and physical health, leaving little room for genuine downtime.

Our sensory systems evolved over hundreds of thousands of years to help us navigate the natural world, not the digital one. The sensory 'software' we still rely on hasn't received any major 'updates' in roughly 50,000 years. This mismatch between our evolutionary wiring and modern lifestyles creates challenges. Our capacity to absorb information isn't limitless, and constant stimulation from multiple sources depletes our energy and attention. This is why when the next social event rolls around you might struggle to enjoy it fully, or when another work issue arises you may not manage it as well as you'd like. Your brain is simply too tired.[3]

Pushing your mental capacity in this way leads to cognitive overload. It's like adding more apps to a device already at capacity and expecting it to operate at peak speed. Social media exacerbates this issue because it feels like a fun way to escape, but it still requires focus that drains your mental energy. Certain platforms are also designed to trigger your brain's ancient reward system, giving you a rush of feel-good chemicals when you receive likes, comments, and pleasing imagery.[4] Positive feelings associated with being wanted, needed, and admired were originally meant to keep us bonded to our tribe for survival, but now they tether us to our screens. The constant influx of notifications and updates initially engages our brains, but ultimately leaves us fatigued.

This dependence can lead to what Dr David Levy from the University of Washington describes as 'popcorn brain'. The term reflects how our attention 'pops' or jumps between different stimuli, much like corn kernels popping in a hot pan. Over time, this state makes the slower pace of real life feel unstimulating. People with popcorn brain may find it harder to focus, and may also feel fatigued or experience anxiety and stress from constantly shifting attention.[5]

Beyond popcorn brain, studies show that people who feel compelled to excessively view social media are more prone to developing conditions such as anxiety, depression and low self-esteem, and young people are particularly susceptible as their brains are still developing.[6]

Daily mental energy is also used to block out unwanted sensory inputs. We are wired to do this to help us focus. Again, this is all about survival; for example, homing in on that deer you were tracking in the forest. The problem today, especially in cities, is that distractions can be relentless. Take noise: whether it's the chatter of colleagues or music from another room, blocking it out requires effort.[7] Even those who appear to be good at tuning out noise are still depleting their mental resources, adding to their cognitive load.

Sleep deprivation is another indicator of sensory overload. Noise pollution, insufficient sunlight during the day, and excessive blue light exposure at night disrupt our natural sleep–wake cycles. For instance, nearly half of Australian adults report sleep-related issues such as poor-quality rest or lack of sleep.[8] This trend is mirrored in other countries, like the UK and the USA. When we don't sleep well, our mental and physical health suffers.[9] Even our sense of taste is affected by modern life. Diets dominated by low-nutrient, high-fat, and high-sugar foods, coupled with late-night eating, disrupt digestion, impact sleep, and negatively influence mood.[10] These lifestyle habits further tax our energy and resilience.

Despite these effects, many people remain unaware of how everyday sensory inputs affect their wellbeing. For those living mainly indoors in urban environments with limited access to green spaces, the disconnect between evolutionary wiring and modern surroundings can be especially jarring. When people ignore the sensory importance of their surroundings and lifestyles, it can lead to a life where times of fatigue and frustration overshadow moments of invigoration and fulfilment.

This book is a guide to reclaiming control over your sensory world. While lighting a scented candle or playing calming music can help, focusing on a single sense often isn't enough. The concept of Total Sensory Wellbeing explores the interplay of the senses (sight, sound, smell, taste, and touch), and explains how to create environments and habits that support your mental fortitude and resilience.

By drawing on research and insights from multiple disciplines, this book will give you the tools to transform your surroundings and lifestyle.

You'll learn how to:
- Recognise your own sensory preferences and those of others
- Use light and colour to evoke desired emotional states
- Use sound and silence to enhance concentration and relaxation
- Integrate scents that calm, energise, or uplift you
- Choose foods that boost mood and cognitive function
- Harness touch, movement, and temperature to improve clarity and resilience
- Create spaces that support you, whether at home or work

Before you continue, take a moment to notice your surroundings. Are you distracted by noise, is the lighting straining your eyes, and are you comfortable? Now settle in and get ready to explore how you can transform your total sense of wellbeing.

Part One: Making Sense

✱✱✱

Your sensory 'software' explained

CHAPTER 1.
SENSORY PREFERENCES

We are unique as well as similar

Sienna and Simon have just moved into their new apartment. Sienna, with her love for vibrant interiors, spends the weekend hunting for bright cushions, scented candles, and an array of house plants to fill their living room. She thrives in a home where colours, scents, and textures create a lively sensory cocktail that invigorates her.

However, Simon prefers a quieter atmosphere. He enjoys the calmness of neutral-coloured walls and minimalistic decor that allow him to unwind after long, stressful days at work. Bold sensory experiences, like aromatic scents or bright lights, overwhelm him, leaving him irritable and uncomfortable.

One evening, Sienna excitedly hangs a brightly coloured painting in the living room. Simon appreciates her enthusiasm, but he's unsettled by the intense colours and the potent scent from the new sandalwood candle. He realises he can't live like this and needs to be honest with Sienna. They are a strong couple, and he's sure they can find compromises to both enjoy the apartment's spaces.

Millions of people worldwide have similar experiences to Sienna and Simon. However, many may not be amicably resolved. Before I embarked on my investigations into sensory wellbeing, I used to put these types of differences down to superficial aesthetic choices, but as I found out, our likes are influenced by our unique sensory preferences. In other words, what calms one may discomfort another.[1] Distinguished Professor Winnie Dunn from the University of Missouri in Columbia, USA, with her expertise in occupational therapy and neuroscience, has spent years researching sensory preferences. She summarised these into sensory profiles: Sensory Avoider, Sensory Sensitive, Sensory Seeker, and Sensory Bystander.[2,3]

These profiles are not rigid categories. We can vary in our responses depending on the type of sensory input. For example, you might prefer bright colours around you (Seeker) but need absolute quiet to concentrate (Avoider). Our sensory profiles can also shift as we age and move through different life experiences.

Labelling people is simplistic and undermines how complex we are. However, these profiles provide a common language to objectively express our preferences and understand the needs of those around us.[4] As you read the sensory profile overviews, consider how they may relate to you and those close to you. This awareness forms the foundation of creating spaces to support harmony in the home.

* Sensory profiles *

Sensory Avoider (Avoiders)

Avoiders actively steer clear of sensory stimulation, seeking controlled, predictable environments. Crowded, multicoloured, or busy spaces can be overwhelming and stressful. As psychologist Izabella Risteski explained, Avoiders feel the need to filter out sensory stimuli, likely due to a highly reactive sensory filtering system in the brain.

Take Josh, for example. Loud or sudden noises unsettle him, so he wears noise-cancelling headphones during his commute and prefers quiet workspaces. Situations like crowded shopping malls or sports matches are highly stressful, so he avoids them.

As a result, Josh often declines invitations to events with a lot of noise and activity, which some may interpret as antisocial behaviour. But if a friend suggested a hike or a day at a quiet beach, you would see a very different Josh.

Sensory Sensitive (Sensors)

Sensors are more attuned to sensory stimuli and may find them engaging or bothersome, depending on their focus in the moment. This is thought to be linked to higher levels of noradrenaline (norepinephrine), as Risteski points out. This enhances alertness, but can also contribute to sensory overload when stimuli become too intense. Sensors comment on things like the volume of music or fabric textures, including pesky clothing tags that irritate them.

Take Lola: she's sensitive to lights. Exposed to office fluorescents and sunlight for too long, she becomes agitated and distracted. To cope, she uses screen filters, wears sunglasses even on moderately bright days, and has soft lighting at home.

Sensory Seeker (Seekers)

Seekers thrive on sensory stimulation. They are easily bored in environments that lack activity or interest. This is believed to be linked to heightened responses in the reward system of the brain (Risteski). Sensory Seekers can be thrill seekers.

Ed, for example, struggles to concentrate in silence and prefers lively, colourful settings. Bright breakout rooms at work or background music boost his focus and energy.

Now, imagine Ed working alongside Josh in an open-plan office. For Ed, the quiet might feel stifling, while Josh would likely find Ed's music and regular chatter disruptive and stressful. These differences could create tension regardless of any shared interests like playing golf or watching zombie movies.

Sensory Bystander (Bystanders)

Bystanders are less conscious of sensory stimuli. They may be quite oblivious to what is happening around them. Sometimes this can give the impression of being inconsiderate of others or disorganised. Risteski noted this may be due to reduced activity in the brain's decision-making and attention-control centre (the prefrontal cortex) responsible for filtering stimuli. As a result, they often appear indifferent to environmental changes.

Take George: he's not fussed with how the living room is set up or how it looks. While he says mess doesn't bother him, it does impact him because he struggles to find things and must sit awkwardly on his couch to watch the TV. Someone visiting George may label him as lazy, despite the fact he works six days a week and volunteers at the local animal shelter.

Our preferences can also vary depending on the type of sensory experience. Emily relishes massages and enjoys hands-on activities like baking, where she can feel the dough between her fingers. These preferences could align with both Sensor and Seeker tendencies, depending on whether she enjoys them because she is highly attuned to sensation (Sensor) or because she actively craves and seeks strong tactile input (Seeker). Meanwhile, her preference for an uncluttered study reflects Sensor traits, as she is particularly sensitive to visual organisation and distractions.

Sensory preferences aren't the sole factor driving emotional or behavioural responses to our surroundings, but they play a significant role.

✴ Insights from neurodivergence ✴

Much of what we understand about sensory needs comes from research into neurodivergent profiles like autism and ADHD. These insights shed light on how we all respond to sensory stimuli. Interestingly, tools developed to support neurodivergent individuals, like weighted blankets and fidget toys, have gained widespread popularity. Weighted blankets, for example, are often used to alleviate stress and improve sleep, while fidget toys, originally designed for those with ADHD, became a global trend in 2017.[5] Many now use them to improve focus and reduce stress in work or study environments. In Chapter 9 we'll explore further the practical benefits of fidgeting.

✶ The sensory lens ✶

You may now start to view those around you a bit differently. I know I have! Understanding people from a sensory perspective helped me see my husband more objectively. No, I don't follow him around taking notes, but I have recognised he is a Bystander when it comes to light and the way things are arranged in the house.

I used to feel agitated coming home to a brightly lit living room and a messy kitchen. Over time, I realised he genuinely didn't notice these things, whereas I am a Sensor in those areas. One memorable example was the day I walked into the kitchen and found every cupboard door wide open while he sat at the table, completely engrossed in his laptop.

When I calmly asked what had happened, he looked up, bewildered. After unloading the dishwasher, it hadn't entered his mind to close the cupboard doors. Thankfully, he's generally very accommodating. Even though these things aren't important to him, he makes an effort because he knows they matter to me. Wise man.

✶ A sensible approach ✶

Throughout this book, you'll see examples that are based mainly on Sensor and Seeker profiles, not because they're more important, but because they provide relatable scenarios to help you better understand your sensory needs and the preferences of those around you.

Reflecting on sensory variances and understanding how sensory triggers help or hinder us means we can actively create environments that support our wellbeing. If we don't take this approach, we will remain unaware and accept many suboptimal experiences as 'normal'. With this in mind, it's now time to understand how sensory experiences influence processes that form your feelings, thoughts, and behaviours.

CHAPTER 2.
HOW WE ARE WIRED

Ancient 'software' in a modern world

In nature, our heart rate, blood pressure, and general stress response is typically lower than in urban spaces. This is because our brains require less effort to assess natural environments compared to built-up areas that are filled with people, cars, and more.[1] With less cognitive demand required, we can use our finite daily energy on other tasks, or simply relax and recharge.[2] If you don't live in a leafy suburb next to a park, don't despair: research shows that spending a total of two hours a week in a natural setting can yield restorative and stress-reducing effects. This can be spread out over several days.[3] Of course, the more time you can spend in nature, the better. But not everyone has easy access to green spaces, which is why understanding how to engage your senses in today's world is crucial for building mental fortitude and resilience.

The positive effects of nature come through our senses, which follow certain physiological pathways that trigger our feelings and behaviours. Being familiar with these pathways helps you understand what prompts your responses. This knowledge can empower you to take deliberate actions to enhance your sensory experiences.

We evolved to respond favourably to sensory triggers that supported our survival. Eating sugar, for instance, provides a rush of pleasure as one of our feel-good chemicals, dopamine, is released. In this situation dopamine functions as an ancient reward system for finding an excellent source of energy. This was a brilliant piece of evolutionary development to motivate us to find food 100,000 years ago, but isn't as necessary for survival today, and yet it still has the same effect on us.[4] This is one of the reasons we can overindulge and why one biscuit is never enough. (Although, I hear the broken ones don't count.)

It's important to note that our sensory processes don't distinguish between physical or psychological triggers.[5] This means it doesn't matter if you're faced with a barking dog or a barking boss, the same stress response process kicks into gear.

Let's explore the key physiological mechanisms that you can influence each day to improve your total sense of wellbeing.

∗ The limbic system: your emotional core ∗

Our brain's emotional and memory processes lie in the limbic system, a complex network responsible for emotional regulation, survival instincts, and motivation. This system ensures we pursue basic needs like food, water, shelter, and social bonds, which are all essential for survival. It also governs the release of chemicals such as dopamine, oxytocin, serotonin, and endorphins that drive pleasure, bonding, and stress relief. Together, these chemicals create what I call the 'Happy DOSE.'

While several areas of the brain contribute to processing sensory and emotional experiences, there are some key players:[6]

- **The amygdala:** Processes emotional responses, especially instinctive reactions like fear and pleasure. It signals the hypothalamus to trigger hormonal and physiological changes, such as the fight-or-flight response.
- **The hippocampus:** Essential for forming new memories and linking emotions to experiences, it works closely with the amygdala to shape how we respond to events.
- **The hypothalamus:** This region acts as the brain's command

centre for the autonomic nervous system, which regulates processes like body temperature, hunger, sleep cycles, and the stress response. It plays a crucial role in translating emotional input into physiological reactions.

Often called the 'primitive brain', the limbic system operates instinctively, while the **prefrontal cortex**, another region of the brain, manages complex decision-making.[7] It controls our critical thinking and is often referred to as the 'executive function'. The limbic system and the prefrontal cortex collaborate to determine how we feel, think, and behave. However, when we are particularly fatigued and stressed, our limbic system can dominate because we are all about survival.

∗ Sensory assessment and decision-making ∗

The prefrontal cortex draws on the emotions and memories in the limbic system to help us form thoughts and take actions. Here's an example of how we could respond to sensing some rough fabric on a couch:

- The **amygdala** flags emotional irritation in response to the physical discomfort registered by sensory receptors in your skin.
- The **hippocampus** retrieves past experiences to help you understand why the fabric feels unpleasant.
- The **prefrontal cortex** synthesises this sensory, emotional, and memory information to prompt an action, like deciding to use a throw or change the fabric.
- The **hypothalamus** processes these cues and may initiate physiological responses, such as increased heart rate or muscle tension.

If you don't take some sort of action, your response can shift from irritation to frustration and beyond. For instance, a colleague who worked long, stressful days once told me how he drove home one night to find his electric garage door was broken and he had to manually lift it. He was too mentally exhausted to do anything about it for weeks, until he exploded in a rage. That was his push to fix it. He told me it took ten minutes. Up until that point, he'd been too fatigued to prioritise any action, until his amygdala escalated his emotional reaction to resolve the issue.

First-world problem? Sure. But whether it's a broken garage door or something more serious, whenever we experience a stressful event the physiological pathway is the same. **The hypothalamus** triggers our responses through the **autonomic nervous system.** This is split into two parts: the **sympathetic nervous system**, responsible for fight-or-flight responses (including excited energy), and the **parasympathetic nervous system**, which promotes relaxation and recovery. In the case of my colleague and the garage door, his heightened frustration was accompanied by a faster heart rate and an increase of stress chemicals.

Because stress management is such an important topic, let's explore these two aspects of the autonomic nervous system and learn about steps we can take to reduce stress and promote calm.

* The sympathetic nervous system: fight or flight *

The limbic system activates the sympathetic nervous system in response to a physical or psychological threat. For example, your heart pumps faster and the air passages in your lungs expand so you're ready to run if you must.[8]

As part of this process, the adrenal glands release chemicals, including noradrenaline (norepinephrine) and adrenaline (epinephrine), which signal your organs and tissues to continue reacting until the threat has passed.[9] This makes you mentally alert and provides you with energy. Meanwhile cortisol, released more gradually, helps sustain this heightened state of alertness by increasing blood glucose (sugar) levels, ensuring a steady supply of energy for prolonged stress responses.

Say you're walking in the woods and suddenly hear a rustling in the bushes. Instantly your heart races, your senses sharpen, and you're physically prepared to either confront the threat or run away.

However, in our modern world, stressors are often psychological, like tight deadlines, financial worries, or social pressures. For some, a prolonged activation of the sympathetic nervous system can lead to physical and psychological problems such as fatigue, anxiety, and cognitive issues. It's like constantly driving your car at high speed, which fast-tracks wear and tear.

Cortisol

Cortisol is a hormone that gets a lot of bad press in relation to stress. However, it has an important and positive role because it helps us stay alert for everyday activities. In the daytime it helps us focus, make decisions, and complete tasks, as well supporting the immune system and blood pressure regulation.[10] However, it is often referred to as the 'stress hormone'. When stress levels are high, cortisol increases beyond normal levels to keep you alert. This is to enable you to stay vigilant and deal with any threats.[11]

While helpful in short-term situations, chronic elevated cortisol can negatively impact memory and focus, and lead to anxiety and depression.[12] It's understandable: when you're constantly on edge, it's hard to relax and rejuvenate. Hence the expression 'tired but wired'.

Regular high levels of cortisol can also disrupt physical health by shifting the body's focus away from essential functions like digestion and immunity. Over time, this can increase the risk of high blood pressure, heart problems, digestive disorders, and a weakened immune system.[13] Managing our stress response is therefore crucial for our sense of well-being and physical health.

∗ The parasympathetic nervous system: rest and digest ∗

Fortunately, our bodies have a built-in system to counteract stress: the parasympathetic nervous system, often referred to as 'rest-and-digest' mode. This system helps us calm down after stress, promoting relaxation, digestion, and energy conservation.

Think of it as applying the brakes after speeding. The parasympathetic nervous system slows your heart rate and decreases blood pressure, allowing you to return to a state of balance known as homeostasis. Note the first four letters of the word. *Home*ostasis is like driving up to your house. You are home; you can relax.

In short, the rest-and-digest functions keep your body going at a comfortable pace, while the fight-or-flight functions will speed you up when the need arises. The body regulates parasympathetic nervous responses primarily through the vagus nerve, which acts as a communication pathway between the brain and vital organs. In fact, it is often referred to as a 'communication highway' or, as I like to call it, the 'vagus highway'.

The vagus nerve: the relaxation highway

The vagus nerve is a collection of nerves that runs from your brain through to your stomach. There are several 'off-ramps' to other parts of your body. This forms a vast network that plays a role in various processes such digestion, hearing, speaking, breathing, and taste.[14]

As part of the rest-and-digest processes, the vagus nerve releases chemicals like acetylcholine, which promote relaxation.[15] These chemicals return your heart rate, blood pressure, and breathing to normal.[16]

Stimulating the vagus nerve can signal the brain to relax, alleviating stress and anxiety. Techniques like deep, slow breathing, humming, singing, or even gargling can improve your ability to cope with stress.

When you are back in homeostasis, your mind has the capacity to focus on positive and productive pursuits again. It's also easier to stimulate rewarding feel-good chemicals.

✳ The Happy DOSE neurotransmitters: your natural mood boosters ✳

Our bodies produce chemicals known as neurotransmitters that contribute to feelings of happiness and wellbeing. To clarify, a neurotransmitter is a chemical messenger that communicates between different types of cells. Let's refer to them as chemicals from here on in.

As we evolved, these chemicals motivated us to engage in behaviours that promoted our survival and development as a species. This chemical reward system hasn't changed much since humans first began walking the earth, but it's not a green jungle anymore, it's an urban one. For example, we were once driven to seek protection in a tribe, but today this has shifted to seeking camaraderie and respect from peers and friends. In developed countries, we don't need to exhaust ourselves to find a source of water, but we do exert ourselves to work hard to earn a promotion. Our perception of what it means to survive and thrive has changed dramatically, but our core survival drivers and sensory processes still function much as they have for the last 50,000 years. Each Happy DOSE chemical plays a role in this, influencing how we seek connection, pleasure, safety, and reward.

Dopamine

The reward and pleasure chemical: eating delicious food, achieving a goal, or receiving praise can all trigger dopamine release.[17] Originally it motivated us to engage in activities that may have been challenging but which supported our survival. For example, we may have experienced delayed gratification after persevering in making a weapon to kill an animal for food.

You've already read how dopamine is released with high-calorie and sugar-dense foods based on our drive to survive, even though in developed countries we don't need to worry so much about accessing food anymore. Remember, our sensory 'software' hasn't been updated for a long time. There are healthy foods that can also stimulate dopamine more moderately, such as bananas, apples, avocados, oats, brown rice, protein in meats, fish, dairy and eggs, fermented foods, and dark chocolate.

Dopamine hits are one reason people get caught up in addictive behaviours such as shopping, gambling, and constantly looking at social media feeds. These are quick hits of gratification associated with the survival behaviours of acquiring goods and feeling included.[18] If people frequently engage in activities that trigger dopamine and then stop, they can experience a dopamine crash, which can lead to a sense of anxiousness or emptiness because that good feeling they've become accustomed to has disappeared. A common example is the need to constantly look at a device.

You can use dopamine as a reward to form positive habits too. Engaging in a new, beneficial activity that requires some effort might feel daunting at first, but once you feel a sense of accomplishment after you apply yourself, you will stimulate dopamine as well as other Happy DOSE chemicals. If you set up a reward or treat to celebrate your efforts, you can enhance the dopamine effect. This is why setting up milestone achievement rewards, or even acknowledgement, as part of a greater goal can help motivate you to keep going with a task. Let's use the example of wanting to reduce the habit of constantly checking your phone: you could establish a morning routine that starts with making your bed, going outside for a walk, and having a shower, all before you look at your phone. You will feel a sense of achievement for delaying the use of your phone and, over time, the morning actions themselves will become associated with positive feelings.

Dopamine isn't just a reward; it's important for our sleep and ability to focus, which are essential for our wellbeing. All of these effects mean that when dopamine drops after regular highs, it can lead to low mood, reduced concentration, and poor-quality sleep.[19]

Oxytocin

Known as the love hormone, oxytocin fosters connections through exercise, music, touch, social interaction, and shared experiences.[20] Hugging a loved one, spending time with friends, or even spending time with a pet can boost oxytocin levels.

The urge to connect and form bonds with others benefits the survival of our species because it encourages us to stay together. Think how much easier finding food, shelter, or fending off attacking animals would be in a group versus alone.[21]

Familiar voices can trigger the release of oxytocin too, but sending text messages just doesn't have the same feel-good effect. The more virtually we live, the more we deprive ourselves of the benefits of bonding, such as feelings of inclusion and affection, and the greater the chance of experiencing anxiousness and loneliness.[22]

Serotonin

This chemical is responsible for our overall sense of wellbeing and happiness. It influences mood, appetite, sleep, and memory. Sunlight exposure, physical activity, and positive social interactions can increase serotonin levels.

Serotonin helps us to feel calm and positive, which is particularly important when we want to focus and make important decisions. It's triggered by activities that prime us to function at our best, such as sleeping well, keeping a consistent sleep routine, exercising, and eating healthily.[23]

It's an important chemical in our sleep–wake cycle, and you can support its production by exposing your eyes to morning sunlight. This doesn't mean staring at the sun, of course, but it does mean you should have a few minutes of morning light without sunglasses on. With so many people enduring long workdays and sedentary lives indoors, it's easy to imagine that they are missing out on a serotonin boost.

Food can indirectly and temporarily trigger serotonin. Comforting carbohydrates, for example, such as pasta or mashed potatoes, help your body make this chemical. Other foods indirectly linked to serotonin include chicken, eggs, tofu, fatty fish, pineapple, plums, bananas, fermented foods, and dark chocolate.

Endorphins

These are natural painkillers and mood elevators released in response to pain, stress, and pleasurable activities.[24] We experience endorphins when we laugh, exercise, fall in love, have sex, and expose our skin to ultraviolet (UV) light, which is a normal part of daylight.[25] Endorphins are commonly associated with a sense of wellbeing, and even euphoria. This helped our ancestors push through physically difficult situations via a mental buzz that today we call the 'runner's high'.[26]

Certain foods can enhance endorphin levels, such as spicy meals or food that gives us energy to exercise, like fatty fish, nuts, and seeds. Sugary foods can also trigger endorphins, but be mindful of the cycle of craving and overconsumption.

Health care professionals often recommend exercise or a walk in the sun to people who are stressed, anxious, or feeling down, because they know it can stimulate a partial Happy DOSE. Our lifestyles today mean we spend much less time outside than our ancestors did. As a result, we may miss out on these natural mood-boosting experiences.

Understanding how to naturally self-administer a Happy DOSE can significantly enhance your mood and resilience. For instance, you might like to try engaging in regular physical activity, especially with others. This doesn't have to involve formal or rigorous exercise. A lunchtime walk with colleagues or dancing at a club with friends can also work wonders; in fact, even dancing at home can lift your heart rate and your spirits.

Chapter 2. How We are Wired

✻ Circadian rhythm: your internal clock ✻

The circadian rhythm is the body's internal clock, orchestrated by the limbic system. It regulates the sleep–wake cycle, hormone release, the feed–fast cycle, and other bodily functions over a twenty-four-hour period. The circadian rhythm times these processes to correspond with daylight and night-time, as dictated by the sun. Well, that's what's meant to happen.

Light exposure plays a significant role in maintaining a healthy circadian rhythm, because light influences hormones like melatonin and cortisol. In the morning, exposure to sunlight suppresses melatonin production and increases cortisol, promoting alertness. As with serotonin, the brain signals cortisol production when light enters your eyes, so it's best to not wear sunglasses for a short period of time in the morning. In the evening, decreased light allows melatonin levels to rise, preparing the body for sleep.[27]

Disruptions to the circadian rhythm, such as irregular sleep patterns, exposure to artificial light at night, or shift work, can lead to fatigue, mood disorders, and other health issues.[28] Blue light from screens can suppress melatonin production, allowing cortisol levels to stay high, making it harder to fall asleep. Even if you stay away from blue light, staying up late, and eating late, can also prevent you from sleeping well. For most people, it's not feasible or desirable to get up with the sun and go to bed at sunset. This is where practices like taking in sunlight in the morning, reducing screen time before bed, and maintaining a consistent sleep schedule can make a significant difference to regulating your circadian rhythm, which in turn bolsters your mental fortitude and resilience.[29]

While circadian rhythms follow a roughly 24-hour cycle regulated by light, not everyone is biologically wired to rise and rest at the same time. Genetics, age, and lifestyle shape an individual's chronotype, which is their natural sleep–wake pattern. Research in this area suggests there may be several chronotypes beyond the classic early-rising morning lark or the late-night owl.[30] While research is still emerging, it does show that ideal times for rising, working, and resting vary from person to person. The key is to work with your natural rhythm where possible, while still following healthy circadian principles such as getting natural light soon after waking, winding down with reduced sensory input in the evening, and maintaining consistency to help reinforce your body's cues.

Key takeaways

- The **limbic system** is the emotional core of the brain, guiding our reactions and generating feel-good chemicals.
- The **sympathetic nervous system** triggers the fight-or-flight responses during stress, while the **parasympathetic nervous system** promotes relaxation with the rest-and-digest processes.
- **Cortisol** is essential for daily alertness and responding to stress, but can be harmful when levels remain high over time.
- The **vagus nerve** plays a crucial role in activating relaxation responses and can be stimulated through breathing and other techniques.
- The **Happy DOSE neurotransmitters** (dopamine, oxytocin, serotonin, endorphins) contribute to feelings of pleasure, connection, and wellbeing and are stimulated by behaviours that supported our ancestors' survival.
- Maintaining a healthy **circadian rhythm** supports overall health and is influenced by light exposure, eating patterns, and daily routines.

Modern life challenges our sense of wellbeing

Sedentary behaviour, living indoors, excessive screen time, diets with high amounts of sugar and carbohydrates, and reduced face-to-face social interactions can all interfere with the natural production and balance of the Happy DOSE chemicals.

Long days and poor sleep where we never switch off also take their toll. Quality sleep is essential for coping with everything life throws at you. It is a cornerstone of your circadian rhythm.

As well as our lifestyles, the physical environment also affects our sense of wellbeing. Limited access to green spaces, constant noise, poor air quality, and even the layout of our cities, homes, and interiors affect our wellbeing through their sensory influences.

A sense of control

The good news is that knowledge is growing about how our senses interpret the world around us and how our lifestyles and environments can be shaped to improve our mental fortitude and resilience. We will now cover these points sense by sense and explore practical ways to improve our sense of wellbeing.

Part Two:
The Senses in a Modern World

✱✱✱

**How everyday sensory input shapes
your sense of wellbeing**

CHAPTER 3.
REFRAMING THE CLASSIC FIVE SENSES

A fresh perspective for the modern age

For centuries, philosophers and scientists have marvelled at the human senses and how they connect us to the world. The ancient Greek philosopher Aristotle, who lived over 2,000 years ago, first defined the classic five senses: sight, sound, smell, taste, and touch.[1] Not surprisingly, we have learned a lot about the senses since Aristotle's time, including defining different types of senses and understanding how they are triggered, both positively and negatively.

Our senses are powerful gateways to our emotions and behaviours. They are so much more than ways to navigate our physical surroundings; they shape our experiences, influence our moods, and even impact our health. In this section, you'll be able to rethink how you engage with your senses to positively affect your wellbeing.

I have reframed how we refer to the senses so that we might see them through a new lens. Daily sensory experiences should no longer be ignored or considered insignificant. They can be impactful moments that strengthen your mental fortitude and resilience and improve the quality of your life.

✳ Expanding beyond the classic five senses ✳

Consider sight: it's the most dominant of the senses, requiring the greatest processing power from our brains. It's an efficient way to quickly understand our surroundings.[2] However, from a sensory wellbeing perspective, sight encapsulates different sensory aspects that need to be understood. For this reason, the umbrella term 'sight' is not particularly useful. When it comes to bolstering our mood and energy, key aspects of sight that influence us include light, colour, the types of objects around us, and how they are positioned.

Here is a breakdown of how the senses will be referred to when exploring ways to influence your sense of wellbeing:

- Aurora—Light
- Aurora—Colour
- Acoustics—Sound
- Aroma—Smell
- Appetite—Taste and the gut–brain axis
- Action—Touch, movement, and temperature
- Atmosphere—The objects and spatial layout that surround us.

Each of these sensory elements can shape your mood, energy, focus, and emotional strength. In the chapters that follow, you'll explore how to work with them more deliberately, not just to get through your days, but to feel more alive within them.

CHAPTER 4.
AURORA—LIGHT

Lighting the way to wellbeing

Scarlet pulls back the curtains. 'That was pointless', she thinks as she stares at the dark predawn winter sky. She flicks the switch on the coffee maker on her way to the shower. Her bathroom lights are super bright; she needs the burst of bright white light to wake her up. Later, as she pulls into the office, she watches a beautiful sunrise with pinks and yellows emerging, and sighs. Working on a major project with tight deadlines, Scarlet knows this will be a ten-hour day. She's right. It's dark by the time she gets home. Exhausted, she decides to catch up on social media because her work commitments mean she doesn't see her friends much. Before she knows it, it's 10.30 pm. As she gets ready for bed, she prays she will sleep well.

Have you had days like Scarlet's? For some, this is a typical experience. As you read in Part One, your exposure to natural light determines the health of your circadian rhythm. This influences your metabolism, immunity, how clearly you can think, the quality of your sleep, and your mental fortitude.[1] Without the right light at the right time, you may not think, feel, and behave as well as you could. If Scarlet's work life regularly involves days like the one described, I fear it will be an uphill battle for her to maintain her mental energy and sense of resilience.

Poor sleep and disrupted circadian rhythms are symptoms of our modern lives. While we are wired to function with the natural cycle of daylight, it's just not how we live anymore. We spend most of our days under artificial light. It's in our homes, workplaces, shops, streets, and bounces off our screens. To make matters worse, we use artificial light to extend our days beyond sunset, which further interferes with our circadian rhythm. It's not an exaggeration to say that light affects the quality of your life. My sympathy goes to shift workers.

Each person's circadian rhythm will differ a little based on genetics, age and lifestyle.[2] If you struggle in the morning and come alive at night, it's possible your circadian rhythm has been affected by genetics and behaviour changes over time, such as exposure to artificial light, social habits, work schedules, diet and exercise, and sleep hygiene. Being a 'night owl' doesn't automatically make you unhealthy, as each person is different. However, research shows that people who get up earlier and go to bed earlier tend to be healthier and suffer fewer psychological problems.[3]

Natural daylight is like a rainbow in disguise, containing all the colours of visible light that blend to appear 'white' to our eyes. As the day progresses, it shifts its balance. Mornings are packed with blue light, the equivalent of nature's cup of coffee, giving us a refreshing wake-up call. By evening, the light transitions to red hues, which act like a soothing cup of cocoa, helping us wind down and prepare for rest.[4]

Think about how you feel on a bright, sunny day compared to a gloomy, overcast one. Sunlight often boosts your energy and mood, while a lack of natural light over time can lead to lethargy or even symptoms of depression.

In winter, less UV light reaches us, so it's understandable that many people say they don't feel as positive or energetic. However, some people are more adversely affected and may experience periodic clinical depression and anxiety. This is called seasonal affective disorder (SAD). Not surprisingly, light therapy is one of the recommended treatments. These light treatments are very intense and should only be used under the guidance of a health care professional. The climate in some parts of the world makes it very challenging to step outside, even for ten minutes in the morning, but if you can, the rewards to your sense of wellbeing can be profound.

Are blind people or the visually impaired worse off? Not necessarily, because the cells in the eye that register light aren't the same ones used for vision.[5]

Regardless of the issues with artificial light, we need it. It would be annoying and impractical to live without it in the pursuit of the healthiest circadian rhythm possible. So let's use it to our advantage to be energetic, productive, creative, and to relax. To do this, you need to know what to look for in lighting.

✵ Show me the light ✵

Artificial lights are produced to provide different effects, such as colour and brightness. Of course, any light shade can affect the light's appearance.

Common light descriptions

Kelvin (K): Kelvin describes the colour temperature or 'mood' of light, not the actual heat. Imagine it as a spectrum: on one end, you have the cosy glow of a campfire (reds, yellows, and oranges), which we call 'warm' light. On the other end, there's the crisp brightness of a clear winter day (white and blue tones), often labelled 'cool'. Technically, it doesn't affect the brightness, but that's the impression it creates.[6]

Lumen (lm): This measures the total visible light emitted, referred to as brightness.[7] Changing the lumen is like turning a light dimmer up and down. A high lumen is like a dimmer turned up and a low lumen softens the brightness in the space. For example, a candle has a lumen rating of around twelve while a standard light-emitting diode (LED) light may have a lumen of 800.

Lux (lx): This measures the area or coverage of light on a surface.[8] Picture this as the focus of a flashlight: the same beam can spread widely or concentrate on a small area, changing how much light reaches a surface. A sunny day has around 100,000 lux, while a full moon and a candle each provide around one lux of illumination. This affects our perception of light intensity.

In short, kelvin defines the light's colour and mood, lumen dictates the level of light emitted, and lux determines our perception of illumination on a surface. When shopping for lights, look for these specifications so you can make an informed choice.

These lighting effects impact our mood and cognitive performance. For instance, bright, cool lights can keep you alert by mimicking daylight's blue tones, which lower melatonin. On the flip side, warm yellow and orange lights mimic the setting sun and lull you into rest, which helps melatonin take over while cortisol takes a backseat, preparing you for sleep.

Coloured lights

Coloured light can be used to influence your mood and create distinct atmospheres. Depending on your sensory preferences, you may love the stimulation of changing light colours or the ability to evoke an atmosphere.

Coloured lights can come from various sources, like LED bulbs or traditional filtered bulbs. LEDs emit pure wavelengths, which means the colour you see is what you get, while filtered lights may use a coloured casing with a normal white light bulb underneath. This means it won't have the same effect as a pure wavelength.

Even a coloured filtered light can affect you though; whether it feels comforting or energising depends on your sensory preferences, associations with the colour, and how you use it.

When you read about psychological or health effects of coloured lights, the information is typically based on research using pure wavelengths of light. Red light and infrared light, which, ironically, we can't see, have caught the attention of wellness communities for their potential effects on skin, cells, and overall vitality.

Red light, at around 660 nanometres, is visible and reaches just beneath the skin. It is used to support skin repair and collagen production, making it popular in facial and therapeutic LED devices. It doesn't produce heat, and the sensation is usually mild or neutral. It's important to note, more studies are needed to determine how effective red light therapy is, and how best to use it. If you're intrigued, try it under professional guidance for medical conditions, as many home devices lack the strength needed for significant results.[9]

Infrared light is invisible to the eye and penetrates deeper into the body. It also produces heat. The near-infrared range (around 850 nanometres) is of particular interest for its potential to enhance tissue recovery after injury and alleviate joint pain in conditions like osteoarthritis.[10] Emerging research suggests it may also support mood, cognitive clarity, and emotional resilience, especially in people experiencing chronic stress, brain fog, or low mood.[11]

The effects of red and near-infrared light are thought to result from their ability to stimulate mitochondria, the energy-producing components of our cells. While findings are promising, more studies are needed to determine the most effective intensity, duration, and frequency of treatment.

Red and infrared saunas remain popular, even though all the mechanisms are not yet fully understood. That said, if they help you feel more relaxed, comfortable, or energised, then go for it!

In Chapter 11, you will uncover practical ways to select and use light to adapt your mood and energy in different scenarios. You may wish to jump there now to take it all in, or you may prefer to continue with an overview of the senses. The choice is yours!

Aurora in nature is a fusion of light and colour, each playing a distinct role in shaping our wellbeing. We've looked at how light affects us. Now let's turn to colour and its surprising effects on mood, motivation, and mental clarity.

CHAPTER 5.
AURORA—COLOUR

How colour speaks to the brain

Sandra isn't in the mood for today's team meeting. She feels off-kilter, her boss's recent comment, 'You don't seem very engaged', lingering in her mind. Sandra ponders what to wear. Black pants and her comfortable grey sweater seem appealing. She's not sure why, but she thinks that might add to the perception of her lack of engagement. She has a bright yellow dress she loves, but that's too over-the-top for how she's feeling. Eventually she chooses her black dress, pastel green scarf and matching shoes: quiet, composed, but still smart—just like her.

Welcome to the world of colour, where every shade whispers to our emotions and nudges our actions. Colour is more than aesthetics; it shapes our moods and perceptions in ways we often underestimate. Imagine walking into a serene blue room, reminiscent of the ocean on a calm day. Instantly your heart slows, your mind clears, and a sense of tranquillity takes over.[1] Now picture a bright yellow space radiating sunlight's joy. It energises and inspires, until it doesn't. Stay too long and its intensity may leave you feeling agitated. Colour's effects aren't static; they depend on our sensory profiles, moods, and the context in which we encounter them.

Businesses have long recognised colour's psychological power. Red commands action and urgency, while green symbolises health and vitality. These choices aren't arbitrary; they tap into deep-seated associations. For example, across cultures, green often evokes calm and contentment, likely rooted in our evolutionary instinct to associate greenery with nature and the concepts of life, growth, food, and safety.

Beyond natural elements, differences in terrain, cultural beliefs, and societal trends can also influence how we respond to colour. Consider Western perceptions of yellow: they range from joy and energy, linked to the sun's symbolism, to associations with cowardice, jealousy and repulsion. While the origins of these negative connotations are not entirely clear, some suggest they stem from associations with the frailty of aging, such as yellowing leaves, the sallow skin of the elderly, or jaundice caused by alcoholism.[2]

Regardless of how someone reacts to a colour, it still evokes an emotional response. Without it, our world would be drab and emotionally stagnant. In fact, colour profoundly influences our wellbeing, often in subtle ways. Like Sandra, we instinctively use colour to express and support our emotions, even if we're not consciously aware of why certain choices feel 'right'.

Since there are so many potential ways we can respond to colour, the results of a 2020 colour survey covering thirty countries are quite enlightening. People were asked to describe emotions they associated with certain colours. Here are some of the results:[3]

- Black: 51 per cent associated with sadness
- White: 43 per cent associated with relief
- Red: 68 per cent associated with love
- Blue: 35 per cent associated with relief
- Green: 39 per cent associated with contentment
- Yellow: 52 per cent associated with joy
- Purple: 25 per cent associated with pleasure
- Brown: 36 per cent associated with disgust
- Orange: 44 per cent associated with joy
- Pink: 50 per cent associated with love

It's striking how much consensus there is, considering different cultures were surveyed. The responses are even more aligned between countries that share similar geography and language.[4]

Colour, without question, influences our sense of wellbeing.

✻ The 'black-and-white' facts of colour ✻

Psychologists and researchers have explored colour's emotional and behavioural impact for decades. Studying this is no small feat; colour isn't a single entity. Variations in shade, intensity, and brightness all influence perception. For example, light blue might soothe, while a deep navy commands authority. Consider also how challenging it must be to objectively interpret an emotional response like 'happy' or 'calm'. Researchers attempt to overcome these complexities by using standardised tests and physiological measures, like tracking changes in heart rate.

Despite these challenges, and understanding that variations will always exist, we can identify some trends. For instance, blue consistently correlates with relaxation and improved communication, which explains why it dominates the branding of tech giants like Facebook and LinkedIn.[5] Similarly, red's association with strength and urgency is why it often features in sports uniforms and sales banners.

There are three main characteristics that contribute to a colour's emotional impact.[6]

Hue is the basic colour we see, such as red, blue, green and so on. Warm hues like red and orange tend to energise, while cool hues like blue and green evoke calmness. This is why hospitals and medical centres frequently feature blues and greens in their buildings and uniforms. The colour wheel divides the colour spectrum into 'warm' and 'cool' wavelength hues. The dividing line between warm and cool colours is an approximation because colour wavelengths, just like light, blend into each other and form a spectrum. Within a single hue, its vividness or dullness is influenced by chroma.

Chroma measures a colour's intensity or saturation, describing how vivid or pure it appears. Think of a neon sign's vibrancy versus a muted pastel of the same hue. High chroma colours energise, while low chroma tones evoke calm.[7] Compare the energising intensity of Spotify's green to Starbucks's more subdued green. Spotify conveys energy and playfulness. In contrast, Starbucks invites relaxation and comfort. Although chroma refers specifically to the purity of a hue, variations are often created by adding white, black, or grey. These adjustments also affect the colour's lightness. The terms commonly used for these changes are:

- Tint: White is added to a pure hue
- Shade: Black is added to a pure hue
- Tone: Grey is added to a pure hue

When describing a colour, people often use the words 'shade' or 'tone', but with this knowledge, you can walk into a paint store and accurately describe what effect you want.

Value/brightness refers to how light or dark a colour appears. Lighter colours feel playful and uplifting, while darker shades convey seriousness and depth. For example, lighter values are associated with kindergartens, while court lawyers may favour darker-value suits. Some studies have shown how we associate light values with 'pleasant' and dark values with 'unpleasant' emotions.[8] Context is everything, of course. In the courtroom, how you felt about the lawyer's dark suit would depend on whether the lawyer was representing you or cross-examining you.

To summarise the emotional qualities of colour:

- The hue, or colour, determines a level of warmth or coolness, influencing energy and calm.
- The chroma describes colour saturation or purity. High saturation creates vivid, energising colours. Low saturation feels calmer, or even passive.
- The value or brightness represents how light or dark the colour is. Light values convey softer, lighter emotions. Darker values convey a more serious mood.

Besides research, we also have history to tell us how colour was used to silently express emotions and make a statement.

∗ A colourful history ∗

Combining colour and clothing styles has a psychological impact on both the wearer and the observer. Colour also creates an impact in architecture, interior design, objects, and accessories. History shows how colour, and not just styles, reflected the zeitgeist of an era. Colour made statements without saying a word. Here are some examples from recent Western history.

Victorian and Edwardian England held conservative social values compared to today. Yet their interior decor used bolder colours compared to modern standards. Their appreciation of the natural world meant floral and nature-inspired prints were the norm. This makes sense, as the Victorian era overlapped with a period of rapid industrial and technological expansion. The demand for factory workers caused urban populations to swell. This transformed people's lives. They were pulled away from the countryside, the only world they had ever known. Nature-inspired colours and designs kept them connected to the familiar. Wallpapers printed with plants and birds in greens, blues, and vibrant turquoise were particularly popular. This helped to compensate for the grey, uninspiring and dirty world outside their doors.

The Art Deco period, particularly in the 1920s before the stock-market crash, featured high-contrast colour palettes and bold geometric designs. Combinations like black, gold, and silver dominated, reflecting an era of exuberance and technological progress. Metals such as chrome and gold were used to reflect development and sophistication. Jewel colours, like sapphire and emerald green, featured in interiors and clothing. This bold use of colour mirrored societal shifts towards liberation and optimism after World War I. Living spaces and public areas were often decked out in red, black, and white, for example. This was an era of fun, especially as women started to gain some financial independence through work. To balance these dramatic statements and to appeal to different sensory profiles, some interiors used cream and pastel tones, as did some clothing, especially in the daytime. Overall, colours reflected confidence: 'Look at me! I'm capable, sophisticated, and modern.' For the first time, women also showed their calves![9]

Following World War II, similarly to after World War I, there was a noticeable increase in the use of colour in both homes and clothing. People used colour's emotional power to overcome the sombreness and austerity of the previous years. In the late 1940s, earthy colours, such as mustard yellow, helped project quiet strength and stability and a connection to nature: very comforting. Bright colours emerged to express joy and life. Pastels reflected gentleness, lightness and positivity. These colours also painted positive sentiments onto objects. It would have been normal to walk into a kitchen with a black-and-white chequered linoleum floor and see walls painted in pastel pink, accompanied by a turquoise stove and fridge along with a matching Formica table.

Picture the bright and varied colour palettes and prints of the 1960s. They represented a newfound confidence and boldness to live and think differently than previous generations. It was an age of breaking established ways and embracing experimentation. Think how the voices of marginalised groups grew in this time: women's liberation, the civil rights movement, gay rights, and anti-war counterculture groups. Bold colours for brave voices.

* Modern-day homes *

In more recent decades, we seem to have lost confidence with colour. So many opt for white, beige or lightly tinted interiors. Some confidently choose a 'feature wall', while a few disregard trends and use colour freely. Good on them, they know what they need. This reflects the visual Seekers' mindset: they will not deprive themselves.

Chapter 5. Aurora–Colour

Did we truly lose confidence, or is this palette reflecting our emotional needs again? We see these colours as neutral and non-offensive. But think how our lives have changed in the last thirty years. We've become overwhelmed with information thanks to technology that leaves our brains exhausted, and we have reduced our brain recovery time because we work late or stream and doomscroll into the evening. Daily, this disrupts our circadian rhythm and contributes to our fatigue. 'Neutral' colours like white and beige serve a need to feel still and quiet in our own space. These colours can allow our minds to 'catch a breath'. Even so-called neutrals have an emotional effect. As well as a sense of calm, they can create a light and spacious atmosphere that complements a pared-back, simple design. It helps counteract the busyness and complexity of our cities, buildings, and lifestyles. Our ancestors never had to navigate multilayered car parks in shopping malls that stretched across streets, or daily, time-pressured commutes in dangerous machines travelling at great speed. When you consider all these points, it's apparent that rather than a loss of colour confidence, people may just be selecting what their overworked senses need. On the practical side, neutrals mean you can change objects in a space, and they will still 'match'. This can be a cost-effective way to adjust colour in a space.

However, selecting neutrals to make a property easy to sell at some stage may limit your opportunity to create a comforting, supportive environment for yourself. What's worse is craving a colourful space but fearing others' opinions. Social media posts have escalated this. Many may opt for a 'neutral' scheme to avoid being judged.

COVID started a stirring, though. When people were shut in their houses 24/7, some started to feel oppressed by their neutral interiors. They were no longer overstimulated by the outside world or getting Happy DOSE chemicals as before. I believe the white 'sanctuary' began to feel like a padded cell to many, prompting a wave of home projects to literally bring colour back into their lives.

The important thing is, regardless of trends, you should colour your spaces to work for your sensory preferences and individual needs, not for anyone else. Besides your family, other people don't live with you, and it's unlikely they spend their day thinking about your place. They have more important things to think about—themselves.

What's my position on all this? I was among those who adored the concept of the 'feature wall'. I got very excited when we renovated many years ago, but in the end every wall was painted 'Beige Royal'. It is calming, but I chickened out because I didn't have the knowledge or confidence to choose wisely, and I feared making an expensive mistake. Not anymore. When I am able to redecorate, the study will be my first project. Blue on most of the walls will help me relax, focus, and be creative. Turquoise will help me feel inspired and invigorated, and nature scenes and living plants will give me moments of restoration. I will install closed cupboards with some open shelves. I have already started decluttering and have added some plants inside and a golden palm outside.

When you finish reading this book, you will better understand my choices beyond the colours I just described. No doubt you will have made some decisions about your own spaces too.

✶ The silent statement of colour ✶

The same colour can have positive or negative associations. This sentiment is often rooted in survival. For our ancestors, a red strawberry was desirable; red blood was not. One represents energy for our body, the other is a source of life and energy within our body.

The brightness and saturation also influence our response.[10] For example, a bright-red strawberry is far more appealing than a dark, almost black strawberry. This would suggest it might be off.

Today, positive or negative sentiments about the same colour have a lot to do with how and when the colour is used, as well as the quantity. Social trends and marketing can also influence us, even if we don't realise it.

When you search for colour meanings, you'll discover many descriptive words. This makes it hard to know which colours, or variations, may be the most effective at supporting a particular mood and behaviour. In Chapter 12 you can explore colours from different perspectives, such as cultural references, history, and nature. When you overlay these insights with your own lived experience and sensory preferences, you should be in a better position to make more informed decisions about which colours are right for you.

Just as colour surrounds us and quietly shapes how we feel, sound moves through our days, often unnoticed, yet deeply influential. Next, we'll explore Acoustics and how the sounds in our environment can either soothe or overstimulate our senses, affecting focus, mood, and even connection with others.

CHAPTER 6.
ACOUSTICS

The surprising effects of everyday sounds–good and bad

Sigrid jolts upright in bed. 'No!' she exclaims. She can't believe someone is drilling at 6 am! This was her morning to sleep in. The noise stops, and she sighs in relief, hoping to fall back asleep. But no. A low-flying plane interrupts her attempts. It's 6.30 am, so she gets up. While sitting in traffic, she tunes in to a classical station in an attempt to calm down, still ruminating about how her sleep was cut short. But classical music is too calming; she needs something more upbeat to stay alert and focused during her drive.

Arriving at the office, her sense of irritation and fatigue returns when she sees Patricia is in today. Patricia is nice, but she just doesn't stop talking. Ah, the joys of open-plan offices. Sigrid knows she's not going to have a productive day.

Sound is a powerful sense that can evoke a wide range of emotions. From the soothing melody of a favourite song to the jarring noise of city traffic or the aeroplane that woke Sigrid, sounds influence our mood, stress levels, and even our physiological responses. This is because our auditory system processes sound through the auditory cortex in the brain, which indirectly interacts with the limbic system, our emotional hub.[1]

When we hear something unpleasant, the amygdala, our brain's alarm system, can activate the hypothalamus to trigger the fight-or-flight response. In some cases, the hypothalamus may also respond directly to a sound. Even seemingly insignificant sounds can cause such reactions. For example, have you ever felt your irritation rise as colleagues chatter around you, breaking your focus?

✳ Modern sounds and their consequences ✳

Being alert to sounds was essential for our ancestors' survival. It's no different today, except instead of a lion's roar, it could be a loud crash as a waiter drops a tray of glasses. Your body jolts slightly as the sound startles you. It causes you to stop talking, even if it's just for a second. This automatic and instant reaction, requiring no conscious thought, is known as the 'startle response'. While not as intense as a full stress response, it still activates the same fight-or-flight processes. Imagine being startled repeatedly. Alerts from devices, boisterous colleagues, doors closing, and dishes clattering are all examples of how we can experience the startle response.[2] Such events can create a cumulative drain on mental energy and increase frustration, yet most of us see these individual events as minor disruptions and often don't address them.[3]

Drowning in sound

Unlike our ancestors, we now live in a world saturated with sound. Chronic noise exposure doesn't just irritate us; it can lead to serious health issues, including obesity, learning difficulties, and anxiety.[4,5,6]

Even sounds that individuals find annoying can still take a toll. In fact, around 25 per cent of the European Union's population report a decline in the quality of life due to the annoyance of noise.[7] Nobel laureate Robert Koch foresaw this in the early twentieth century, predicting, 'One day, man will have to fight noise as fiercely as cholera and the plague.'[8] His words are more relevant now than ever. The World Health Organization estimates that in Western Europe alone, traffic noise causes a loss of over 1.5 million healthy life years annually.[9] This is simply tragic.

Chapter 6. Acoustics

It's tempting to believe we've adapted to constant noise, but the evidence suggests otherwise. Chronic exposure can erode mental fortitude and emotional balance, leaving us feeling drained. Even low-level sounds, like background TV or a colleague typing, can disrupt sleep or focus. We block out sounds all the time, for example, the hum of the fridge or very low traffic, but when they stop, we notice that too.[10] This indicates that our brains are working to reduce distractions to help us focus elsewhere. While this is a normal brain function, the ongoing effort to block out background noise can deplete our limited daily energy, contributing to fatigue and stress. The research is clear: 'getting used to it' isn't an effective strategy.

The startle factor

The Hearing Health Foundation graphic, Figure 6.1, confirms that sound doesn't have to be at a high volume to be disturbing.

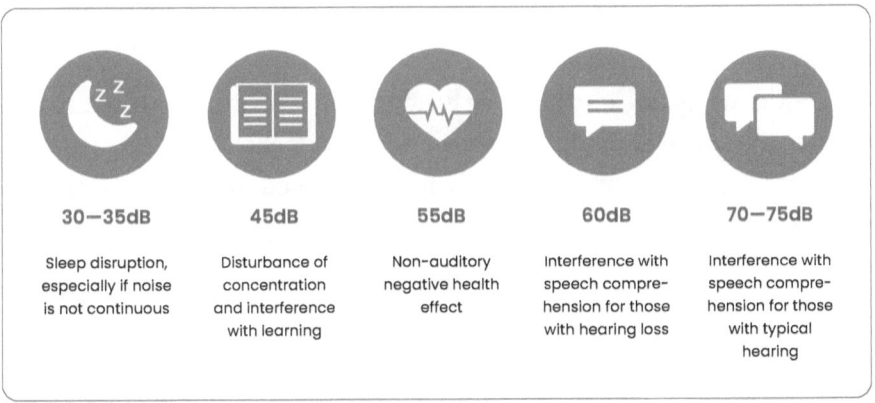

Figure 6.1. Noise disturbance volumes
Courtesy of the Hearing Health Foundation, hhf.org. Volume is measured in decibels (dB).

Curious about everyday sound levels, I downloaded a free dB app and discovered that my typing registered approximately 50dB. This is fine because I am controlling the noise. However, when I worked in an office,

I struggled to focus with people typing or talking nearby. The dB chart confirms I am not an anomaly. Consider home environments as well: even low-level TV or music could affect someone's sleep or study in the next room.

Over time, these 'microbursts' of stress increase cortisol, sap our energy, and impair focus, making us feel drained from even seemingly small disruptions.[11] Yet most of us don't credit these sounds as contributors to our daily fatigue, stress, or reduced productivity. Clearly, sound doesn't have to be dramatic to affect us. It's easy to see how open-plan offices can lead to inefficiency. Research shows it can take up to twenty-five minutes to refocus on a task, and that we often rush through our work just to catch up.[12] No wonder noise-cancelling headphones have become a workplace staple.

Psychologist Izabella Risteski explains that shifting focus, whether due to noise, interruptions, or multitasking, is mentally exhausting because it forces the brain to repeatedly activate and deactivate different neural networks. This cognitive 'gear shifting' consumes significant amounts of glucose, the brain's primary fuel, leading to rapid depletion of mental energy and reduced efficiency.

Besides using noise-cancelling headphones and finding a quiet space, you can minimise interruptions by working in blocks of time where alerts are turned off (job permitting), allowing you to focus properly and reduce microbursts of stress.

Fighting noise with noise

Poor-quality sleep from noise pollution can lead to serious health issues. I, like Sigrid, live in a moderately noisy area with planes frequently flying over my house. I used to use a device to mask them. I experimented with lots of sounds and responded well to sounds of the ocean. That device broke. I then trialled a headband device that paired with my phone. It worked, but for me the sound was too close to my ears. Thank goodness no one could see me because I felt like I was in an eighties exercise video.

Chapter 6. Acoustics

Now I don't use anything. I put this down to making sensory improvements in the areas of Aurora, Aroma, Appetite, and Action, which have contributed to improving the quality of my sleep.

I spoke with Rohima Badri, who holds a PhD in Audiology and Hearing Sciences from Northwestern University in the United States. She is a regular contributor to the Hearing Health Foundation website. She confirmed that when it comes to our wellbeing, the annoyance factor of sound is just as critical as the impact of sound volume and duration. An individual's annoyance can be influenced by a number of variables, including their sensory profile, personality traits, attitudes, and life experiences.

* Your unique profile *

That rings a bell

The hippocampus in the limbic system records memories that shape how you feel and behave. For example, a song may make you smile because it reminds you of a wonderful holiday, yet for someone else it may represent a break-up or a tragic event. A friend once told me how he threw himself on the ground at the sound of a loud bang while he was touring a factory. None of his colleagues did, because they weren't ex-army like him.

Sensory preferences

With effort and practice, we can learn to shut out noise to a certain degree, and some can do this more effectively than others. I would classify myself as a sound Sensor, which means I struggle to block out background noise.

There are also people that thrive with background noise. A friend of mine can't focus unless she can hear something. She told me she would interrupt people at work just to hear some sound because it was too quiet. Finally she started listening to music and her productivity skyrocketed.

Music not only helped her focus, it also quieted her internal chatter. She is likely a sound Seeker who uses music to block external and internal distractions to help still her mind. She still expends mental energy to do this, but for her, it's worth the cognitive effort because it allows her to focus.

Parents who worry that their children won't study properly while listening to music may want to consider that background noise might benefit their sensory profile. Their grades may give insight into this.

For those who do prefer background noise, it's important to know that it still has the potential to distract you and compete with your cognition and working memory.[13] In Chapter 13 we'll review how to use sounds and music to ensure they work for you, not against you.

Speak up

Our hearing declines as part of the aging process and through noise exposure. I have no doubt much of my natural hearing loss is self-inflicted thanks to live music concerts and loud music blasting in my car or home.

Hearing loss isn't just a physical disadvantage, though. It has been well documented that those who suffer hearing loss can experience a greater degree of depression and cognitive decline than those whose hearing isn't impaired.[14] Please don't have a stereotyped image of an elderly person bent over a walking stick. These findings have been documented in working adults too.[15] Sadly, elevated levels of anxiety and depression have been found in adolescents with hearing loss as well.[16]

According to the United States federal agency the National Institute for Occupational Safety and Health (NIOSH), an individual should not be exposed to noise levels of 85 dB or higher for more than eight hours a day.[17]

Decibel range (dB)	Examples of sounds	Impact on hearing
20–70	Ticking watch (20); leaves rustling, whisper (30); background music (60); average room noise (30-50); average office noise (70)	Sounds at or below 70 dB are safe, but can still distract
75–100 dB	Landscaping equipment (from inside a house) (75); vacuum cleaner (80) city traffic (from inside a car), noisy restaurant (85); hairdryer (90); food processor, DJ'd school dance, crowing rooster (95); approaching subway train, car horn at 5 metres (95-100); hand dryer, motorcycle (100+)	Even sounds around 75 dB can be harmful with prolonged exposure
105–140 dB	Trombone; dog barking in ear; nightclubs and bars; leaf blower; jack hammer; rock or pop concert; siren; jet engine from 90 metres	Sounds in this range can cause immediate harm to hearing

Figure 6.2. Noise levels – Courtesy of the Hearing Health Foundation, hhf.org.

Headphones are a common way to help block unwanted interruptions and enjoy music, streaming, or gaming. However, there is evidence that inappropriate use leads to avoidable hearing loss. To protect your hearing, avoid earbuds in favour of over-ear headphones and limit exposure to sixty minutes at a time. Of course, volume is everything, as it affects your hearing, concentration, and stress levels.[18]

✽ Human sounds ✽

It's nice to hear your voice

In Part One we saw that the spoken voice can reduce stress and foster connection, while texting can have the opposite effect.[19] Think about how often you text instead of making a quick call; 'text conversations' can be a missed opportunity for genuine connection and clarity. At work, phone calls or online catch-ups strengthen bonding, alignment, and decision-making far better than emails or texts do.

People who default to text and email may experience more loneliness and anxiety, missing out on the benefits of oxytocin and stress reduction. Whenever possible, make the call and enjoy a more calming and connected experience.

Laughter *is* contagious

Think about laughter in a group: when someone laughs, we instinctively smile and want to laugh with them. This is known as the 'contagion effect'.[20] This has nothing to do with diseases; it's about 'catching' emotions from other people.

During tough times, people often seek humour and find solace in laughter. It feels like a release. This is instinctive behaviour that stimulates the vagus nerve, triggering the rest-and-digest processes. Remember, the vocal cords are reached by one of the 'off-ramps' of the 'vagus highway'. This means that laughter helps reduce cortisol and gives us a Happy DOSE.[21] You can imagine how laughter helped us connect to the tribe and feel positive and calm. Conversely, when we hear someone crying, we are likely to feel concern and empathy, which make us want to help.

Vocal sounds

Beyond laughter, when you sing, hum or chant, you can stimulate your vagus nerve as well. This can create a sense of calm and makes it easier to generate dopamine, serotonin, and endorphins. You can add oxytocin to create a full Happy DOSE if you engage in these activities with others.

Whether it's speaking, laughing, or humming, generating vocal sounds and listening to others can have a profoundly positive effect on your wellbeing. So simple, so powerful, and yet so many moments to experience these benefits are lost with our online lifestyles. Online activities can be convenient, but a life lived too virtually is counterproductive to your sense of wellbeing.

Music and emotion

No doubt you have had times when you have been swept up in music, whether it's at home or in the car, or singing along with friends. Music moves us because it has the ability to arouse and calm us, both physically and mentally.[22]

This is why it evokes a range of emotions, from joy to sorrow. For example, when you find music stirring, it's stimulating dopamine.[23] If it makes you happy, serotonin is being released.[24] It's not surprising that studies have repeatedly shown that music can reduce stress.[25]

Music can be a powerful tool to grab our attention, with no effort required. It can transport us to a happier place away from our current doldrums, because it can trigger memories. For example, you may recall the best summer you had with friends, or the music your parents played on repeat that you secretly now like because it reminds you of them. In that moment, you can't stress about the deadline, the dog, or the debt. Because of this effect, it makes sense to listen to music to uplift your mood. It won't make a problem go away, but it will give your brain a break and a lift, which gives you the opportunity to think differently. When you are down you may not feel like putting music on, but do it and your limbic system will do the rest.

Sometimes when you're upset, listening to an upbeat and happy song is the last thing you want. It's like when someone tries to be positive and cheery and all you can think is, *Are you serious? Where is the empathy?* When you do experience empathy, you think, *You get me, you understand what I'm going through.* This allows you to connect with people and you can start to transition to a more positive headspace. It can be the same with music. It's known as the Iso Principle. When you're sad, listening to a sad song resonates with your current emotional state.[26] The sad music allows you to grieve for a time, which helps you move on. It's like the music 'gets you'.

Have you experienced joy and elation while listening to live music? Listening in a group can be more powerful than listening to music alone. Believe it or not, our emotional response is partially due to the synchronisation of our brainwaves with the music and even with others in the audience. Everyone is experiencing the same beat, frequency, and melody, and those whose brainwaves synchronise more closely with others enjoy the experience even more![27] The music experience doesn't have to be at rock concert decibels either.

Music combined with a positive crowd experience, as well as dancing and singing, has the potential to bring great joy on many levels. I know this is strictly more than sound alone, but that is the beauty of the interplay of the senses. It's no wonder music is called the universal language. At a gig, we don't need words to connect, we just let our brainwaves align, while the music supports the release of a Happy DOSE.

* The call of the wild *

Nature is a multi-sensory delight, from pleasing and relaxing vistas to fresh and fragrant aromas and an array of soundscapes, such as birds singing and waves rolling into shore.

We can't all escape to nature every day to help us relax, but the good news is that recorded sounds of nature can help us unwind. Studies show that blood pressure, heart rate, and breathing can all reduce just from listening to nature sounds. This is compared with normal urban noise and even quiet environments.[28] Varied natural soundscapes appear to be the most effective, but selecting nature sounds that are pleasing to you is the most important thing. It can offer a kind of auditory 'breathing space' for your mind to focus, reduce stress, and improve your mood.

Chapter 6. Acoustics

✽ How does this sound? ✽

Did you know that when we hear sound, we are processing pressure waves that pass through a medium? For example, the medium could be air, water, or even our own bodies. These pressure waves are measured in hertz (Hz), which are the number, or frequency, of pressure waves emitted per second.[29]

High-frequency sounds, or rather fast-pressure waves, sound high to us and we often refer to this as high-pitched. Think of sounds like chirping birds and whistles. Conversely, drums and rumbling thunder represent low-pitched sounds.

The pitch of the human voice influences you, whether you realise it or not. In English, we use higher-pitched sounds to express fear, surprise, and happiness, while lower-pitched sounds tend to communicate authority, seriousness, sadness, or anger.[30] This is why lower-pitched voices often command more attention and respect. Leaders with higher voices, male or female, may struggle to convey authority.

Different noises and music clearly have a profound effect on our sense of wellbeing, ranging from pleasure and calm through to anxiety and even depression. In Chapter 13, we'll explore how to incorporate beneficial sounds and music into daily life, to support stress relief, sharpen focus, restore energy, and bring emotional balance.

Now it's time to tune into a quieter influence, one that travels directly to the emotional centre of the brain and can shift our mood in seconds, often without us even realising it: Aroma.

CHAPTER 7.
AROMA

How scents shape your sense of wellbeing

Selina clutches the cellophane around the giant bouquet of colourful flowers. The scrunching sound and the sensation of her grip reflect the tightening of her throat as she enters the hospital. The calming wall colours and modern, relaxing interiors don't make up for that familiar stench of disinfectant that fills her with sadness. The grief of previous visits comes flooding back. As she walks down the corridor, she raises the bouquet and buries her nose in it to inhale the soothing lavender and geranium scents. To some it may have seemed an odd combination of floral shapes, but Selina has selected these flowers specifically for their calming aromas. They are for her as much as they are for her father, who lies behind the closed door in front of her.

Selina reminds us how powerful aromas can be. They evoke memories and emotions tied to people, locations, circumstances, and our past selves. Aromas affect us this way because they register in our limbic system, where emotions and memories are formed. This gave our ancient ancestors a survival advantage too; for example, the smell of rotten food may have reminded them of a time they had eaten it in the past and been sick, so they knew to avoid it a second time. Aromas act as silent alarms and signals that shape our thoughts and actions.

Of course, smells today are vastly different, from tarmac to traffic and factories through to sophisticated aromas wafting from restaurants and perfumeries. Aromas affect our feelings and behaviours today just as they have always done; they can create feelings of malaise, unease, or pleasure, influencing us often without our awareness. History provides valuable insight into how people discovered and harnessed the power of aroma to enhance their lives, lessons that continue to benefit us today.

* Ancient aromas *

Before humans understood how smell worked, they relied on what they sensed and what they observed. Egyptian hieroglyphics indicate that people used essential oils and plants for healing and spiritual purposes. They used scents from cassia, cinnamon, frankincense, and myrrh for mummification because of their rich lingering fragrances.[1] Essential oils benefited living people too. A well-known aromatic blend was kyphi, which was often burned in temples. It created a heady, relaxing effect. One blend consisted of calamus, mastic, cassia, cinnamon, juniper berries, wine, raisins, frankincense, honey, and myrrh. This complex recipe involved multiple steps and was prepared over several days.[2] Interestingly, one ingredient, calamus, was reputed to have narcotic effects. Many countries now regulate or ban calamus due to its potential health risks, including carcinogenic properties. It's not recommended in modern aromatherapy.[3]

The Greeks continued to appreciate and evolve the use of oils and burnt offerings, including kyphi. Other cultures, such as Indian and Chinese, also embraced the benefits of oils for wellbeing.

Ancient India included what we know today as Southeast Asia. This meant it enjoyed an array of fragrances thanks to the bountiful foliage. One of the most valued aromas from this region is the warm and spicy sandalwood. Other popular fragrant oils included patchouli and jasmine, and the spicy scents that we associate with Indian food;[4] the vibrant and energising aromas of cardamom and cinnamon not only uplift the spirit but also tantalise the tastebuds, blurring the line between scent and taste. It's no wonder these fragrances make me feel both uplifted and a bit hungry!

Arab nations valued the benefits of aromas and developed sophisticated plant and flower oil-extraction techniques. Sadly, in the West, the decline of the Roman Empire marked the start of the Middle Ages. Not exactly known as a fun or progressive time in Europe. In the Middle Ages fragrances were viewed by the church as frivolous, although their medicinal properties were valued, especially when waves of the black plague came. People believed that sickness was carried in the air and that breathing in the bad smells could directly affect their brain. They were right about an aroma going directly to the brain, even if they didn't understand what that meant for our health. Doctors wore beak-like devices filled with a variety of scents, such as mint, lavender, and myrrh. They believed this would not only protect them, but had the potential to heal as well.[5]

The use of scents throughout history for physical and psychological wellbeing is fascinating and many books are dedicated to this subject. This extends to the use of aromas in spiritual and ceremonial practices across cultures as well.

* Heaven scent *

In Chinese and other Asian cultures, people burn incense to remember and show respect to ancestors, deities, and even spirits. Prayers and messages are believed to ascend through smoke to connect with the spiritual world.

The Roman Catholic Church uses incense to symbolise many sentiments, such as purification. They will often use heady aromatics such as frankincense, myrrh, and benzoin. These evocative aromas add emotional significance to a service and, perhaps occasionally, lend a little extra 'spirit' to a delivery that might otherwise feel less inspired.

Some Indigenous communities around the world practice ancient ceremonies using the evocative power of aromas. For example, many

Indigenous people of North America burn sage for cleansing and healing. Smoking ceremonies are also common in Australian Aboriginal cultures, where they're used for welcoming people, commemoration, and mourning.[6]

New Age spiritual practices also use aromas. For example, certain essential oils are associated with specific chakras, which are considered energy centres in the body, to influence emotions, perceptions, and behaviour.

Regardless of beliefs, the use of incense and essential oils is commonplace in homes today as people want to facilitate a sense of calm and joy in their environment. You will often find them used in secular as well as spiritual meditation practices because some aromas can aid focus and introspection.

This comes back to the power of aroma over our limbic system. As we move from ancient spiritual practices into modern times, let's explore how our understanding of scents has evolved and what science tells us today.

∗ Scents of healing ∗

Modern aromatherapy originated in nineteenth-century France. One of the reasons French researchers became interested in the properties of essential oils was the observation that most workers who processed herbs and flowers didn't contract tuberculosis, a respiratory disease common at the time. While herbal medicine is ancient and global, these early studies helped shed light on the properties of plants and flowers that could be responsible for health benefits, such as antibacterial effects.[7]

Today, while many people associate essential oils with lovely aromas and emotional balance, there's a growing body of research exploring their medicinal properties. Validating the research is challenging, though. Unlike medications that have specific ingredients, plants contain multiple compounds, and their concentrations can vary depending on growing conditions and subspecies. Therefore, even though certain essential oils have active compounds that affect bacteria, viruses, fungi, the limbic system, and the nervous system, it would be almost impossible to 'guarantee' the exact strength of what is in the bottle. Products that make medical claims must also be backed by multiple robust trials that require the investment of millions of dollars. Another fundamental challenge in aroma trials is that participants may recognise the oils from their scent, and this could influence their reported feelings and behaviours.

These obstacles mean that research to date hasn't provided adequate proof to recommend the use of essential oils in mainstream medicine. Consequently, aromatherapy remains a complementary therapy and can be used alongside modern medicine but should never replace the guidance or treatment protocols provided by qualified health care professionals. A truly holistic approach would embrace the benefits of both disciplines and ensure all health practitioners are informed about every treatment you're using.

Regardless of research, essential oils find their way into home remedy first-aid kits because people have benefited from using them. For example, Australian households commonly use eucalyptus oil for colds in a steam inhalation preparation, as it helps alleviate respiratory congestion. The key molecule, 1,8-cineole, works by relaxing cells in the respiratory system.[8]

Anyone can buy essential oils, but they can be harmful if used incorrectly. If you wish to use essential oils for a specific condition, seek guidance from a certified aromatherapy practitioner. Natural doesn't always mean safe. With this in mind, let's delve into the world of essential oils and uncover how they enhance our sense of wellbeing.

∗ Exploring essential oils ∗

In terms of assessing the effects of aromas on our mood and behaviour, 100 per cent pure essential oils have been researched the most, compared to aromas produced by plant smoke, incense sticks, and potpourri.

This doesn't mean these forms of scents can't have some sort of effect on people. It's just difficult to assess.

Essential oils are also unique compared to other aromas because they contain volatile active compounds that have the potential to create therapeutic and psychological effects. Think of it this way: just as active yeast makes bread rise, active essential oils can lift our spirits and affect us physiologically. If the oils lose their potency, they may still smell nice, like a synthetic perfume, but their beneficial properties diminish, just as deactivated yeast results in flat bread.

The volatility of essential oils means they lose their fragrance faster than synthetic fragrances when exposed to the air. Commercial perfumes use additives and preservatives, much like food manufacturers add stabilising agents to products to prolong their shelf life.

Regardless of artificial, non-active ingredients, synthetic aromas can still trigger memories and emotions, but they lack the complexity of essential oils to significantly influence our psychological and physiological wellbeing.[9]

I was intrigued to understand how essential oils affect people and this is why I qualified as an aromatherapy practitioner. During my studies I learned that evidence about their effects on psychological wellbeing does exist, but the research is in its infancy and trials show mixed results.

As mentioned, validating the effectiveness of an essential oil is challenging. A Cleveland Clinic article sums this up by noting that aromatherapy may offer psychological benefits for conditions like anxiety. However, for clinical illnesses, study results are conflicting or inconclusive.[10] This suggests that evidence is more convincing for situation-based conditions like sadness or stress, rather than clinically diagnosed illnesses such as depression.

From my exploration, I believe aromas can affect behaviour and mood. Here are some intriguing findings that showcase how different scents can influence us.

Chapter 7. Aroma

✷ Modern insight into the effects of essential oils ✷

Getting a good night's sleep is particularly challenging when you are unwell. A review looked at several studies to see if essential oils could improve the quality of sleep for hospitalised cancer patients. The review concluded that single-scent essential oils improved sleep quality, while blends did not.[11] Although more robust studies are needed to validate this, it's interesting that single scents were more effective. It's also encouraging that this was an overall finding after reviewing several studies. Today, people often mix essential oils to create pleasing sleep blends. However, with this information, you might try a calming single oil like lavender, which has been a sleep aid for centuries. In Chapter 14 you will find guides on essential oils to support sleep as well as various moods and behaviours.

Another review explored studies that looked at brainwaves to assess the effects of essential oils on sleep and anxiety. This included some studies on rats, who clearly can't fake their behaviour. The review highlighted rose, lavender, lemon, and peppermint as oils that helped reduce symptoms of anxiety. It also identified lavender, sweet orange, bergamot, jasmine, and frankincense as oils that could improve sleep quality.[12]

Further brainwave studies looked at the effects of essential oils on relaxation, focus, and creativity. For instance, lavender, lemon, and jasmine increased theta waves, which promote relaxation and creativity. Sandalwood had a similar effect. Rosemary, on the other hand, boosted alpha waves, linked to calm alertness, and reduced beta waves, associated with intense thinking and high alertness. This aligns with rosemary's long history of stimulating a calm mind and supporting memory. No wonder it symbolises remembrance.[13]

Oils like jasmine, ylang-ylang, rose, and peppermint reduced both alpha and beta waves, which can really calm the mind and ease stress. Meanwhile, neroli and grapefruit decrease alpha waves and boost theta waves, encouraging deep relaxation, introspection, and creativity.[14]

You might wonder how the same essential oil can make someone feel both sleepy and productive. The effects depend on how much you use, when you use it, and your current state of mind. For example, if you're tired late at night, lavender can enhance this state and help you sleep. But in the morning, if you're feeling wired and agitated, its calming properties can help you focus. Similarly, grapefruit's relaxing effects can soothe agitation during the day, boost creativity, and help you drift off to sleep at night. This effect is linked to grapefruit essential oil's ability to increase theta waves.

Interest in essential oils for cognitive health is increasing as individuals seek natural methods to combat fatigue, reduce mental stress, and improve alertness and productivity. With a focus on longevity, people want to maintain mental sharpness and enjoy life to the fullest, regardless of age.

A University of California study looked at whether aromatherapy could help older adults perform better on cognitive tests. None of the people in the study had any memory problems. Half of them received single-scent essential oils to use each night, while the other half received aromatic oils without active ingredients. They were asked to diffuse a different oil each night for two hours before bed.

The group using active essential oils showed a 226 per cent improvement in a verbal learning test compared to the group that used the simple aromatic oils. Brain scans also showed positive changes in an area that connects emotional processing and decision-making.[15] It's amazing to think that simply smelling certain active aromas could help enhance our brain function. This is an example of how essential oils with active ingredients affect us physiologically in ways synthetic aromas can't.

The essential oils used in the study included rose, orange, eucalyptus, lemon, peppermint, rosemary, and lavender. Oils like peppermint and rosemary have long been used to help with energy and mental clarity. Interestingly, using these essential oils in the evening didn't seem to interfere with sleep. This might be because scents like peppermint and lemon can help you feel alert in a calm way. Once again, the body's underlying state will play a significant role.

While more research in broader and larger populations is needed, it's promising to see that certain essential oils can affect behaviour and productivity as shown through brainwaves, sleep quality, and test results. Although these reviews suggest single scents may be more effective, this doesn't rule out the potential benefits of certain blends. For instance, could combining the energising properties of peppermint with the calming qualities of lavender help someone achieve a state of calm alertness, improving mood and productivity? May the research continue.

Love is in the air

When it comes to attractiveness, studies show that pleasant odours don't make someone more attractive to us. However, an unpleasant odour can have a negative effect. This doesn't mean you should throw your colognes and perfumes away, though. As you will see, they can play a role.

In one study, participants viewed pictures of people while being exposed to different scent scenarios: no scent, a pleasant scent, or an unpleasant scent. The results revealed that individuals were rated as less attractive when paired with an unpleasant odour. People's verbal responses were also validated by brain scans that showed heightened activity in the amygdala, which processes emotions and reactions to sensory stimuli.[16]

Besides the question of physical attractiveness, have you ever thought about how a fragrance you wear influences how others perceive you? Some research suggests it can.

A study explored the effect of scents on how positive traits like attractiveness spill over into unrelated areas, such as intelligence or sociability. Participants rated male faces while exposed to either a gender-congruent scent (for example, traditional masculine cologne for male faces), an incongruent scent (such as traditional feminine perfumes paired with male faces), or no scent. Results revealed that gender-congruent fragrances amplified positive perceptions of traits like confidence and social competence, even if they didn't boost attractiveness itself. In contrast, incongruent scents had no such effect.

These findings show how fragrance can shape impressions in subtle but powerful ways. A well-chosen scent that aligns with your identity might not change how physically attractive you appear, but can enhance how others perceive your character.[17]

Sometimes, less is more. A study discovered that when people were unaware of a scent, they found someone more attractive compared to when the scent was noticeable.[18] This is a good reminder for everyone: using too much cologne or perfume can be overpowering and therefore counterproductive.

I have certainly made initial judgements based on someone's fragrance, such as when I was introduced to a man at work who was wearing an overpowering cologne. To me it smelled cheap because of its high alcohol and sweet overtones, plus it was overpowering. Without realising it, I made reactive assumptions about his personality, such as 'he's brash and unsophisticated'. Of course, getting to know someone can undo these amygdala-based assessments, but the immediate impression was made. Next time you choose a perfume or cologne, remember: it might do more than complete your look. It could shape how others see you.

While we actively choose essential oils and artificial fragrances to benefit us, there are aromas around us all the time that can either enhance or diminish our sense of wellbeing. Let's look at how we can embrace or reduce their effects.

✴ Something in the air ✴

Spending time in nature offers many benefits, like improved mood and reduced stress. These benefits have been confirmed by research that shows time in nature can reduce blood pressure, cortisol, and heart rate. Part of this can be due to the natural aromas we experience outdoors. Trees like pine, spruce, and eucalyptus release active compounds that can promote feelings of calm and wellbeing.[19] Some of these include α-pinene, β-pinene, d-limonene, and 1,8-cineole.[20]

The smell of rain in nature can be pleasing too. Known as 'petrichor', it is caused by oils being released from plants and soil-dwelling bacteria when raindrops hit the ground.[21] This scent evokes feelings of freshness and nostalgia, linking us to our evolutionary connection to water and nature. While it is possible to get some of these benefits from urban rain, it won't be the same due to additional compounds from asphalt, pollution, and urban vegetation.

For many who live in cities, regularly getting into nature isn't always possible. However, you could create a sense of calm by diffusing essential oils that are high in the natural compounds identified. For example, you could try lavender, sweet orange, rosemary, and frankincense.

City living means we're often exposed to unpleasant or harmful odours that affect us, so it's important to understand some ways we can improve indoor air quality too.

Clearing the air

Most of the urban scents we encounter, whether we notice them or not, are artificial because city dwellers spend about 90 per cent of their time indoors.[22,23,24] We often think we are used to indoor odours, but are we really? When I enter my home, I'm often greeted by an unpleasant damp smell. Although I can't see any mould, the odour suggests it might be present. This doesn't create a welcoming or relaxing environment. Over time, my nose adapts and I stop noticing the smell, but it's still there. Some mornings I wake up congested or groggy without an obvious reason. This can prompt a spring clean, which I often neglect to repeat until the congestion begins again.

One aspect of indoor air quality is the balance of negative and positive ions. These are created when naturally occurring molecules undergo a slight alteration in their structure.[25] Nature creates negative ions through phenomena like sunlight, moving water, and after thunderstorms. They are more abundant in cleaner air and can improve air quality by causing pollutants to clump together and settle out of the air we breathe.[26] Studies have linked higher levels of negative ions to stress reduction, better sleep, and an improved sense of wellbeing.[27] There's even evidence they may help people with seasonal affective disorder.[28]

Positive ions are often associated with higher levels of pollutants and allergens.[29] Factors like temperature, humidity, and time of day can affect ion levels too. While being in natural environments with higher negative ion concentrations can benefit our wellbeing, installing negative ion generators at home isn't a practical or safe solution; excessive negative ions indoors can lead to respiratory irritation and static build-up, disrupting the natural balance of air quality.[30]

In city and urban living, it's challenging to eliminate all unhealthy odours from sources like petrol fumes, mould, wood smoke, and gas. But there are practical steps you can take to minimise indoor air pollution, especially from sources within your home:

- **Improve ventilation:** If feasible, open windows regularly to allow fresh air to circulate, especially when cooking or after using artificial cleaning products. Use exhaust fans in your kitchen if you frequently cook with gas.
- **Control moisture and humidity:** Use dehumidifiers in damp areas to prevent mould growth. Fix any leaks.
- **Regular cleaning:** Keep your home clean to reduce dust, pet dander, and other allergens. Use a vacuum with a High Efficiency Particulate Air (HEPA) filter.
- **Use natural cleaning products:** Opt for cleaning products with natural ingredients to reduce chemical pollutants.
- **Avoid synthetic fragrances:** Limit the use of air fresheners and artificially scented candles that may emit harmful compounds.
- **Introduce houseplants:** Certain indoor plants can help purify the air by absorbing pollutants. From a Total Sensory Wellbeing perspective, having plants in your home, especially if you don't have a garden or balcony, is a must. However, you would need hundreds of them to genuinely purify your home.[31] They will help, but they can't do the job alone. Some examples of plants

Chapter 7. Aroma

known for their air purifying qualities are spider plants, bamboo palms, and rubber plants. Note: rubber plants are toxic to cats and dogs!
- **Test for carbon monoxide:** This is relevant if you are concerned about adequate ventilation and frequently use gas stoves, heaters, fireplaces, wood-burning stoves, or have attached garages where cars might idle.
- **Use air purifiers:** Consider using air purifiers with HEPA filters to reduce airborne particles.

The cleaner the air we breathe, the better we feel, physically, emotionally and cognitively. Smells definitely influence our mood and behaviour, and this fact is not lost on the commercial world.

✻ The smell of success ✻

Businesses understand that smell helps to shape our impressions of places, objects, food, and people. It's no accident that department stores commonly put the perfume section near the entrance; it lures you in and makes you feel good. If you're sensitive to aromas or avoid them, it may encourage you to move to other departments faster.

Real estate agents often use uplifting aromas like fresh coffee to enhance the experience of home inspections. Shops and hotels will commonly deploy diffusers as well. These investments would not be made if there were no return. The benefit doesn't have to be a sale, although that is always welcome. A positive impression of a place, company, or person is equally valuable because it can lead to customers returning and positive online reviews and recommendations, which can all generate more business.

As you know, when emotions are affected, so is behaviour. A study showed that floral scents in a casino increased people's gambling time by 50 per cent![32] A *Business News Daily* article discusses another study that found single scents influence consumer behaviour more effectively than combination scents or no scent at all, boosting sales by 20 per cent.[33] The researchers believe single scents are less complex and therefore easier for our brains to process. The less energy and effort required to interpret sensory information, the more relaxed we tend to be and the more we can focus on something specific, like deciding whether to buy something.

The influence of aromas on the limbic system means that besides emotions and behaviours in the moment, our response to an aroma can trigger memories, just like Selina experienced when she smelled the odours of the hospital. How we respond to an aroma is based on our lived experiences, current situation, and sensory profile.

In Chapter 14, we'll explore ways to prepare essential oils for specific emotional and behavioural effects so you can narrow down which scents make sense to you.

Now let's look at a sensory experience we actively have several times a day: food. It's not just fuel; it's a powerful influence on our thoughts, behaviour and sense of self. Hence the term Appetite, to highlight how food shapes not only our physical state but also our emotions and overall sense of wellbeing.

CHAPTER 8.
APPETITE

How food fires and fries your brain

Stacey and Sebastian glance at the catered lunch table, a familiar sight at these meetings where schedules always run over. Colleagues hurriedly pile their paper plates with white-bread sandwiches stuffed with processed meats and calorific fillings, and mindlessly eat as they respond to emails. Stacey sighs. She hates these lunches. The starchy bread and rich fillings are undeniably tasty, but they often leave her feeling even more drained. Worse, they tempt her to eat far more than she needs, derailing her healthy eating plan for the day.

With her resolve depleted, Stacey grabs a plate. What the heck, she thinks, adding a chocolate brownie to her selection. I'll need the sugar rush just to get through the afternoon.

Sebastian, meanwhile, takes a different approach. Turning to Stacey he says, 'I knew they'd serve this food again. That's why I brought my own lunch.' With that, he walks away from the table.

Stacey stares at her plate of food, frustrated by her lack of willpower. She packed her own healthy lunch too, but the allure of the sugary treats and indulgent flavours was too strong.

People like Sebastian treat food as fuel, selecting options that help their bodies perform at their best. Stacey, on the other hand, knows what she *should* eat but often finds herself drawn to foods that are hard to resist.

Her cravings feel like a failure of self-discipline, but the truth is more complex. Stacey's body and brain are under constant stress, leaving her cortisol levels elevated, a biological state she's unaware of. Her lack of sleep and demanding workload intensify her body's craving for a quick energy boost, driving her towards sugar, refined carbohydrates, and calorie-dense foods.[1] What she interprets as weak willpower is actually her brain and body trying to cope with overwhelming demands. It doesn't help that Stacey is a food Seeker, someone naturally drawn to rich flavours and tempting textures.

* That gut feeling *

Our understanding of the expression 'you are what you eat' resonates more deeply than ever, thanks to ongoing research that demonstrates how profoundly food shapes not only our physical health and appearance, but also our brain health.

Just like our other senses, our sense of taste has evolved over millions of years, shaped by both innate wiring and learned experiences. Throughout history, humans have instinctively adapted their eating habits to survive. This includes the enduring notion of food as medicine, a concept deeply rooted in ancient practices.

Recipes discovered on ancient Mesopotamian tablets (dating back to 3500–2300 BCE) highlight this connection. These early recipes, originating from the regions now known as Türkiye, Syria, Iran, and Iraq, included breads, pies, stews, cakes, and porridges. Ingredients such as garlic were believed to treat respiratory infections, while barley was used to aid digestion. To date, the science behind garlic remains inconclusive, though some studies suggest mild antimicrobial effects. Barley, however, like other wholegrains, is known to support digestion due to its high fibre content. These ancient culinary recipes also reveal that aesthetic presentation was important, suggesting food has long held emotional significance to us.[2]

The idea of food as medicine is echoed across cultures. In India, Ayurvedic practices dating back to around 1500 BCE used food to balance the body's systems, or 'doshas'.[3] Turmeric, for example, was recommended for inflammation, digestion, and skin health; its benefits are supported by modern research.[4] Similarly, in traditional Chinese medicine (circa 200 BCE), *Huangdi Neijing (Yellow Emperor's Inner Canon)* listed foods to balance 'qi'. This referred to the body's vital energy. As an example, ginger was prized for its ability to ease nausea, aid digestion, and alleviate colds, and it still remains a staple remedy today. Around 400 BCE, the ancient Greek physician Hippocrates, known as the father of Western medicine, also championed the connection between food and health.[5]

Modern research has validated many of these ancient practices by identifying the active compounds in foods like turmeric and ginger. However, not all historical theories have withstood scrutiny. For instance, the doctrine of signatures, which refers to the age-old belief that a plant resembling a human body part would benefit that part, has been debunked. For example, walnuts, long thought to benefit the brain due to their shape, do contain brain-boosting nutrients, but their resemblance to the brain is purely coincidental.[6]

Today, we are fortunate to have robust and ongoing research into how food affects our overall wellbeing. While much of the focus has been on food's role in physical health and appearance, interest and research into food's profound impact on brain health is growing. We now understand that the body and mind are intrinsically connected and communicate in a dynamic loop that travels from gut to brain and back again.

✶ Your gut-brain ecosystem ✶

Microbiome refers to the community of trillions of bacteria living in your gut. These bacteria play a vital role in extracting nutrients from food, supporting overall wellbeing and fuelling the brain. In fact, the brain is one of the body's most energy-hungry organs, requiring about 20 per cent of your daily calorie intake.[7]

The gut–brain connection has become a focal point for health research, offering exciting insights into how diet influences mood, cognition, and mental health. However, much of this research is still in its early stages, with many studies conducted only on animals. As a result, health professionals caution against expecting miraculous changes from microbiome-focused diets or stool analyses. It's an exciting and promising area, but findings and recommendations are not yet definitive and should therefore only be explored under professional guidance.[8]

Probiotics are ingestible products designed to contain beneficial microorganisms with the goal of adding these to your existing gut bacteria population. Probiotics have become a thriving industry. However, their actual impact on the microbiome is often overstated. With trillions of bacteria already in your gut, adding a few billion from a probiotic supplement is like pouring a cup of water into a swimming pool. Additionally, stomach acid may destroy many probiotic bacteria before they reach the gut. Many experts agree that probiotics are unlikely to make a meaningful difference if you're healthy and eating a balanced diet.[9]

That said, emerging research shows promise in their use for brain health. For example, some studies suggest that probiotics may alleviate mild to moderate depressive symptoms. However, inconsistencies in the types of probiotics used make it difficult to draw firm conclusions.[10] Once again, the research is currently too limited to provide people with advice that will produce specific results.

Probiotics also occur naturally in foods. Fermented foods are excellent sources of probiotics and include sauerkraut, kimchi, kefir, yoghurt, miso, and kombucha. When buying fermented products, check the sugar content as recipes vary and excess sugar can counteract some of the benefits.

Prebiotics are typically high-fibre foods that feed your microbiome. The bacteria ferment the fibre, producing by-products known as short-chain fatty acids that have far-reaching effects on our overall health.[11] For instance, one of the substances they produce, butyrate, has the potential to improve sleep and reduce inflammation.[12]

Prebiotic fibres are found in foods such as garlic, onions, leeks, asparagus, bananas, and legumes. While fibre is the most common source of prebiotics, other foods like tea, coffee, and red wine contain these beneficial compounds as well, offering additional ways to nourish your gut bacteria (in moderation). A comprehensive list of foods that support gut and brain health can be found in Chapter 15.

So, what's the best approach to gut health? At this stage, a varied diet rich in a diverse array of wholefoods (think wholegrains, leafy greens, vegetables, and nuts) is the best way to support a healthy microbiome. Each type of beneficial bacteria in our gut thrives on different nutrients, so the more variety you include, the better. Reducing your intake of inflammatory and processed foods is equally critical.

A diverse gut microbiome is now widely recognised as essential for overall health and mental wellbeing. We'll further explore the fascinating two-way connection between the gut and brain, known as the gut–brain axis, in Chapter 15.

✳ Fibre: Fuel for your gut and brain ✳

When we think of fibre, it's often associated with 'keeping us regular' and protecting bowel health. But fibre does much more, especially when it comes to supporting your gut and brain. Fibre is a carbohydrate that comes in various forms, each with specific benefits.

- **Feeding gut bacteria:** As outlined above, certain types of fibre, known as prebiotics, serve as food for beneficial gut bacteria.
- **Regularity:** Insoluble fibre is a kind of roughage that passes through the digestive system whole, helping to keep bowel movements consistent.
- **Slowing digestion:** Soluble fibre absorbs water in your gut, slowing the digestion of carbohydrates. This helps regulate blood glucose levels and reduces the likelihood of inflammation. In turn, it supports brain health by preventing glucose spikes that can impact mood, energy, and focus.

To ensure your diet supports both gut and brain health, include a variety of fibre containing foods daily.

Flavonoids: Natural brain boosters

Flavonoids, a group of plant-derived compounds, are celebrated for their protective and anti-inflammatory properties. Notably, certain flavonoids can cross the blood–brain barrier, supporting brain health by enhancing memory and cognition. They also play a role in regulating serotonin and dopamine levels, contributing to mood balance and helping you stay calm and focused amidst daily challenges.[13]

Best sources of flavonoids

Flavonoids are abundant in many foods and beverages. Excellent sources include:
- **Berries:** Blueberries, strawberries, and blackberries are rich in flavonoids that support memory and cognitive function.
- **Teas:** In descending order of concentration: Matcha, green tea, black tea, and white tea.
- **Coffee:** A popular source of flavonoids that also offers a moderate energy boost.
- **Red wine:** Contains flavonoids, but should be consumed in moderation.

The wine factor

While red wine has flavonoids, its alcohol content can disrupt brain health. Overconsumption may:
- interfere with serotonin and dopamine levels
- disrupt your circadian rhythm, leading to poor sleep and cognition
- negatively affect stress regulation.

However, moderate wine consumption is part of many social traditions. For better sleep and mental clarity, it's best to avoid alcohol at least three hours before bedtime.[14]

Incorporating flavonoid-rich foods and beverages into your diet is an easy and enjoyable way to boost your brain health while managing stress. Moderation and balance are key to reaping the benefits.

* Ultra-processed foods *

Through gut health research, we have not only learned which foods fuel the body and brain the best, we also understand more comprehensively why food can literally make us feel bad.

Ultra-processed foods are designed to dazzle the senses. Their bright packaging, intense flavours, and long shelf lives make them convenient and tempting, but beneath the surface, these foods can disrupt our well-being. Many of these foods are loaded with high levels of sugar, unhealthy fats, and salt, which can overwhelm the natural balance of our systems, leading to overeating and long-term health challenges.

How they are prepared also has an impact. When foods are cooked at high temperatures, such as during frying or grilling, the structure of fats and sugars changes. This is especially so when oils are used many times over, such as in restaurants and takeaway food outlets. This process creates unstable molecules called free radicals. Free radicals are highly reactive and can damage healthy cells, leading to a range of physical and mental health issues.

In addition, refined carbohydrates and sugars in ultra-processed foods cause rapid rises in blood glucose, which can also impact energy regulation and cause cell damage. This happens because refined foods lack fibre, which is critical for gut health and reducing inflammation. Some preservatives and additives in these foods may also disrupt the gut microbiome, further exacerbating inflammation and cell damage. High salt levels, another hallmark of ultra-processed foods, can interfere with the body's natural defences, making it harder to counteract damage.[15]

In short, a diet high in ultra-processed foods can lead to an increase in free radicals, excessive glucose spikes, a disrupted microbiome, and compromised immune function.

The eating habits of developed nations tell a concerning story. To use my home country of Australia as an example, a 2023 report from the Grattan Institute revealed that 38 per cent of Australians' average energy intake comes from unhealthy, non-essential foods, while vegetable consumption remains at just half the recommended amount.[16] In the USA, it's worse: more than 50 per cent of an adult's energy intake comes from ultra-processed foods.[17] If we think of our microbiome as a garden, it's like we are tipping garbage on it instead of feeding it the nutrients it needs to foster a flourishing array of plants. Junk food can create a junkyard.

Even though we know these foods aren't healthy, resisting them is difficult. Manufacturers design ultra-processed foods to be hyper-palatable; in other words: delicious and moreish. The high levels of sugar, fat, and carbohydrates trigger the brain's reward system, which served our ancient ancestors well, driving them to seek energy-rich foods for survival. Food manufacturers worked this out decades ago and have been perfecting the sugar–fat–carbohydrate combination ever since. This perfectly delicious and addictive mix is known as the 'bliss point'. In today's world, where convenience foods are everywhere and physical activity is limited, these hyper-palatable options exploit our ancient wiring and lead us down an unhealthy path of overconsumption.

Steps to curb unhealthy foods

- **Start small:** Swap out one ultra-processed item each week for a wholefood alternative. For instance, replace sugary breakfast cereals with porridge or muesli topped with fresh fruit.
- **Cook at home:** Preparing meals allows you to avoid harmful additives and experiment with healthy cooking techniques like steaming or baking. Highly organised people might like to block

out weekend time to batch cook and prepare in advance. If this isn't you, that's okay, just try one day first, or cook double quantities on a couple of days. Experiment with strategies that work for you.
- **Focus on fibre:** Add more wholegrains, vegetables, and legumes to your diet to support your gut health and reduce inflammation and cell damage. For example, try making homemade baked beans. I'm sure you won't look at canned versions the same way again.
- **Limit high-salt and sugary snacks:** Check labels and opt for lower-sodium and low sugar alternatives to support your body's natural protective processes.

By taking small, manageable steps, you can begin to break free from the grip of hyper-palatable foods and nourish your body and brain with the nutrients they need to thrive. Life is wabi-sabi, it's about progress, not perfection.

✱ Why eating can make you tired ✱

Feeling tired after eating is common and often depends on what and how much you eat. Meals high in refined carbohydrates, like white bread or pastries, can cause rapid blood glucose spikes followed by dramatic drops, leaving you fatigued and irritable. This would be Stacey's fate after reaching for these foods during her work lunch. Her desire to improve her energy would quickly backfire, leaving her even more sluggish.

Tryptophan: Myth vs reality

Tryptophan, a protein building block known as an amino acid and found in foods like eggs, turkey, and oats, supports serotonin production, which can influence mood and relaxation.[18] While serotonin can convert into melatonin to aid sleep, several factors affect whether tryptophan effectively reaches the brain:[19]

- **Nutrient competition:** Tryptophan competes with other amino acids to cross the blood–brain barrier, limiting its effects unless specific conditions are met.
- **Carbohydrate pairing:** Eating tryptophan-rich foods with carbohydrates can enhance its availability by triggering insulin, which reduces competition from other amino acids and makes it easier for tryptophan to enter the brain.

The time of day, food pairings, and activity levels all influence whether tryptophan promotes energy or relaxation:

- **Daytime eating:** Tryptophan-containing foods like oats or eggs at breakfast won't make you tired when paired with nutrient-dense sides, such as vegetables or wholegrain toast. These balanced meals align with natural cortisol peaks, helping you stay alert, ideally supported by a good night's sleep.
- **Evening eating:** To support better sleep, try tryptophan foods like turkey with complex carbohydrates, such as sweet potato. This combination aids the serotonin-to-melatonin conversion, encouraging relaxation. Complex carbohydrates support the steady release of insulin. Be mindful that while fattier cuts of meat, such as lamb or fatty chicken, contain tryptophan, eating heavy foods just prior to bed can disrupt your sleep because of the effort required to digest these foods.

Preventing daytime fatigue

To maintain steady energy levels and avoid post-meal crashes:

- **Balance nutrients:** Pair proteins like chicken or fish with high-fibre vegetables and healthy fats to stabilise blood sugar. For instance, an egg salad is a better choice than an egg sandwich made with refined white bread.

- **Limit refined carbs:** Avoid sugary snacks, processed foods, and refined grains that cause energy spikes and crashes.
- **Watch portions:** Overeating even healthy foods can overburden digestion, which can leave you feeling sluggish.
- **Stay hydrated:** Water is essential for optimal brain health. Even mild dehydration can impair concentration, memory, and mood, because the brain relies on adequate hydration to maintain energy and support neurotransmitter function. Incorporate water-rich foods like cucumbers, oranges, and watermelon alongside regular water intake to support overall wellbeing.

Tailoring food choices for energy and sleep

By aligning your food choices with your daily schedule and pairing tryptophan and melatonin-rich foods thoughtfully, you can enhance your daytime energy and support restorative sleep at night. Melatonin-rich foods like tart cherries, grapes, and walnuts are excellent for evening meals to promote restful sleep. However, be aware that consuming these in large amounts during the day may contribute to fatigue when you need to be alert.

✻ What time is dinner? ✻

When we eat can significantly influence our circadian rhythm. While the body's master clock resides in the hypothalamus, several other systems, including the gut, have their own circadian rhythms. Just like the brain, the gut evolved to support energy needs during daylight hours, making digestion most efficient during the day.[20] However, modern habits such as long workdays and evening activities often lead to later meals and the consumption of refined foods. Unfortunately, our sensory 'software' was designed for a different environment and doesn't function optimally under these new habits.

This means the earlier you finish eating, the better your body manages digestion and insulin resistance, which helps maintain blood glucose control. This reduces oxidative stress, which damages cells. Oxidative stress is more likely to occur with frequent late-night eating, disrupting sleep quality and mood.[21] Eating most of your food later in the day and eating late at night can compromise metabolism, making it harder for your body to regulate energy efficiently. This increases the likelihood of developing metabolic problems, including obesity.[22] While stopping eating by sunset might be ideal for circadian alignment, it's not practical for the way most of us live. Instead, focus on eating dinner as early as possible and minimise after-dinner snacks to optimise sleep quality and mood regulation. It's also healthier for your metabolism to consume most of your calories earlier in the day.[23]

Fasting and its benefits

Fasting, especially intermittent fasting, has gained popularity as a weight-loss strategy, but its benefits can extend beyond shedding kilos. I remember receiving a book on fasting from my mother for my birthday. Initially, I wasn't sure how to take this 'thoughtful' gift, but after reading it, I followed the advice. While I did lose weight, I also gained something: I found that delaying my first meal made me feel more alert and productive, especially if I did some form of exercise. However, when I had a poor night's sleep, I struggled to delay eating. Much like Stacey, my resolve dwindled.

One of the reasons fasting helped me feel more alert is because it allows the body to focus on repair and regeneration for longer. This includes a process called 'autophagy', the body's natural process of breaking down and recycling damaged or unnecessary cellular components to promote cellular repair and maintain overall health.[24] This can help to improve mood and clarity while also reducing stress.[25] I liken autophagy to the night-time office cleaners who take out the rubbish and wipe everything down so the office is clean and fresh the next day. It's important to note that human research into autophagy is still evolving, and additional studies are needed to fully understand this process.

However, fasting isn't without its challenges. Extreme fasting or prolonged calorie deprivation can deprive you of essential nutrients, leading to fatigue and poor mental health. Secondly, if you develop a fasting pattern that sees you eating all your calories too late in the day, it's possible you could negate some of the potential benefits by going against your natural circadian rhythms.

Various fasting approaches exist, including sustained fasting, which is not about calorie deprivation but instead focuses on metabolic and brain health. Research is inconclusive on which sustained fasting approach is best. Many recommend eating windows ranging from eight to twelve hours, and some suggest even longer. If you're considering fasting, consult a health care professional to tailor the practice to your needs and ensure it aligns with any underlying health conditions.

In short, establishing a regular eating pattern within a defined window, finishing meals earlier, and giving your body adequate time to rest and regenerate can provide physical and mental benefits, but balance and personalisation are key.

With the foundations laid for how everyday food choices shape your energy, mood, and gut health, Chapter 15 will explore the evidence and strategies that show how food can bolster mental fortitude, resilience, and general wellbeing.

After all that food, it's time to get things moving—literally. In the next chapter, we shift focus to Action: how the sense of touch, movement, and even temperature shape your wellbeing. You'll discover how to work with these physical sensations to feel energised, grounded, and bring clarity to your daily life.

CHAPTER 9.
ACTION

How touch and movement influence your day

Sean sighs as he steps into the warm shower after a weights session. The heat eases his muscles, which are slightly sore, but in a good way. He is relaxed and content. Later, as he sinks into bed, pulling the thick duvet around him, Sean feels enveloped in comfort and calm, a perfect end to his day.

Now, imagine the opposite: a pulled muscle from exercise, a lukewarm shower thanks to a faulty water heater, and a stiff, rough towel waiting for you. Instead of relaxation, the discomfort would result in frustration, making it difficult to unwind. These contrasting experiences show how physical sensory factors shape our emotions and wellbeing, often without us registering the influence they have.

The sense of touch, diverse movement modalities, and sensitivity to temperature are often overlooked pillars of wellbeing. These sensory experiences work through the somatosensory system and are deeply woven into our mental and physical health.[1] Action is not just about doing; it's about physically experiencing the world through skin, muscle, and temperature, and understanding how to use these elements to energise, calm, or restore ourselves.

In this chapter, we'll focus on the tangible Actions of touch and movement, physical elements of daily life that we can actively influence.

By contrast, temperature is a more ambient and passive sensation, something we typically experience and respond to, rather than initiate. For this reason, it is explored separately in Chapter 16.

Let's begin with the tactile world at our fingertips.

✳ Touch ✳

Our senses are so intertwined with our emotions that we frequently use them to describe feelings and cognitive actions. This is especially so with the sense of touch. Terms like 'rough patch', 'soft spot', 'painful experience', or 'to grasp an idea', are just some examples. Such phrases exist in many languages, underscoring how universal the link between touch and emotion is.

The personal touch

Your sensory profile intertwines with your culture and lived experiences to shape your touch preferences. Seekers thrive on physical connection, from hugs to high-fives. Others, like Avoiders, may shy away from physical contact, finding handshakes or hello kisses uncomfortable. These preferences even extend to our interactions with objects and materials; some adore the feel of cosy weighted blankets, while others prefer crisp, cool sheets. For instance, I love cotton bedding, but my husband swears by flannel.

Recognising your touch preferences can enrich your life. Imagine slipping into a soft sweater and unconsciously smiling as your hands glide over the sleeves. This experience creates a sense of comfort and relaxation. But how do we register an object as pleasant to touch? For example, we don't 'ooh' and 'ahh' when we pick up a piece of cardboard. The difference lies in how our brains interpret touch signals.

What the brain 'feels'

Our palms and soles are free of hair, which makes them ideal for assessing texture, vibration, and pressure.[2,3] For instance, when you feel something rough, your brain processes the sensation based on the pressure points activated on your skin.[4] This intricate system allows us to interpret whether an object feels pleasurable, protective, or potentially dangerous.

The emotional side of touch

Touch isn't just about physical sensations; it triggers emotional responses too. This is because hairy skin contains receptors that send signals to the limbic system.[5] This explains why a massage can release oxytocin, reduce stress, and leave you feeling euphoric.[6]

Even the hairless skin on our palms can create positive feelings through memory association. Think how you might smile as you hold a soft toy, or the sense of release you might feel as you sink into a plush couch. These sensation memories are influencing your emotions in the current moment.[7]

Research confirms that touch really does have the power to calm and comfort us. For instance, slow, steady stroking of the arm can lower heart rates and evoke pleasant emotions, even when performed by a stranger.[8] This suggests that touch doesn't need to be intimate or familiar to have a profound effect.

It's possible that when you're highly stressed, you don't want to be touched at all. This could be a symptom of an elevated fight-or-flight response, where even well-meaning actions feel overwhelming and intrusive. It's like the body is saying, 'I'm just too exhausted to handle the experience.' But even in these scenarios there can come a point when a silent, non-judgemental hug can do a world of good.

The silent language of touch

Touch speaks when words fall short. Imagine comforting an upset friend, not with solutions or advice, but with a reassuring hand on their shoulder. This simple gesture can bridge emotional gaps, offering support when logical reasoning might fail.

Human touch is so powerful because it's our first sense of comfort and connection as babies. It releases oxytocin, fostering bonds that make life seem easier and more enjoyable, a survival mechanism that still holds true today.

When human touch is absent, we experience 'touch deprivation', which can heighten stress and negatively impact mental and physical health.[9] Regular, meaningful touch can improve immune function, enhance sleep, and reduce cortisol levels, reinforcing its importance for overall wellbeing.[10]

Those who prefer minimal human contact can still benefit from tactile experiences. Weighted blankets, soft slippers, or a pet's fur can provide calming sensations. For example, a study showed that hugging a pillow while talking to a stranger on the phone reduced cortisol and a sense of stress more effectively than a conversation alone.[11]

A lack of human touch can exacerbate poor health and create a sense of loneliness.[12] So what does this mean for people who live alone?

A sense of belonging

Loneliness can be experienced by those who live with others as well as those who live alone. Touch isn't a cure-all to loneliness, but a conscious focus on touch can make a difference. Beyond contact with a loved one or friends, the sensation of textures and certain objects can also reduce stress and improve mood. This means we should all create opportunities for positive touch experiences.

The first step is to be aware of your own touch likes and dislikes. Here are some practical considerations:

- **Home:** Pay attention to how you respond to different materials and textures in your home. Do you have some that you don't like? Could you switch these for more pleasing fabrics? For example, would you benefit from items like throws, cushions, or weighted blankets? You might even splash out on more comfortable furniture. At the very least, bedding should be comfortable and comforting. Establish a routine of changing into relaxing clothes at the end of the day. This sends a signal to your brain that it is also time for your mind to relax.
- **Comfort beyond aesthetics:** Don't underestimate the power of materials and textures to soothe you. When we are down, we are more emotionally affected by the feel of an object than the look of it.[13] There are two key theories about this: first, it is thought to link back to when our ancestors faced threats and instinctively sought security in closeness,[14] and secondly, when we have a sense of danger, the awareness of our immediate surroundings is heightened.[15]
- **Pets:** If it's feasible, consider adopting a pet, not just for companionship, but for the benefits of touch. Stroking a dog, cat, or rabbit, for example, can lower stress and bring a sense of calm and joy. Some people find it rewarding to volunteer at animal shelters. This can provide the benefits of owning a pet while also helping and engaging with others. It is also a great way to self-administer a Happy DOSE.
- **Personal reset:** Simple techniques like placing a hand on your heart or gently rubbing your arms can reduce cortisol levels and create a sense of safety.[16]
- **Professional touch:** A massage, manicure, or even a haircut can provide tactile comfort. These activities don't need to be high-end or take hours to relieve stress and improve mood.

Culture

Touch varies widely across cultures. In some Asian and Arabic communities, men holding hands is a common display of platonic affection, while Western men may reserve such gestures for romantic partners and may prefer to bear hug, slap arms and backs, and ruffle the hair of male friends.

Even within cultures, individual comfort levels differ. Sensory preferences, along with our upbringing and experiences, shape how we engage with touch.[17] For example, I found the cheek kisses of Australia's Italian and Greek communities a culture shock when I first arrived, but I've since grown to appreciate them—well, most of the time.

Touch also has practical implications in social and professional settings. A firm handshake, a pat on the back, or even a light touch on the arm can foster connection and influence how others perceive us. Research shows that people tend to find others more agreeable if there is some form of accepted physical contact, even in situations with strangers such as a customer and shop assistant.[18] If the physical contact seems appropriate, we can't help but be impacted by the smallest of gestures.

Many people feel uneasy about any physical contact at work. A touch on the arm after a funny joke could be an uncomfortable moment for someone. I always found it difficult to know how to greet a colleague I hadn't seen for some time; should we shake hands, say hi, or do the cheek kiss? I've blown it several times; my hand has gone out when they have wanted to give me a quick hug, and I've ended up planting a real kiss on some cheeks without meaning to. Awkward.

Social contact boundaries are there to make people safe and comfortable, which is a good thing. We just need to make sure we get the benefits of touch in our social settings and through materials in our home.

If you are fortunate to benefit from a hug, it has been shown that a ten- to twenty-second hug eases sadness, reduces a sense of fatigue, and boosts the immune system![19] That is powerful, so if it feels right to you, embrace the embrace.

Children and the importance of touch

Touch is a vital part of a child's development, influencing their emotional, social, and cognitive wellbeing. Professor Tiffany Field, a leading researcher in this area, has shown that touch, including gentle massage, enhances neurological development, weight gain, and cognitive abilities in premature infants.[20] Further research by Field suggests that cultures where adolescents engage in more physical affection, such as hugging, leaning in, or casual touch, tend to report lower levels of peer aggression. In contrast, reduced social touch, particularly during adolescence, may be linked to higher levels of verbal and physical aggression and difficulty with emotional regulation over time.[21]

The importance of touch in childhood is so profound that its absence can lead to delayed development and long-term emotional challenges.[22]

Simple, everyday actions, such as cuddling or even a friendly hand on a shoulder, can help children feel safe and connected. These physical gestures support the release of oxytocin, which is vital for building secure emotional attachments. Daily affectionate touch has the power to bolster a child's sense of connection and security, which in turn helps them thrive developmentally and emotionally.[23]

Complementary therapies: Exploring the benefits

Touch-based complementary therapies offer practical and accessible ways to support wellbeing. Massage is a well-established starting point, with studies showing it can reduce cortisol levels, enhance sleep quality, and promote a deeper sense of calm.[24]

Massages using moderate pressure and slower strokes are particularly effective. Physiological effects can include lowered blood pressure, a slower heart rate, and an increase in theta brainwaves associated with deep relaxation. Techniques such as Swedish massage often focus on common tension areas like the neck, shoulders, and back. These methods not only release muscular tightness but also activate the vagus nerve, which plays a key role in calming the nervous system. Overall, a moderate pressure massage can leave you both physically soothed and emotionally uplifted.

Massages are commonly provided in spa environments. Spas intentionally create a multi-sensory environment that amplifies a sense of relaxation.[25] Besides the Action of the massage, you're greeted by ambient Acoustics; essential oil Aromas fill the spaces and are used in treatments; Aurora low lighting and calming colours relax you; and herbal teas stimulate your sense of Appetite. The interplay of the senses creates an inviting and tranquil Atmosphere. Smart!

While massage is now firmly in the mainstream of the wellness industry, some other popular touch-based therapies, such as reflexology and acupressure, incorporate aspects of traditional Chinese medicine (TCM), particularly the concept of meridians. These refer to a network of invisible pathways or channels that transport what TCM refers to as the life energy, or qi, throughout the body. According to TCM, there are twelve main meridians, each corresponding to an internal organ (such as the liver, heart, lungs, etc).[26]

Reflexology targets the feet, hands and sometimes the ears, while acupressure focuses more broadly on meridian points. The aim is to restore qi and bring balance and harmony to bodily functions.[27] While evidence on their clinical efficacy is not considered reliably effective in Western medicine, many people report feeling relaxed and invigorated after sessions. At the very least, they may benefit from the massage-like touch experience.

Tactile reset techniques such as tapping (also known as emotional freedom technique, or EFT) involve rhythmic tapping on pressure points while repeating positive affirmations.[28] The location of the tapping has traditionally followed the meridian points in Chinese medicine.[29] As with reflexology and acupressure, study results about the efficacy of this technique are mixed. Some believe that any positive effects achieved likely come from the visualisation and phrase repetition aspects of the treatment.

While scientific findings vary across therapies, there is consistent evidence that touch itself has tangible benefits for reducing stress and improving wellbeing. The important thing is to find what works best for you.

As with any therapy, you should only seek treatment with someone who is qualified. Whatever you try, if you feel unwell, always consult a medical practitioner and inform them of any treatments you are receiving. A holistic approach can only be effective when people providing care have all the relevant information.

✱ Movement ✱

Think back to the last time you moved with purpose. Maybe it was a morning run, a walk in the park, or even dancing in your kitchen to music. Movement is not only about physical fitness; it's an emotional and cognitive reset button that helps us navigate stress, find focus, and connect with ourselves and others.

From traditional exercise to creative expression, movement serves as a bridge between body and mind. The good news is you don't need to be a fitness fanatic to strengthen your mental fortitude and resilience.

Motion creates emotion

Movement activates multiple systems in the body and brain that influence emotions and thought processes. For example, a Happy DOSE can be stimulated in response to movement and this helps to reduce stress, elevate mood, and improve focus.[30]

Physical activity also boosts neuroplasticity, the brain's ability to adapt and rewire itself in response to challenges. For instance, regular exercise has been shown to increase the size of the hippocampus, the region associated with learning and memory.[31] Let's look at different Actions you can take to benefit you on a day-to-day basis.

Repetitive movements

Repetitive movements such as walking, swimming, or rowing have a unique ability to quiet the mind and induce a meditative state. These activities create rhythmic patterns that focus attention and soothe the nervous system, much like a mantra in meditation.

Studies suggest that walking, in particular, enhances problem-solving and creativity. For instance, a Stanford University study found that participants who walked were 60 per cent more likely to generate creative ideas compared to those who sat.[32] This effect is attributed to the stimulation of the brain as it processes the rhythm of movement. Walking, being a slower form of movement, creates a rhythmic pattern that facilitates a calming and reflective mental state, thereby enhancing your thought processes and problem-solving capabilities.

You can access these benefits with a simple fifteen-minute walk. Personally, I find walking or jogging extremely beneficial for creative thinking and just feeling more positive. I've always said that walking is good for the soul. It's nice to know the science validates the benefits, if not my metaphor.

Regular exercise: Building the stress muscle

Aerobic exercise: Increasing your heart rate creates physical stress that triggers noradrenaline and adrenaline.[33] These hormones boost alertness and deliver a surge of energy. When aerobic activity lasts for around thirty minutes, cortisol also rises, not in a harmful way, but as a means to sustain energy during exertion.[34] We can experience a Happy DOSE too; dopamine rewards us for the effort, serotonin 'thanks' us for the long-term physical health, and endorphins help relieve pain by giving us a euphoric feeling. When we connect with others through any form of group exercise, we can also stimulate oxytocin. With consistent aerobic exercise, your brain starts to reframe the physical signs of effort, such as, a pounding heart, faster breathing, sweat, and even sore muscles, as part of a positive, life-enhancing experience rather than a threat. In essence, you're rewiring your response to stress.

Resistance training, like lifting weights or using your body weight, similarly stresses the body and can induce an aerobic effect. Pushing through challenging movements stimulates dopamine, while the discomfort can trigger a wave of endorphins that leave you feeling strong and euphoric. This type of exercise can increase confidence and improve mental resilience.[35]

Remember, your body doesn't differentiate between physical and psychological stress when activating the stress response. The same neural pathways are involved, the same surge of adrenaline, the same rise in cortisol. But with regular physical training, your nervous system learns to respond and recover more efficiently. It gets fitter, not just physically, but also emotionally. So when you face everyday stressors like deadlines, conflict, or uncertainty, your body and brain are better equipped to bounce back. Think of aerobic exercise as training your 'stress muscle', increasing your capacity to handle life's challenges with more resilience and mental fortitude.

Aerobic intensity: A simple way to gauge whether you're exercising at high or moderate intensity is to use the 'talk test'. If you can talk with some effort but can't sing while exercising, the activity is moderate in intensity. If you can only say a few words before needing to catch your breath, you're working at a vigorous intensity.

If you feel that your aerobic fitness is low, don't forget that walking is still very beneficial. Besides the cognitive benefits already outlined, walking offers a change of scene to help clear the mind and gather your thoughts, especially if you focus on something outside of yourself. This can interrupt a negative thought pattern, even if you're only gazing at front yards or shop windows.[36]

If exercising outside the house is challenging, look for online exercise that you enjoy. This includes dancing, which has been shown to improve cognitive ability more than walking.[37] The point is to move for your mind. Spending your day at a desk and your night on a couch will only exacerbate your potential to feel sluggish and stressed.

Mind–body movements: Bridging calm and cognitive growth

Movements that blend physical effort with mindful intention, such as yoga, tai chi, and Pilates, offer unique benefits for mental and emotional health. Yoga in particular focuses on aligning breath with motion and involves an element of strength training, creating a harmonious connection between the body and mind. Being mindful of your body's movement and sensations keeps you in the present moment. This can help to interrupt the stress cycle and start to break it.

Studies show that yoga reduces the stress hormone cortisol and increases GABA, a neurotransmitter associated with relaxation.[38] Tai chi has been linked to improvements in cognitive thinking, especially in older people,[39] while Pilates has been linked to better stress management and confidence.[40]

Slower, focused practices may be challenging for modern minds that are overstimulated with dopamine, but they could be the answer for those who want to experience more calm rather than agitation or perceived boredom driven by dopamine highs and lows.

The evidence is clear: whether it's aerobic activity or focused deliberate movements, regular exercise has been proven to reduce stress, anxiety, and even depression,[41] as well as improve cognitive function. Cultivating a list of activities you enjoy is one way to stay engaged and avoid the temptation to skip taking Action. But movement goes beyond formal exercise and includes other brain-healthy Actions that keep you mentally and emotionally energised.

Beyond exercise: Mind–body integration

Action extends to movements that cultivate a state of 'flow': a mental state where focus and creativity peak.

For example, writing allows you to process emotions and externalise worries. It's a way of organising mental clutter into something tangible and manageable. You will engage more cognitive thought processes if you write with your hand (this includes a digital pen), compared to typing.[42] Handwriting has been shown to stimulate alpha and theta waves, but typing doesn't do this as effectively.[43] Remember, alpha and theta waves support calm, clear and creative thinking associated with flow.

Different forms of writing can engage different thought processes as well:

- **Gratitude writing** promotes the release of dopamine and serotonin, enhancing happiness and wellbeing as you deliberately focus on details, even small ones, that were positive in your day. This has been linked to increased resilience and improved coping skills.[44] Best results have been found when writing in the morning and evening.
- **Expressive writing** might seem contradictory because it involves detailing frustrations and negative experiences, but this method helps to articulate and externalise issues. This can reorganise your thoughts and release bottled-up stress.
- **Creative writing** is another way to put your stress and negative thoughts aside and daydream with your words. For example, you might write a poem or a short story. This free-flow approach lets you explore your imagination and enjoy the escapism.[45]

I must confess that before I understood the cognitive power of writing on wellbeing, I was rather dismissive of terms of like 'journalling'. I had syrupy visuals in my head of somebody writing, *Dear diary*, and I saw it as a fluffy trend. However, the research, and personal experience, has now convinced me otherwise.

Mind mapping: When it comes to creative thinking, problem-solving, and memory recall, visualising and 'mind mapping' ideas can be highly effective, more so than traditional writing. This is thought to be due to its ability to engage different parts of the brain.[46]

Mind mapping is simply creating a diagram, outlined any way that works for you, with a key idea or problem at the centre. From here you, or a team, can identify and link related subtopics to build a picture of a situation. There really is something in the phrase 'A picture paints a thousand words.'

It's clear that relying solely on devices and keyboards can limit our creativity and problem-solving abilities. Writing, with its proven benefits for learning, memory, and critical thinking, isn't outdated—it's essential. To enhance our thinking even further, both personally and professionally, we should embrace visual tools like mind mapping and vision boards, which help us better understand and navigate complex situations.

Here are some other Actions that can relax your body and mind.

Controlled deep breathing: Different techniques are common in practices like yoga, mindfulness, and meditation. They can help combat shallow unconscious breathing, which can form part of the stress response. Controlled breathing aids relaxation because it stimulates the vagus nerve.[47] This can reduce stress hormones. By concentrating on your breath, you also stay in the moment instead of your thoughts.

It's interesting how breathing, meditation, and mindfulness, once viewed as 'alternative' or purely spiritual in the West, are now mainstream and recommended for a healthy lifestyle. You can find them taught in schools and corporate settings. They are another example of ancient sensory practices that people across the world have long benefited from but took some time for Western science to validate.

One breathing technique you could try is box breathing. This is a simple technique to employ as part of your daily routine, such as winding down before bed or helping you to alleviate a sense of overwhelm or a creative block. Here's how it's done:
- Inhale deeply for a count of four.
- Hold the breath for four counts.
- Exhale slowly for four counts.
- Hold again for four counts.

Hobbies: These are activities that are fun and engaging without being stressful. They allow you to take a mental break from anything negative in your life. It could be cooking, reading fiction, seeing a show, doing woodwork, learning something like a language, or even colouring in pictures. Colouring in repeated patterns, such as mandalas, can be quite therapeutic; beyond any spiritual reason, the brain likes repeated patterns because they are easy to interpret. More about this in the Atmosphere chapter.

Forest bathing (*shinrin-yoku*): this Japanese practice from the 1980s is designed to counter stress and depression, inspired by traditional concepts like *yugen* (awareness of beauty), *komorebi* (sunlight through leaves), and *wabi-sabi* (appreciating imperfection). This sensory-focused activity involves observing your surroundings, engaging deliberately and slowly with what you see, hear, smell, and touch. It provides benefits like improved mood, reduced stress, and enhanced brain function, thanks in part to better air quality. While not everyone has access to forests, the principles can be applied in parks, gardens, or tree-lined streets to enjoy similar benefits.

Fidgeting: 'Stop fidgeting!' is a refrain many of us heard growing up, yet research suggests these small, seemingly unconscious movements have surprising benefits. Fidgeting can improve focus and reduce stress, particularly for those with ADHD or high anxiety. These movements may help discharge nervous energy, allowing the mind to stay engaged.[48]

Fidgeting could even be an innate coping mechanism, one many of us suppress due to societal norms. Now fidgeting is recognised as an effective way that people may be able to maintain focus and reduce tension. If it works for you, don't hesitate to spin that fidget device, squeeze that stress ball, and jiggle your leg (perhaps not all at once, though!).

* The case for taking micro-breaks *

In our productivity-driven world, we're often encouraged to *push through*, to keep working even when our focus fades or stress builds. But working through fatigue or frustration is often counterproductive. Short, intentional breaks can actually improve concentration, uplift mood, and help regulate emotions.

The most effective breaks involve a change in sensory input. A brisk walk, gentle stretches, or standing by a window and taking slow, controlled breaths can reset your nervous system and boost mental clarity. These small Actions aren't just pauses, or a waste of time, they're strategic resets that enhance cognitive performance.

* Action at any age: The younger, the better *

Students, especially those who move away from home, face stressful episodes with exams, new living arrangements, perhaps poor eating and sleeping habits, along with the challenge of finding new friends and communities. A review of studies concluded that moderate or high-intensity aerobic exercise and yoga could reduce this anxiety.[49] Because physical activity enhances cognitive function, improves memory retention, and boosts focus, children who are physically active are more likely to feel capable, balanced, and confident than those leading mostly sedentary lives.[50]

The key to sustaining movement at any age is to find actions you enjoy. If some of these can be with others, you'll reap an extra dose of oxytocin and serotonin as you connect with your 'tribe'. Here's a recap on the key benefits of exercise and how to access them:[51]

- Aerobic exercise: Improves mood and energy, lowers anxiety, and sharpens focus.
- Strength training: Boosts confidence, builds resilience, and reduces the risk of depression.
- Yoga and stretching: Enhances mindfulness and reduces cortisol, which supports calmness and clarity. It is particularly effective at reducing anxiety.
- For adults, the WHO recommends at least 150 minutes of moderate aerobic activity weekly or 77–150 minutes of more vigorous

Chapter 9. Action

activity, or a combination of moderate and vigorous activity. It also recommends two strength-training sessions a week.[52]
- Repetitive actions, even walking, especially in nature, can relax the mind and boost cognitive thinking, including creativity.
- Include non-exercise Actions such as writing and hobbies to bring calm and contentment into your life.

Figure 9.1 lists a few ways to embrace regular exercise. If you get bored, move on to something else. Never stop taking Action.

Aerobic rhythmic	Aerobic complex	Resistance	Focused and calming
Running	Gym classes	Resistance bands	Tai chi
Cycling	Dancing	CrossFit	Yoga
Swimming	Boxing	Lifting weights	Meditation practices
Nordic walking	Pilates	Specific yoga poses	Pilates
Walking and hiking	Rock climbing	Reformer Pilates	Walking and hiking
Rowing	CrossFit	Rock climbing	Chanting
Stair climbing	Mountain bike riding	Rowing	Controlled breathing
Elliptical training	HIIT (high-intensity interval training)	HIIT (high-intensity interval training)	Muscle relaxation exercises

Figure 9.1. Exercises to support mental fortitude and resilience

After exploring Chapter 16, which focuses on the third somatosensory action, temperature, you will have seen how touch, movement, and temperature can enhance your sense of wellbeing.

Now, it's time to consider how elements of your environment, the layout of your spaces, and the objects that fill them work together to create an atmosphere that influences your overall sense of wellbeing.

CHAPTER 10.
ATMOSPHERE

Understanding our instinctive response to spaces

Stan is on autopilot as he pulls into his street and parks his car. Exhausted, all he wants is to switch off. The moment he opens his front door, a smile crosses his face; Otto is looking up at him, wagging his tail. Unfortunately, the joy is fleeting; entering the open-plan living area, Stan's mood shifts as he notices the kitchen bench splattered with pasta sauce and piled high with dishes. The open dishwasher, with its empty trays, only heightens his frustration. He can feel his heartbeat quicken and an eruption of anger spills out. His daughter looks up from her phone, utterly confused by his outburst. What's his problem?

This scene is familiar to many of us who share our living spaces with partners, family members, or flatmates. Our homes are an intersection of varying sensory needs and preferences, which can make it challenging to create an environment where we can truly relax, focus, or feel inspired. In Stan's case, he desperately needed a sense of order to unwind and recharge after a stressful day. His daughter, however, felt perfectly comfortable in a state of disorder. She might be a Bystander who doesn't register the mess and therefore isn't bothered by it. This disconnect in sensory preferences can lead to tension and frustration, making it essential to consider spaces that support everyone's wellbeing.

Balancing different sensory profiles can be tricky, but it is possible. By recognising the profiles of others and by following certain design principles, we can create interiors that support us while minimising friction between household members.

Regardless of sensory profiles or aesthetic tastes, the most fundamental design principles that influence our sense of wellbeing are found in nature, because that is where our sensory wiring was refined over millions of years.

Humans evolved in natural environments, relying on cues like light, airflow, and spatial arrangement for survival. These instincts subconsciously guide how we respond to modern spaces as well. Today, with many people living in cities and removed from natural environments, there is an increased awareness and appreciation that elements of nature should be brought intentionally into our surroundings to reduce stress, enhance focus, and foster creativity.

Beyond house plants and green paint, ongoing research in human behaviour and design continues to identify elements of building structures and interiors that can improve the quality of our lives. This chapter explores some of these findings so you can understand your innate response to a space, which until now, you may have struggled to articulate beyond vague but common expressions such as, 'I don't know, something just doesn't feel right.' With these insights, you will move closer to pinpointing what you need, and don't need, to create a great Atmosphere. So, let's start at the beginning.

* Instinctive aesthetics *

Our ancestors survived by recognising environments that provided safety, sustenance, and spaces to rest and revitalise. Understanding these responses to nature has been a key research field in environmental psychology. One influential theory is the 'habitat theory', developed by Gordon Orians in the early 1980s. This theory suggests that humans have an innate preference for open, meadow-like spaces with scattered trees, like an African savanna, because these landscapes provided our ancestors with food, water, and shelter and were relatively easy to move around in.[1] Today this theory is commonly referred to as the 'savanna hypothesis'.

Building on this, environmental psychologists Rachel and Stephen Kaplan developed the 'information processing theory'. They proposed that our attraction to certain environments is based more on cognitive assessments, that is, how our minds interpret and make sense of the surroundings, rather than just instinctive reactions.[2]

This doesn't mean they diminished the value of aesthetic reactions. Instead, the Kaplans believed we learned to like environments and find them pleasing when they offered opportunities for survival, and this encouraged exploration. Therefore, we use both aesthetic judgement and rational thinking to evaluate the suitability of spaces.[3] This is another example of our sensory wiring evolving to trigger a Happy DOSE if a behaviour benefited our survival.

Kaplan and Kaplan developed the preference matrix to highlight the features humans are drawn to because they aid survival and development.[4] This research significantly influences landscape, architecture, and interior design today. To understand how these principles apply, let's see how they translate from our ancestral times to modern life:

- **Coherence:** A sense of order and harmony. 'Things fit together and I can comprehend what's going on without much effort.'
- **Complexity:** Visual interest and stimulation. 'There is a good mix of environments here. I can find shelter, water and a variety of food sources.'
- **Legibility:** Clear organisation, landmarks and predictability. 'I can see how the environment is laid out; I know where I am and can move around easily.'
- **Mystery:** The promise of discovery and exploration. 'I wonder what's down that winding track, or beyond that mountain range. It looks enticing.'

Instincts for interior spaces

Coherence
- Does anything feel out of place or jarring?
- Are the shapes, colours, and materials in harmony, or do they clash?
- Is the layout logical and easy to work with, supporting how you use the space?

When a room is coherent, your mind can relax and focus on what matters. For example, a bedroom with a consistent colour palette and balanced furniture arrangement encourages calm, whereas mismatched tones or cluttered layouts may create unnecessary mental strain because they lack clarity. A lack of coherence would have been one of the triggers to upset Stan when he got home; pasta sauce and dirty plates 'don't belong' on a benchtop.

Complexity
- Is the space too bare or overly busy?
- Does it feel underwhelming, interesting, or overwhelming?
- Are there engaging elements, like textures (a soft throw, a woven rug) or patterns that create variety without chaos?

Complexity adds stimulation and interest. A living room might feel inviting with a mix of natural materials, such as a wooden coffee table paired with textured cushions, while a wall with bold artwork offers visual engagement with a colour scheme that complements the furniture. The goal is to strike a balance that suits your sensory preferences.

Legibility
- Is it clear how to navigate the space without confusion or effort? For example, are pathways unobstructed, and does the furniture placement guide movement naturally?

- Is there a clear focal point, like a piece of art, a rug, or a fireplace, that helps you orient yourself?

Legibility makes a space intuitive. For instance, in a kitchen, a well-lit counter with easily accessible items that are frequently used can increase the satisfaction of cooking, while a cluttered or poorly laid out kitchen can feel chaotic and tiring, and increase frustration.

Mystery
- Does the space spark curiosity and invite exploration, or does it lack intrigue and feel uninspired?
- Are there design elements that encourage a second glance, like layered lighting, partially obscured views, or unique designs, materials and textures?

Mystery creates interest and excitement. Even in open-plan spaces, you can introduce mystery with subtle design choices, like a glimpse of greenery through a window, an obscured reading nook behind a screen, or layered decor that draws the eye. In a home, a hallway with art could lead you towards the next room.

By reviewing your spaces with the framework of the preference matrix, you can start to understand why certain areas may feel supportive and engaging and others do not. This way of thinking has been at the forefront of many interior design styles.

✣ Modern-day benefits of nature-inspired design ✣

Designers from many disciplines are focused on incorporating the proven health and wellbeing benefits of spending time in nature. They understand the sensory overload of city living such as noise, and air and light pollution, which can be layered on top of the cognitive overload from 24/7 news and social media and an always-on work culture. All of this occurs within complex city environments where people may lack access to parks, backyards or national parks that can actively reduce stress, both emotionally and physically, making people feel less anxious or angry.[5] This is why translating restorative elements of nature into our homes can make a significant difference to our wellbeing. Fortunately, research confirms that even viewing natural environments like grass or a few plants can help our minds recover from mental fatigue.[6] Images of nature can also benefit wellbeing; though not as effective as the real thing, they can make a difference.[7]

One Western design approach that has embraced lessons from environmental psychology is biophilic design.

Biophilic design: Reflecting nature indoors

Biophilic design merges our affinity for nature with practical interior solutions to improve the quality of life within built-up environments. Key features include:

Direct nature experiences[8]

- **Light:** Harness natural light for energy and circadian support. Use artificial lighting with adjustable warmth for functionality.
- **Airflow and temperature:** Use fans and open windows to emulate natural breezes, enhancing air quality where feasible. Understand temperature control to support cognitive clarity and reduce stress.
- **Plants:** Create a sense of calm and improve air quality. For some, though, they may bring unwanted humidity to a space.
- **Water features:** Fountains or aquariums can create tranquillity through sound and visuals. This may not be beneficial indoors if there are already issues with damp and humidity.
- **Fire:** Candles or fireplaces evoke warmth and relaxation. Today, indoor fires are discouraged from an environmental and health perspective, but enclosed electric alternatives can still provide warmth and create an atmosphere.[9]

Indirect nature experiences[10]

- **Natural materials and textures:** Natural materials add a tactile element, such as soft, comforting fabrics like wool or cotton, or grounding elements like wood grains. People typically use hard materials like wood, bamboo, metal, stone, slate, and marble for floors, walls, and furniture. Natural materials can be fashioned in any number of ways to help shape the atmosphere you want. For example, natural wood creates a relaxed, rustic feel, while lacquered wood lends a more luxurious, elegant look. Softer materials like rattan, jute, wool, cork, and leather can be used for soft furnishings such as seating, curtains and rugs, as well as on walls for decorative accents and improved acoustics.
- **Organic patterns:** Forms found in nature can be calming and restorative as we associate them, even subconsciously, with being in nature. Fractal patterns repeat the same pattern at varying scales, making them easy for the brain to process. A snowflake is one example of this. Any repeating pattern, such as honeycombs, leaf veins, or dragonfly wings, can have this effect; the simplicity allows the brain to relax. In homes, this can be reflected in simple repeating pattern wallpaper, or slatted wood dividing a room space, mimicking trees in a forest.

Shapes

- Rounded and curved shapes can promote calmness and joy. Think babies, a smiling face, and the sun. They are also the opposite of sharp.[11]
- Sharp angles can heighten stress. This might be because in nature, sharp objects reflected danger: animal horns, sticks, or jagged rocks could all inflict harm. For this reason, these shapes don't often feature in nature-inspired designs, which aim to relax and rejuvenate people.
- Triangles, a form of structured straight lines, can symbolise dynamic energy, evoking mountain ranges or leaves.

- Wavy lines suggest water and sand dunes, adding a sense of fluidity and creativity.
- Spirals, while also dynamic, suggest contemplation and rest because of their curved, inward repeated nature. In Māori culture, a young fern frond with its spiral shape is used to symbolise perpetual movement, such as a journey, a new beginning or growth. It is known as a koru. Spirals can also be seen in the form of galaxies, which are dynamic and can fill us with wonder and awe.
- Squares and rectangles reflect solidity and sturdiness, like rocks.
- Columns reflect strength and support, like tree trunks.

Colours

There are obvious associations of blues with the sky and water, or green found in lush landscapes, and browns reflecting the sturdiness and protection provided by trees. However, nature's colour palette is vast; you only need look at a vibrant bunch of flowers to realise this. Consider too the rich hues found in marble or granite, or the striking mix of feathers on tropical birds. The key is to select colours that support you in your space. For example, in a bedroom, lighter, tinted colours are typically more restful to the mind.

Colour can affect temperature perception as well, not just mood.[12] Chapters 5 and 12 explore colour in more depth.

Imagery of nature

Nature can appear in our interior spaces through artwork, photographs, and design elements like nature-inspired rugs, wallpapers, and curtains. Including nature imagery is key to creating a calm, restorative environment in spaces without a green outlook.

The more we live apart from nature, the more we miss out on its rejuvenating benefits. This means design principles like biophilic design are not fads, but essential schools of thought that we need to embrace for our wellbeing.

Chapter 10. Atmosphere

✶ Design for wellbeing ✶

Merging our affinity for nature with practical interior solutions is not a new concept; it has roots in design principles used across cultures for centuries.

For example, the Alhambra, built in the thirteenth century in Granada, Spain, is a stunning example of biophilic design. This architectural masterpiece incorporates natural elements like water, light, and airflow to create tranquil and harmonious spaces. Intricate patterns inspired by nature, such as repeating hexagonal motifs from beehives and floral designs, enhance the sense of calm and balance.[13] These features were also common in ancient Arabic spaces designed for learning, where the soothing environment supported focus and creativity.[14]

Similarly, renowned architect Frank Lloyd Wright championed the idea of harmonising buildings with their natural surroundings. His designs featured flowing spaces, earthy colours, and abundant use of natural materials like wood and stone to foster a deep connection to the outdoors. He died in 1959, but his philosophy of integrating people, land, and architecture remains influential today.[15]

These examples highlight that the principles of biophilic design have long been recognised as vital to our wellbeing and will continue to evolve as our needs change.

Today, nature-led design is valued across segments of society. For example, biophilic design has been embraced in homes, workplaces, schools, and health care settings because of its effects on wellbeing. This approach underpins the rewilding techniques that have become common in cities, where plants adorn buildings' walls and rooftops.

There are other approaches to design that are dedicated to improving how we live and work. Neuroarchitecture, for example, studies how building design affects brain function and emotional wellbeing. It considers sensory factors like lighting, acoustics, and spatial geometry to create environments that promote positive mental states.[16] Human-centred design is another; this approach prioritises the needs, desires, and limitations of the end user. It aims to make spaces not only functional but also emotionally satisfying.[17]

As approaches evolve, building design, materials, and interiors will increasingly prioritise the health and wellbeing of occupants through the sensory experience of a space, with nature continuing to serve as the benchmark.

You can find endless inspiration for your home through interior magazines and designers, manufacturers of paint, furniture or wallpaper, different cultures, and of course, high profile people. So how do you decide what's right for you?

✽ What is your design style? ✽

Our aesthetic tastes are a combination of our evolutionary survival instincts, where and how we grew up, and our sensory profiles.[18] However, many of us may not have had an opportunity to identify what aesthetic qualities make us feel relaxed, rejuvenated and so on, because we've gravitated to what's on trend or what we're familiar with. We may never have thought to question how the space around us influences our sense of wellbeing—until now.

In Chapter 17, we will expand on how design elements can be incorporated into spaces to improve wellbeing, including insights from other cultures. These examples will help you identify the features and elements that matter most to you.

With a sensory overview in place, it's time to explore how you can use each sense more deliberately to improve your mood, focus, energy, and resilience in everyday life.

Part Three:
Shape Your Sensory Experiences

✳✳✳

**Practical ways to enhance everyday life
through your senses**

CHAPTER 11.
ILLUMINATE YOUR WORLD

Brighten your day, naturally and artificially

While we are captivated by awe-inspiring auroras of coloured light in the night sky, we barely consider how natural and artificial light profoundly affect us every day.

In Chapter 5 we explored how natural and artificial light affect mood and overall wellbeing. This chapter offers practical insights to help you select and position lighting to suit your needs, whether it's creating focus in a study, relaxation in a bedroom, or balance in shared spaces. By understanding how to work with light, you can make thoughtful choices that support your daily activities and enhance your sense of wellbeing.

✶ Light sources ✶

Before delving into aspects of artificial light that support your sense of wellbeing, I cannot overstate the importance of natural light. Experiencing morning light, with its higher levels of blue light, plays an essential role in your day. It provides healthy doses of energy by elevating adrenaline and cortisol and helps maintain the health of your circadian rhythms.[1] It also stimulates the production of serotonin and endorphins, which support a positive mood.[2] It also stimulates vitamin D, low levels of which have been linked to fatigue and poor mood regulation.[3] Although optimal timing varies by location, you can generally benefit from a morning boost of blue light between 6 a.m. and 9 a.m., while the best time to stimulate vitamin D synthesis is close to noon.

If you're inside most of the day, try to step outside a few times for a couple of minutes. Besides taking a cognitive break, you can experience the re-energising effects of daylight. Weather permitting, daylight typically holds blue light through to the early afternoon.

When it comes to artificial light, LED (light-emitting diode) is fast becoming the most used type of light source. It's cost-effective, more environmentally friendly than older sources, and continues to advance in terms of light-wave quality and smart applications such as voice control and light-wave colour changes. It's also possible to dim LED lights, but if you have older light fittings with dimmers, first ensure they are compatible with LED lights.

When buying a light, see if the packaging shows the colour rendering index (CRI). This will tell you how close the colour of the light is to the same colour under natural daylight. A CRI of eighty is normal, while greater than ninety is excellent. Figure 11.1 outlines the most common light sources.

Light source	Overview
Incandescent bulbs	Phased out of production in most places. They are not energy or cost-efficient
Halogen	Used for spotlight and accent lighting. Think kitchens, bars, and outdoors. They are dimmable and more efficient than incandescent lights, but less efficient than LEDs. They can generate a lot of heat, but mimic natural light well
Fluorescent lamps and tubes	These are 70% more efficient than incandescent bulbs and have a longer lifespan. They contain mercury, so do not throw them away in the normal rubbish bin. They can flicker with dimmers
LED	The most energy-efficient light. LEDs use 90% less energy than incandescent or halogen lights. They emit very little heat and are measured in lumens and kelvins. The main issue is blue light emission, but this is improving as LEDs evolve

Figure 11.1. Light sources

Chapter 11. Illuminate Your World

* Lighting is personal *

There is no exact solution to improve lighting; it's more like balancing ingredients in a recipe. Light runs on a spectrum, so its effects shift gradually in the same way that carefully adding spices can subtly shift the flavours in a dish. The impact of artificial light also depends on the 'ingredients' you work with: factors like room size, natural light levels, and whether you use dimmers or light shades. This makes finding the 'right' lighting a mix of art and science.

Your sensory preferences play a significant role in determining which light temperature and brightness work best for you. For example, a small study found people selected various options within a range that was offered to them. The range spanned from 2,200 kelvins to 5,300 kelvins. The majority gravitated to around 3,400 kelvins with a high level of intensity/illumination (lux). This combination equates to a 'neutral' white light.[4]

Despite these variances, guidelines are still useful because they show ranges that tend to work well in different situations. They serve as a starting point to consider what could work best for you.

The guides below have been laid out using various scenarios to help you select lighting that supports your daily activities and overall wellbeing.

* Light behaviour guide *

Invigorating and uplifting

Natural daylight is unparalleled for its dynamic range, from the warm tones of morning to the cool brightness of midday. However, artificial lighting can provide effective alternatives when natural light isn't accessible.

- **Dim white light isn't enough:** Studies show that dim artificial white light fails to stimulate alertness or wakefulness.

- **Bright, cool white light:** Artificial light that mimics daylight (5,000K–6,500K) is invigorating and uplifting, particularly for those with SAD.
  - **Devices for SAD:**
    - Light boxes emitting 10,000 lux mimic bright white daylight. Their intensity means they are typically used for a limited timeframe due to possible side effects.
    - Alternatives include light-emitting glasses, visors, and lamps, which may be more convenient.
    - Tip: Consult a health care professional to select an effective device to avoid misuse or wasting your money.

Focus and clarity

Cooler and brighter light supports mental focus, making it ideal for task-oriented spaces.
- **Neutral white light (4,000K–5,000K)**
  - **Description:** Energising and suitable for concentration.
  - **Applications:** Common in open-plan offices, technical workspaces, brainstorming areas, and meeting rooms.
  - **Why it works:** Balances clarity and comfort.
- **Cool white light (5,000K–6,500K)**
  - **Description:** Crisp and energising, simulating bright natural daylight.
  - **Applications:** Ideal for detailed tasks, such as in art studios, laboratories, or spaces requiring precision.
  - **Tip:** Prolonged exposure may feel harsh or cause glare indoors. Use for short, focused tasks or specific work areas.
- **Specialised cool blueish-white light (6,500K+)**
  - **Description:** Extremely bright and crisp.
  - **Applications:** Best for specialised environments, like spotlighting products in retail or in medical research facilities.

Relaxed but alert

For spaces that require both relaxation and attentiveness, warm-to-neutral white light is the best choice.
- **Warm-to-neutral white light (3,500K–4,000K)**
  - **Description:** Visually comfortable with a balance of warm and cool tones.
  - **Applications:** Suitable for casual breakout areas, lunch rooms, client engagement spaces, and interview rooms.
  - **Why it works:** Encourages a calm, welcoming atmosphere while maintaining alertness.

Working late

Blue light from devices and office lighting can disrupt your circadian rhythm. To mitigate its effects, especially when working late, adopt these strategies:
- **Use blue-light filters**
  - Download apps for your laptop or set devices to 'night mode' (also known as 'dark mode').
  - Use screen covers or glasses with blue-light filtering.
- **Adjust lighting**
  - Use light bulbs around 3,000K–3,500K in lamps for late-night reading.
  - Choose e-reading devices with 'night mode' or colour temperature adjustments. E-ink readers emit significantly less blue light and are gentler on your eyes.

Relaxation and sleep preparation

Lighting can help transition your body and mind towards rest.
- **Warm light for relaxation (2,000K–3,000K)**
  - **Description:** Muted yellow and orange tones support mela-

tonin production and create a cosy atmosphere.
  - **Applications:** Ideal for bedside lamps, accent lighting, or evening activities.
  - **Tip:** Overhead lights with cooler tones (4,000K or higher) should be avoided at night.
- **Candlelight (1,900K)**
  - **Description:** Soft, amber tones for a soothing ambience.
  - **Tip:** Always extinguish candles before sleeping.
- **Night lighting**
  - Use low-kelvin, low-illumination lights (2,000K or below) with motion sensors to provide safe but unobtrusive lighting during the night.

∗ Home lighting guide ∗

Relaxation spaces

- **2,000K:** Mimics candlelight, perfect for creating a calming effect.
- **2,700K:** Provides a warm, relaxing ambience.
- **3,000–3,500K:** Offers a comfortable, warm white effect, suitable for reading or casual dining.

Bathroom

- **Ceiling light (4,000K):** Neutral white for general illumination and an invigorating start to the day.
- **Vanity light (4,000K–5,000K):** Neutral-to-cool white for precise tasks like makeup application or shaving. This range provides more accurate colour rendering and reduces shadows.
- **Accent light (3,000K):** Warm tones to create a spa-like, relaxing atmosphere.

Kitchen and eating areas

- **Cooking area (4,000K–5,000K):** Bright, cool white light for precise tasks.
- **Dining area (2,700K–3,000K):** Warm tones for a cosy, inviting dining experience.
- **Combined spaces (3,500K):** Dual-purpose lighting for eat-in kitchens without dedicated zones.

Study

- **4,000K:** Supports sustained computer work and reading with a calm, productive mood.
- **5,000K:** Suitable for detailed tasks, but prolonged use may cause eyestrain. Use task lights that can be repositioned or turned off.
- **3500K:** For late-night tasks, reduce the kelvin and intensity to avoid overstimulation. This could be achieved by using dimmers or even throwing a scarf over a lampshade.

∗ How lumens and kelvins combine to influence characteristics of light ∗

Lighting is highly versatile. Figure 11.2 shows how certain combinations of kelvins and lumens can optimise spaces for different purposes.

Lumens (approximate)	Kelvin	Colour description and lumen effect	Light effect guide	Location examples
1,000lm–1,500lm	10,000K+	Clear, intense blue-white light. Very cool and bright	Highly stimulating; mimics intense daylight; use cautiously to avoid disrupting circadian rhythm	Light box to treat seasonal affective disorder (SAD)

Lumens	Kelvin	Light description	Effect	Typical use
1,000lm–1,500lm	6,500K–7,500K	Crisp, cool white light (daylight at noon, very bright)	Promotes alertness; prolonged use may cause eye strain or reduce relaxation	Industrial workspaces, laboratories, detailed tasks
800lm–1,200lm	5,000K–6,500K	Bright, neutral-to-cool white light (morning sunlight)	Stimulating; ideal for task-focused environments or work requiring precision	Technical offices, warehouses, hospitals, car parks
800lm–1,000lm	4,000K–5,000K	Moderate brightness with neutral white light (daylight tone)	Efficient and focused; balances brightness and clarity for extended use	Offices, dedicated kitchens, bathroom vanities, libraries, schools, shops
600lm–800lm	2,700K–4,000K	Soft to moderate brightness, warm-to-neutral white light	Friendly and inviting; calming in lower ranges for social or casual environments	Eat-in kitchens, living rooms, reception areas, cafes
300lm–500lm	2,000K–2,700K	Dim, warm orange-white light (sunset or firelight glow)	Relaxing and intimate; enhances comfort and reduces stimulation for winding down	Living rooms, bedrooms
200lm–300lm	1,900K	Very dim, deep warm amber light (candlelight)	Soft ambient lighting; creates a calming, cosy atmosphere for restful spaces	Restaurants, spas
100lm–200lm	1,000K	Soft, warm, low red light (subtle glow)	Low red lighting; promotes sleep	Night-time use, spas, clubs

Figure 11.2. Kelvin and lumen light characteristics

✳ Lighting effects ✳

Where a light is positioned is just as important as the type of light it is. It will either enhance or disrupt the mood you want to create. For example, a cosy lounge could be achieved with a few lamps that have warm-kelvin bulbs. This means you don't need to put on overhead lighting, which may be bright and would destroy a relaxed atmosphere.

Designers generally recommend having at least two of the following lighting effects. This supports a variety of moods and functions within a single space.

General lighting: Also referred to as 'ambient lighting', this is your room's main source of light. Besides natural light, overhead lights, recessed and track lighting are some examples that fit this category.

Accent lighting: This is used to highlight features, like an actor spotlighted on a stage. Think architectural details, artwork, or a textured wall. It can also help with a sense of zoning while adding depth and intrigue.

Task lighting: Whether you're chopping vegetables or analysing a spreadsheet, a task light shines a focused beam to support precision and productivity. At home, lamps with movable heads work well for this purpose. In kitchens, direct overhead lighting is particularly effective for food preparation.

Combining these types of lighting ensures your space isn't just functional but also inviting and dynamic. A pro tip is to avoid using multiple lights in the same area at the same time if they have different kelvin ratings because this can confuse the eye and cause stress. The aim is to de-stress, not to complicate things.

Now it's time to consider how you can apply these insights in your own home.

WHAT MAKES SENSE TO YOU?

This section will appear at the end of every chapter in Part Three. I've created a free template guide for this section called 'Shaping Your Sensory Experiences'. You can access it under 'Total Sensory Wellbeing Resources' on my website, Nriched Living.

If you prefer, set aside a notebook or create a digital file called 'Total Sensory Wellbeing'. Either way, this is your opportunity to reflect on each sense, and to come up with practical considerations for your own life. Of course, you can choose to read through the book first and come back to this when it suits you.

To start, create a 'Room Review' section. I suggest focusing on just one space when you read this book for the first time. If you use a notebook, allocate a few pages to this section so you can add additional sketches.

Room Review

Create a basic sketch of your room's current layout. You can use simple shapes to represent the position of furniture, light fittings, windows, and doorways. They don't need to be accurate images. You could also use photos. The purpose is to help you assess the space.

As we review key sensory experiences within a space, it will be tempting to jump ahead to all the issues and possible solutions, but the goal is to break down what's happening one sense at a time. This will help you see your environment with fresh eyes to identify opportunities to improve your sense of wellbeing.

Room overview questions:

- **Activities:** Does the space serve multiple functions? List them all. For example, a living room could be a play area for young children in the day, a study for students at night, or a space for watching television, or for hobbies. Mark on the room layout where these activities take place

- **Mood and energy:** What feelings and behaviours do you need to support each of these actions? For example, if the purpose is work or study you may write 'calm and focused'.

Lighting-specific section:
- Write down the position of all the lights in the room, such as overhead, wall lights, or standing and table lamp lights.
- Consider the light quality and light position. Describe how well each light serves the function it is used for.
- Does any of the lighting force you to operate in a way that isn't ideal? For example, the dining table is the only space with good task lighting, so someone sits there to do a hobby while someone else is trying to work on their laptop. Hypothetically, would one of these tasks be easier to do elsewhere if adequate lighting were in place, either somewhere else in the same room or in a different room? Make a note of what currently prevents this from happening.
- Write down the kelvin or known light strength of each light source in the space. Is a light shade dulling the light intensity or changing the light effect? This is important to consider for future purchases.
- Use the Light Behaviour Guide to write down what you think the ideal kelvin range for each activity in the space could be.
- Are there other activities you would like to do in the space, but the lighting is preventing this? For example, you would like to read in the evenings, but the lights are inadequate or in the wrong position, so you either don't bother to read or go to the bedroom instead.

Overall, can you see opportunities to make improvements? Note these down under 'Lighting Potential Improvements'. Write them all down, even if they seem outlandish. These are your thoughts and ideas, not final decisions.

Some changes in lighting can be quick and fairly inexpensive.

> For example, you might try a warmer or cooler bulb to resolve an issue you have identified. If potential improvements require more money and time, I recommend waiting until you have read the whole book to see what other changes you may want to make and how everything can fit together in a cohesive way.
>
> I suggest creating Pinterest boards to seek inspiration and collate images. This could be in the form of separate boards for each sense, which you can compile into an overall Total Sensory Wellbeing board to bring your ideas to life.

With these illuminating insights in place, it's now time to add some colour to your life.

CHAPTER 12.
EMBRACE A COLOURFUL LIFE

Use colour for emotional and cognitive needs

When we interact with colour, our current emotions often dictate our response. A vibrant orange might energise you one day but feel overwhelming the next.[1] This variability is why it's essential to evaluate colour choices not only for their general effects but also for their suitability to your current state and sensory profile.

The colour descriptions below allow you to see the colour through the lens of nature, research, history, and culture. This will give you different perspectives to think more deeply about your response to colour.

If you disagree with some explanations, take this as an opportunity to explore why. Maybe you associate the colour with unpleasant memories. Perhaps the cultural meaning affects you. For example, people in the West typically see orange as a fun and vibrant colour, even if they don't want it all over their living room walls. However, many people in Northern Ireland may associate it with nearly thirty years of conflict in a period known as The Troubles. Another factor to consider is that people may dismiss the suitability of a colour in their home because they don't like wearing it.

The following colour insights should help you confirm your position on certain colours and possibly tempt you to broaden your palette.

✳ Blue ✳

Nature's palette and psychological effects: You smile as you walk on the beach. It's a beautiful day and the sky is bright blue. It's warm now, so you jump into the refreshing blue water and relish the coolness. The weightlessness of your body seems to release the weight on your mind. You zone out as you watch the waves form and roll in.

It's no wonder that variations of blue repeatedly top the list in colour preference surveys. In 2015, blue was the most preferred colour in a survey that covered ten countries across four continents.[2] Another survey conducted in 2017 across 100 countries found deep teal was the most preferred colour.[3] Teal combines blue and green. The appeal of blue is not new, as blue was also the favoured colour in an 1897 survey.[4] There will, of course, be cultural variances and changes of perception with time, but blue clearly has a significant effect on our sense of wellbeing.

A bright blue sky on a sunny morning boosts your energy and mood for the day by stimulating cortisol, serotonin, endorphins, and vitamin D. Blue water is soothing and life-giving. It seems as open and vast as the sky, and the rhythmic, fractal patterns of ocean waves have a calming effect on the mind. The vastness of the sky and water have driven our curiosity and spurred our imagination through the ages: 'What's up there?', 'What lies beyond or beneath this water?' 'What is beyond the blue horizon?' With its overall positive, calming, and inspiring effects, it's no wonder that people use blue in environments where they desire relaxation or inspiration, such as bedrooms and schools.

The blue we associate with the sky, water, and the horizon is not due to a pigment, but due to light scattering. Short blue wavelengths scatter more, which is why large volumes of air and water appear blue to the human eye. We cannot grasp the blue in water, and as we chase the blue horizon, we will never arrive to see it. This adds an element of intrigue and curiosity. The famous German writer Johann Wolfgang Goethe, who also studied colour, wrote, 'We love to contemplate blue, not because it advances to us, but because it draws us after it.'[5]

Conversely, the phrase 'feeling blue' represents this colour's downside. In Greek mythology, the god Zeus was said to make rain when he was sad, symbolising tears. Rainy, cloudy skies often appear blue-grey, linking the colour blue to melancholy. The origin of the phrase 'feeling blue' is often debated, but one association is with the seventeenth-century sailing practice of raising a blue flag when an important crew member had died.

Historical and cultural influences: In Western cultures, blue is often associated with masculinity and social power (think: 'blue for boys') but this trend only became popular in the mid-twentieth century. Prior to the mid-nineteenth century, all babies were dressed in white. When pastels were first introduced in the nineteenth century, there wasn't any distinction between the sexes. Initial ideas on suitable colours for a boy or girl may surprise you; in 1918 the trade publication *Earnshaw's Infants' Department* claimed the 'generally accepted rule is pink for the boys, and blue for the girls. The reason is that pink, being a more decided and stronger colour, is more suitable for the boy, while blue, which is more delicate and dainty, is prettier for the girl.' After World War II, the opposite notion took hold as children's clothing became more about mimicking adult dress.[6]

Because of where blue features in nature and its association with life, many cultures associate blue with calm and positivity. In Japan, for example, blues represent tranquillity, harmony, and purity, and appear in traditional kimonos as well as the arts to reflect these qualities. Indigo is a favoured hue.

Many writers used blue as a symbol of melancholy and romantic longing. Love can be like the unobtainable blue horizon. Goethe did this with powerful effect in his 1774 novel, *The Sorrows of Young Werther*. The main character, Werther, was wearing a blue coat when he fell madly in love with a woman who was already engaged. The blue coat symbolised his sadness. In the tragic end, he takes his own life. The book became a sensation across Europe, and many young men emulated the main character by wearing blue coats. Several tragically took their own lives. This created such concern that Goethe added a new last line spoken by Werther's ghost: 'Be a man, and do not follow me.'[7]

Spirituality: In many religions, the blue sky is associated with interpretations of heaven and godly figures. For example, in Christianity, blue is associated with the Virgin Mary, representing purity and divinity. In Hinduism, blue represents the god Vishnu, symbolising cosmic harmony and protection. In Buddhism, blue robes are worn by the god Vairocana to symbolise wisdom and enlightenment, whereas Bhaisajyaguru wears blue to represent healing.

A symbol of divine connection in Judaism is the blue techelet thread. Across various Middle Eastern and Mediterranean cultures, the 'evil eye' is commonly depicted in blue or turquoise and serves as protection against ill wishes.

The throat chakra in Hindu's tradition of tantra is blue. It's associated with communication and the ability to express oneself clearly and truthfully, as well as listen. Chakras are used in various ways across spiritual beliefs to symbolise energy centres in the body. Each chakra is thought to influence different aspects of wellbeing.

These examples demonstrate how blue has held similar meanings throughout history and across cultures with very different belief systems. Many of these associations are prevalent in everyday Western society, such as the banking sector's use of blue to portray knowledge and protection; the notion of healing and calm in health and wellbeing centres; and knowledge, communication, and calm demonstrated in school and police uniforms.

Business: You will see blue used when a business wants to convey trust, knowledge, dependability, and open communication. This includes banks, learning institutions, the health industry, and technology. For example, Facebook and LinkedIn are two technology companies that focus on connection and information sharing. Blue is also used to represent opportunity, or forward thinking, which reflects our curiosity and imagination. Hence the phrase 'blue sky thinking', often used to describe a creative brainstorming session.

It's impossible to summarise every variation of a colour. Use the colours listed as an enticement to explore and uncover what is right for you. You may see the same colour appear under different colours. This is because of colour mixing. For example, you can have turquoise blue and turquoise green.

Examples of blue: Baby blue, sky blue, powder blue, turquoise, cyan, aquamarine, cornflower blue, cerulean, azure, French blue, sapphire, teal, cobalt.

Colour characteristics:[8]
Light blues: Positivity, friendliness, caring, openness, creativity
Bright blues: Energising and uplifting, especially in the blue-green range
Dark blues: Knowledge, a sense of authority. Focus, concentration, luxury
Negative characteristics: Cold, too serious (dark blues)

✳ Red ✳

Nature's palette and psychological effects: Red is the rose, red is 'that dress', and red are flushed cheeks of arousal or embarrassment. Red screams emotion and action, not logic. Its long wavelengths mean it is very vivid to the human eye. Evolutionarily, this was beneficial. Imagine scanning greenery for something edible and spotting bright red berries. You experience dopamine bursts with anticipation and relief as your hunger is satiated.

Red signals danger too, such as blood or the person next to you turning red with anger as they realise you've eaten all the berries. Hopefully, those berries gave you a glucose spike, because it's time to run. Early humans associated red with fire and heat. All these natural reference points mean we associate red with energy.

Research shows that red can project strength and dominance.[9] Sports studies show that when teams are evenly matched, those wearing red uniforms win more than those in other colours.[10] This dominance may extend beyond a psychological effect, as the colour has been shown to increase blood pressure, heart rate, and metabolism, potentially enhancing physical strength.[11] It is a colour of action and emotion over intellect.

Historical and cultural influences: Well before any studies, the ancient Romans associated red with Mars, the god of war. Red reflected blood and battle. This also symbolised strength and power. Soldiers often donned red tunics, and people used it in festivals and ceremonies to represent power, courage, and victory.

Nobility (such as Roman and Chinese emperors) often used red in formal dress to exude authority, a tradition that continues today in many royal families worldwide.

Red appears on many flags, symbolising strength, bravery, and sacrifice. In modern Western settings, red represents energy and strength; many sports teams incorporate red, and red cars are associated with speed. We use red for warnings, such as in stop signs and fire trucks, because it's highly visible and associated with action.

In Western culture, wearing red can empower, projecting strength, confidence and a sense of action. Because of its emotional impact, it can also create arousal. Red lipstick often symbolises sex appeal.

In China, red is the traditional colour for wedding dresses, representing good luck, prosperity and happiness. In India, brides wear red saris or dresses as symbols of auspiciousness, life, and fertility.

Despite red's association with energy, power, and arousal, certain chroma effects can evoke warmth, as seen in Victorian England, where deep, dark reds were popular in interiors, creating a sense of richness and intimacy.

Spirituality: In Hinduism, red is associated with the goddess Shakti, who represents power and energy.

In Japanese culture, red is associated with life force, vitality and energy. It is used in festivals, celebrations, and religious ceremonies.

The Indigenous people of Australia and America often use red ochre with spiritual references to the earth and life force.

In Hinduism, Buddhism, and yoga, the root chakra is red. It is a grounding energy that represents stability and connection to the earth.

Universally, red has a primal physical and emotional effect, but social connotations may lead to different emotional responses. For example, the major left-wing party in Australia uses red in its logo, but red is the colour of the major right-wing party in the United States. Here we use our emotions to characterise what this means. For example, if I voted left, I might see the Australian left-wing party as 'action oriented' and 'progressing change', but if I were a left-wing voter in America, I would associate the red of the right-wing party with 'aggressive' and 'irrational' characteristics and the blue of the left-wing party with 'intelligence' and 'thoughtful, caring decision-making'. Either way, colour is shaping an emotional response.

Business: If a company wants to portray energy, excitement, and vitality, they may use a saturated, vibrant red. This is common in the fast-food and drinks industry. Coca-Cola and KFC are two examples. The red conveys 'fast' food and invites you to 'act now', as you drive past the sign. This is the same effect as a red sales banner. It creates a sense of urgency: 'act now or you will miss out'. For these reasons, high-chroma (vivid) red is often associated with affordable, low-cost items. If high-end brands want to use a high-chroma red, they need to invest heavily in upmarket imagery of strength, power, or allure to avoid appearing cheap. The trademark red-soled shoes by Christian Louboutin is one example.

Examples of red: Electric red, strawberry red, vermillion, watermelon, rose, blush, blood red, carmine, cherry, crimson, ruby, scarlet, brick, burgundy, maroon, raspberry, russet, terracotta, tomato.

Colour characteristics:[12]
Light reds: Romantic, youthful, playful
Bright reds: Energetic, creative, strong, exciting, confident, alluring
Dark reds: Luxe, cosy, confidence, resilience, seductive, elegant
Negative characteristics: Loud, overpowering, cheap, aggressive, overexcited, salacious

✷ Purple ✷

Nature's palette and psychological effects: Purples and violets can appear in auroras and in the cosmos, though they are less common than greens or reds. This is because purple and violet occur at higher altitudes and require darker skies to be seen. Our ancestors surely gazed up in wonder. Purple would have appeared mystical, especially as it is not prevalent on earth in such radiant forms. We now understand how these colours form, but it doesn't diminish the mesmerising delight we still feel when we look up.

People sometimes use the words 'purple' and 'violet' interchangeably. Purple isn't a pure colour; it's a mix of red and blue. Violet is a pure colour. You can see it in the rainbow. It has the shortest wavelength of visible light and sits next to X-rays and gamma rays, which are outside our visible range. This can make it hard for us to discern violet. The purple we see in the night sky is a combination of red and blue light.

The composition of blue and red in purple makes it an emotionally in-between colour. This means people can find it calming or energising, depending on the blend. In nature, purple foods include grapes, eggplant, and heirloom carrots (before they were bred to be almost exclusively orange). The light-purple colours of wisteria, lilac, and lavender flowers are associated with more romantic sentiments, and the way they grow in clusters creates an appealing and calming sense of abundance. Lavender oil has compounds that relax us, adding to the idea of blissful romanticism. Wisteria has a gentle, pleasant fragrance, but its oils are toxic. Aurora and Aroma combine to make us associate these lighter purples with sweet sentiments, besides the toxic element, which can lend itself to a sense of melancholy romance.

Purple not only mixes an energetic and a calming colour, its components, red and blue, also represent wavelengths from opposite ends of the spectrum. Metaphorically, this reflects the range of impressions purple can have on us; beyond the mystical and romantic, purple reflects inspiration, creativity, peace, meditation, and introversion.[13]

Historical and cultural influences: Purple's strongest historical associations with power and divinity emerged in Phoenician, Roman, and Byzantine cultures, where Tyrian purple, an extraordinarily expensive dye, was made from molluscs such as murex sea snails.[14] It was reserved for royalty, emperors, and high-ranking religious figures. Its rarity made it a global symbol of status and exclusivity. Historically, purple dye was extremely expensive to make and was the reserve of nobility and religious leaders. Many European countries include it in their coat of arms. It is also prominent in the Thai and Japanese royal families. In Chinese culture, it is traditionally considered auspicious and honourable.[15]

Because of its rarity and association with the elite, purple can exude an expensive quality in the right setting. Some hues can be seen as cheap, although in branding today that can imply 'cost-effective'. The notion of cheap quality dates to the revolutionary production techniques that saw purple explode into the marketplace. For innovators and modernists, it was exciting, while traditionalists viewed it as vulgar because some of the final colours could run or fade.[16]

Mysterious, heavenly, innovative, calm, energetic, regal, or even cheap: Purple is polarising. In recent history, the late singer Prince used purple as his signature colour. He personified many attributes of the colour: a gifted musician who played more than twenty instruments, a creator of original music, a talented singer, but also a reclusive personality who disliked being in large groups. He was unique and a bit mysterious.

The LGBTQI+ community readily adopted purple as a key colour, perhaps due to its controversial nature and its ability to blend both ends of the colour spectrum. It initially represented 'spirit.'[17]

Spirituality: Purple features in Christianity, especially at times of reflection such as Lent and Advent. It is also associated with the highest order of Japanese Buddhist monks. It represents both spirituality and wisdom. In ancient Chinese myths associated with Taoism, fairies would often dress in purple.[18] In Hinduism, purple is associated with royalty and spirituality. The crown chakra is linked to violet or white light, symbolising enlightenment and higher consciousness.

Business: Asprey, a luxury goods company, uses rich, deep purples to reflect luxury. When brands use lighter, brighter purples, they are conveying fun but do run the risk of appearing 'cheap'. The streaming platform Twitch focuses primarily on a younger gaming audience. In this setting, purple encapsulates fun, escapism, and innovation. Although not new, Yahoo was an innovative search engine when it first launched; its purple branding reflecting its creative energy. In 2019 it changed to indigo, a blend of blue and violet. The influence of blue now reflects experience and knowledge, giving it a more sophisticated look, while the purple/violet still retains a sense of innovation.

Examples of purple: Lavender, lilac, periwinkle, orchid, iris, mauve, amethyst, violet, magenta, puce, mulberry, plum, pomegranate, aubergine, wine, royal purple.

Colour characteristics:[19]
Light purples: Calm, romantic, meditative
Bright purples: Creative, fun, innovative, bold
Dark purples: Luxurious, warm, reflective
Negative characteristics: Cheap, eccentric, lacks seriousness

✻ Pink ✻

Nature's palette and psychological effects: A mix of red and white, pink is a happier and softer version of red. In nature we see pink in warm sunsets, flowers, sweet fruits, earth, and rocks. Pink animals include flamingos, dolphins, and galahs. It's associated with calm, care, and gentleness. Pink is also associated with springtime and new beginnings, symbolising growth and renewal. This can be seen in the pinkish hue of some newborn animals or pink blossoms on some trees and shrubs.

Historical and cultural influences: Pink has become polarising and political thanks to twentieth-century marketing. Many men shied away from pink as they saw it as emasculating. Because of pink's association with softness, several studies have used different tones of pink to determine its ability to reduce aggression in incarcerated men.[20] They produced mixed results, however. In 2011 researchers conducted a rigorous four-year study with a specific pink and found that it did reduce aggression. The hue was called 'cool down pink'. However, the prisoners found the experience degrading, as they associated the colour with young girls.[21] They wouldn't have felt this way if the experiment had occurred before the baby clothing marketing strategies of the nineteenth century! For example, pastel pinks were worn by both men and women in the eighteenth century, particularly in the Rococo period.

Designers in the 1980s tried to restore the overall appeal of pink by introducing pastel colours for both men and women. At this time it was cool for men to wear pink. Just google *Miami Vice*, a slick police action show. However, many women began rejecting pink because of its association with weakness and outdated stereotypes of a woman's role in society.

Attitudes have shifted again, and pink has become bolder. Women have started to embrace pink as a colour of empowerment, such as in the 'Me Too' movement, and in 2023 Pantone released Viva Magenta as their Colour of the Year. The 2023 *Barbie* movie also embraced pink across the genders, with messages of strength and change for all.

In non-Western cultures, while you will find pinks associated with the expected symbols of beauty, love, and delicacy, you can find other meanings. In China, it's associated with happiness and prosperity; in Japan, thanks to the famous cherry blossoms, pink is associated with spring, fleeting beauty, elegance, and tranquillity. Men in Barbados embrace pink in their attire because it reflects the pink sandy beaches of their environment.

Spirituality: In Christianity, the fourth Sunday of Lent is known as Laetare Sunday, or Rose Sunday. Pink symbolises joy, hope, and anticipation as Christians approach Easter. Seasonally, this can coincide with the end of winter and the early signs of spring. In Hinduism, Lakshmi, who represents wealth, fortune, and prosperity, is often depicted wearing pink attire.

In New Age spirituality and metaphysical practices, pink is often associated with love, compassion, and emotional healing. It's considered a heart-centred colour that promotes harmony, balance, and inner peace. Many people believe that pink crystals, including rose quartz, possess properties that aid in emotional healing and self-love.

Business: Pink is still used to promote services and products to women. Besides the element of femininity, it speaks of fun and freshness. In food and beverage, pink is associated with sweetness, thanks to berries in nature. Pink in its variations has a renewed popularity in women's clothing and apparel now that it is associated with female independence.

Examples of pink: Baby pink, cotton candy, blush, dusty pink, peach, strawberry, bubblegum, flamingo, carnation, rose, orchid, magenta, hot pink, cerise, fuchsia.

Colour characteristics: [22]

Light pinks: sweet, gentle, feminine, romantic, caring, warm
Bright pinks: energetic, strong, bold, fun
Dark pinks: calm, confident
Negative characteristics: fragile, weak, loud

∗ Yellow ∗

Nature's palette and psychological effects: To our ancestors, the yellow sun was a source of life and warmth. Yellow springtime wildflowers and vegetation represented vitality and new life as colder weather subsided. They would have felt more optimistic about their chances of survival. Today, yellow evokes happiness, fun, positivity, and energy. Because of its joyful associations, people often use yellow in children's play areas.

Like red, yellow has longer wavelengths, making it stand out. It's used to attract attention, such as the yellow postboxes in Germany and Australia, or crime scene warning tape. While yellow is optimistic, its overuse can backfire, creating agitation and anxiety. As an example, pure lemon yellow reflects a lot of light, and excessive exposure can irritate our vision and psyche.[23]

Research supports these polarising emotional responses. When people were asked to select a colour reflecting upbeat music, the majority chose yellow.[24] However, studies also show bright yellow can create disagreeable emotions, such as overwhelm.[25] With any colour, hue, chroma, value/brightness, placement, and quantity all influence the effect it can have.

Historical and cultural influence: In ancient Egypt, the sun god Ra was associated with yellow and orange, representing light, warmth, and life-giving energy. In China, yellow was the most prestigious colour, worn by emperors to symbolise power and prosperity. Throughout the ages, people across Asia and Europe used yellow as a sign of wealth and power, because it was associated with the sun, divinity, and gold.

Ancient Egyptians painted tombs yellow, making it a symbol of mourning.[26] In modern-day Mexico, yellow (and orange) marigolds are used during the Day of the Dead festival. The Aztecs used marigolds to guide the souls of the deceased back to the world of the living.[27]

In Thailand, yellow is the lucky colour for Monday, and it's considered the most important colour of the week because it represents the king. In many African nations, yellow is worn by people of high rank because of its close resemblance to gold. Yellow is also significant to some Indigenous American nations. It's the colour of gold and corn, and therefore reflects wealth and prosperity.[28]

While yellow is mainly associated with positive emotions, it does have some negative historical symbolism. In ancient Greece and Rome, disreputable people, including prostitutes, were made to wear yellow clothing. In the tenth century, the French painted the doors of traitors and criminals yellow. In the Middle Ages, people linked yellow to cowardice and crime. A more recent disturbing example of using the colour yellow to label people occurred during Nazi Germany, when Jewish people were forced to wear a yellow Star of David on their clothing marking them as outsiders and targets of persecution.[29] Some believe yellow was used in these situations because of its association with the unpleasantness of aging and disease, weakness, and infections with yellow pus. These unsavoury symbols, along with its vivid wavelength, made yellow a convenient colour to label people and make them stand out.[30]

Overall, the symbolism of yellow is positive and energetic, reflecting its emotional impact. Harvey Ball beautifully represented this through the iconic round smiley face he created in 1963. This design came from an assignment to create a motivational logo for an insurance agency.[31] No, he didn't have a patent. Sad face.

Spirituality: For Hindus, yellow is a sacred colour that represents knowledge, wisdom, and learning as reflected in the goddess Saraswati.[32] It represents the solar plexus chakra, representing confidence and power. This aligns with the emotional effects of optimism, and the sense of feeling uplifted and vibrant.

In Christianity, yellow is often used to represent enlightenment, depicted by halos. On the negative side, artists often paint Judas in yellow to symbolise his betrayal of Jesus and his status as an unwanted outsider.

Business: Yellow expresses fresh, fast, vibrant, optimistic, fun, and creative. You will often find it on food packaging, such as Lipton tea and McDonald's branding. Mailchimp, a company that sells online marketing software, uses yellow to represent innovation and the idea of standing out to your customers.

Examples of yellow: Champagne, cream, custard, lemon, maize, pineapple, banana, butterscotch, canary, corn, marigold, saffron, sunflower, amber, honey, mustard, citrine, topaz.

Colour characteristics:[33]
Light yellow: Youthful, playful, happy
Bright yellow: Energetic, creative, fun, positive, confident
Dark yellow: Earthy, warm, friendly
Negative characteristics: Agitating, anxiousness

* Orange *

Nature's palette and psychological effects: In nature we see orange in fire, sunrises, and sunsets. We see it in rocks, stones, and in food such as modern carrots, mangos, pumpkins, sweet potato, and of course, oranges. In flora, orange stands out to pollinating birds and bees with flowers such as marigolds, lilies, and tulips. Animals like tigers and frogs use orange as camouflage. Monarch butterflies use is it as warning signal, whereas snakes, lizards, insects, and birds use orange to attract mates.

A blend of red and yellow, orange is a warm colour that stands due to its long wavelength, second only to red. Overall, it has the active energy of red and the happy emotions of yellow.

Historical and cultural influence: In ancient times, the sun rising and setting was an act of the gods. It was often linked to vitality and fertility. Its association with divinity and heaven has remained a constant.

In the Middle Ages, orange pigment was difficult and expensive to make so it became associated with wealth.

In Europe during the Renaissance and Baroque periods, people embraced the vitality of orange and used it as a symbol of energy, power, and creativity. William of Orange, born in the Netherlands, derived his title from the Principality of Orange in southern France. This association led to the adoption of the colour orange as a symbol by the House of Orange-Nassau, which still influences the Dutch national identity today.[34]

Orange fell out of favour in the United Kingdom during the Victorian era, especially after Queen Victoria entered lifelong mourning following the death of Prince Albert in 1861 The trend for darker clothing spread to British colonies and even to the United States.

In recent Western history, orange has reflected varied sentiments, just as its use in nature ranges from blending in to standing out. In the early twentieth century, the link to luxury still resonated and it was associated with avant-garde artists and designers, which reinforced its tie to creativity. After World War II, it was associated with optimism and modernism. Earthy orange colours were prevalent in the 1970s, reflecting a link to nature. The vibrant 1980s didn't embrace these earthy themes; any orange had to be vivid. In recent times, variations of orange have been used to symbolise energy, creativity, and youthfulness.

In parts of Africa and Asia, people use orange in textiles and celebrations to represent joy, good luck, and prosperity. The Chinese often exchange oranges, tangerines, and mandarins as gifts during festivals and celebrations to bring luck and blessings, especially during the Lunar New Year.

Among certain Indigenous American cultures, orange signifies harvest, abundance, and renewal.

Spirituality: In Hinduism, orange is associated with the sacral chakra, which is believed to govern emotions, creativity, and sexuality. In Ayurvedic treatments, practitioners sometimes use orange-coloured foods, spices, and herbs to promote balance and vitality.

In Hinduism and Buddhism, monks wear saffron-coloured robes. The colour is sacred and represents the search for enlightenment and inner transformation. The saffron robes also represent humility and detachment from materialism.

The dual symbolism of orange, from the heavenly life-giving sun to the earth, is also reflected in some Australian Aboriginal cultures through the use of ochre pigments.

All humans across cultures and throughout the ages see the sun rise and set, and see orange-tinted flames, vegetation, flowers, and wildlife. It is therefore unsurprising that so many diverse cultures hold similar emotions about orange and share its symbolism.

Business: Orange is used to showcase qualities of innovation, energy, playfulness, and freshness. Like red, more vibrant oranges can appear in call-to-action situations like 'click here' and 'buy now'. With its longer wavelength, it helps a campaign or brand to stand out. Brands like Fanta convey fun and energy. Brands like Timberland use warmer tones to suggest natural ingredients or connections to the outdoors.

An interesting combination is a logo I saw for I-MED Radiology. They used the expected blue to represent care and competence as a medical company, but they also used orange. This matched their marketing message about using up-to-date technology. The orange helped to express their innovation and technological advancement.

Examples of orange: Apricot, peach, cantaloupe, clementine, papaya, tangerine, mandarin, sunset orange, ginger, saffron, goldfish orange, marigold, persimmon, coral, carrot, burnt orange, pumpkin, amber.

Colour characteristics:[35]
Light orange: Fun, youthful, playful
Bright orange: Energetic, bold, creative, innovative
Dark orange: Natural, earthy, spiritual, calm, warm
Negative characteristics: Immature, silly

✸ Green ✸

Nature's palette and psychological effects: Green is the grass and the leaves of trees, plants, and food. To our ancestors, and therefore to us, green represented life, protection, growth, and abundance, qualities that evoke feelings of positivity, stability, and calm.

Green's middle position in the colour spectrum, sitting between the warm and cool colours, also links to the concept of harmony and balance. This middle wavelength means we need less effort to adjust our eyes to it in relation to other colours. We can see more shades of green than any other colour. Given these positive attributes, it's unsurprising that research has validated green as a positive colour, especially shades found in nature.[36]

But some greens can have negative effects. A green-yellow hue can remind people of vomit, making it unappealing.[37] This negative emotion is a physiological warning, just like some very dark or muted greens may be off-putting because they can be associated with decay and the breakdown of vegetation that could make us ill if we ate it.

Overall, the calming and rejuvenating effect of green makes it ideal for relaxing spaces and fostering collaboration and connection.

Historical and cultural influence: Green's association with healing is an ancient one. Green vegetation symbolised health and vitality, and many edible greens were foraged for nourishment. Due to the importance of vegetation for survival, green's association with health and growth is universal across cultures. In various countries, agricultural festivals celebrate with the colour green. For example, in China, there is the green-thumbed God of Millet.[38] In the Indian flag, green symbolises faith and fertility, reflecting cultural and agricultural richness.[39] In countries like India and China, green is linked to prosperity, while in Japan, the focus is on harmony and balance.

The expression 'green with envy' links to the ancient Greeks, who believed an overproduction of bile caused jealousy, resulting in a greenish complexion.[40] In ancient folklore and mythology, otherworldly creatures were often depicted as green. This continued into science fiction, with Martians portrayed as green. Shrek's greenness follows the folklore tradition, marking him as an outsider.

The universal symbolism of green has also seen it embraced by social and political movements focused on environmental awareness.

Spirituality: In Hinduism, in the festival of colours known as Holi, green powder is used to represent the arrival of spring.

In Islamic culture, green symbolises paradise and is traditionally associated with the Prophet Muhammad. People also wear green during celebrations and festivals, such as Eid al-Fitr and Mawlid al-Nabi (the Prophet's birthday).

In both Buddhist and Christian traditions, green is associated with life, renewal, health, and harmony. The Christian Garden of Eden, often imagined as a lush and fertile paradise, mirrors Islamic descriptions of paradise as rich with greenery and flowing water.

In Hinduism, the heart chakra is green. This is associated with harmony, balance, and healing, as well as love, compassion, connection to others, and divinity.

Regardless of the country or culture, green's symbolism and emotional impact strongly align due to its importance and prevalence across the natural world.

Business: Green represents health, balance, harmony, nature, the environment, and sustainability. The Land Rover vehicle (the name says it all) uses green to demonstrate its suitability for driving in rural areas. The Body Shop promotes ethical and sustainable products with a deep earthy green. Bayer, a global pharmaceutical company, uses vibrant green for vitality, and blue, showing knowledge and care.

Examples of green: Mint, sage, celadon, seafoam, lime, chartreuse, shamrock, grass, fern, olive, avocado, moss, hunter pine, veridian, emerald, teal, Kelly green, jade, forest.

Colour characteristics:[41]

Light green: Restorative, calm, balance
Bright green: Refreshing, energetic, growth
Dark green: Natural, earthy, harmonious
Negative characteristics: Stagnation, boredom

✳ Brown ✳

Nature's palette and psychological effects: In a forest we see an abundance of brown in tree trunks. Forests provide a protective canopy for a variety of plants and animals. When we lived in these environments, we would have viewed trees as useful to build shelters, hide, use as fuel, or climb for a better view. However, if the trees were too densely packed we could easily become disorientated, overwhelmed, and engulfed by claustrophobia.

Brown also represents the earth that provides abundant crops. When the rains come and the weather turns, they can become a muddy trail that is difficult to move through.

These experiences illustrate the emotions brown can elicit. Tree trunks and wood evoke feelings of being grounded, safe, and warm, but too many can make you feel hemmed in. Brown can symbolise being 'down to earth' and natural as well as stagnant and dreary. No one wants to be labelled as 'stuck in the mud'.

Historical and cultural influence: Historically, hunters and warriors used brown clothing and materials to blend into their environments.

Brown was also linked to poverty, since workers on the land were frequently covered in soil and mud. It is not typically considered a glamorous colour and people rarely choose to wear brown to stand out.

Many Indigenous cultures associate brown with the earth and use it in rituals and ceremonies to honour the land and ancestors. For example, brown ochre is prominent in Aboriginal art. Land, or 'Country', often represents a sense of belonging, connection with ancestors, and life.

In the 1970s, brown was associated with the hippy movement due to its connection to nature. However, it became less prominent in the 1980s when the focus shifted to economic growth, favouring bright, shiny colours. People considered brown to be the opposite of innovation and technology. Now, with its variations, brown can represent a bolder image, with shades like bronze, cognac, cinnamon, and chocolate. Today, people embrace brown to symbolise environmental awareness and natural products, reflecting an organic, sustainable lifestyle. It can also hold an 'antitech' social appeal.

Spirituality: In certain Buddhist and Christian traditions, monks wear brown robes as a symbol of piety and humility.

Many Indigenous cultures use brown in practices related to healing, protection, fertility and grounded reflection. These typically arise from associations with the earth as a source of life.[42]

Business: American delivery company UPS uses brown in its brand colours. It was introduced in 1916, because brown trucks showed less dirt. This has developed to symbolise a sense of reliability and security.[43]

While green and blue dominate in health care, disciplines that advocate natural approaches often include brown, as seen in some complementary therapy practices. Organic or naturally focused food and products frequently feature brown. Skincare brand Burt's Bees is just one example.

Examples of brown: Beige, ecru, almond, buff, wheat, tan, camel, sand, taupe, oat, tawny, mocha, cinnamon, sienna, caramel, russet, auburn, chocolate, mahogany, chestnut, cocoa.

Colour characteristics:[44]
Light brown: Restorative, calm, balance
Bright brown: Warm, relaxing, friendly, vitality
Dark brown: Natural, earthy, protective, grounded
Negative characteristics: Dull, unsophisticated, claustrophobic

✱ Black ✱

Nature's palette and psychological effects: For our ancestors, darkness evoked fear of the unknown, but it also gave them opportunities to hide from predators or conceal themselves from surprise attacks.

Black is achromatic, meaning it is technically not a colour, as it absorbs all light rays, reflecting none.

In daylight, black appears in rocks and stones like onyx and jet. In fauna, it is associated with powerful animals like panthers, bears, and rhinoceroses. It's also seen in birds like swans, cockatoos, ravens, and crows. Black helps animals blend into the background; for example, a panther can hide in the dark jungle and leap on unsuspecting prey.

While black is rarely associated with food, examples include black beans, black garlic and black rice.

Our emotional response to the dark night and shadowy places often leads us to view black as threatening, mysterious, and powerful.

Historical and cultural influence: To the Egyptians, black was a positive colour associated with the underworld, where plants germinated, the sun recharged, and the dead were reborn. Black symbolised protection and life.[45]

The ancient Greeks linked black with darkness and death. Their underworld was ruled by the stern and unemotional Hades, but he wasn't inherently evil. Greeks sacrificed black animals to the dead, and mourners wore black. The Romans continued to associate black with bereavement and death.[46]

Christianity used terms like 'light' and 'darkness' to reference good and evil. Later this expanded to include white and black. In the Middle

Ages, black became linked to evil. Women wearing black were often associated with witchcraft, as were black cats.[47] Depending on where you live today, black cats can still hold a notion of bad luck or good luck.

In the West, black is associated with negative emotions, including depression and sadness.[48] British Prime Minister Winston Churchill referred to his depression as 'the black dog', an expression rooted in literature about feeling lost in the dark.[49] Studies today show that people still associate black with evil and death and perceive black colours as the least pleasant.[50]

Despite this, the fashion industry views black as sophisticated and elegant. The fashion designer Coco Chanel helped shape this perspective in the 1920s. A black evening dress or work suit exudes confidence and authority. Fashion shows us how the context and placement of a colour shapes our emotional responses. Black clothing can still intimidate though, like Darth Vader's menacing presence in *Star Wars*. If he had worn a cape of baby blue, I just don't think he would've been perceived as very threatening.

The camouflage quality of black also holds true in clothing; it says, 'don't focus on me'. Waitstaff often wear black to avoid standing out, just like the animals hiding in the foliage. This means black can also create an impression of being standoffish: 'I'm hiding, don't approach me.'

Black has represented counterculture movements like Goths, as well as protest movements such as the Black Panther Party for African American rights, symbolising defiance and strength. Disruptive political groups like Italian fascists and the Nazi SS also used black.

In Japan, darkness and black are embraced for their mystery and ambiguity. This view influences Japanese religion, architecture, and art, as seen in lacquerware today.[51]

For a non-colour, black evokes powerful responses, empowering, impressing, and intimidating us. It also conveys a sense of escape and withdrawal.

Spiritual: While the West associates black with death and the occult, in many cultures, the strength associated with black gives it protective powers. In India, for example, people often use black as a protective colour, especially for newborn babies and pregnant women.

Some Middle Eastern and African cultures believe that black wards off the evil eye or other forms of negative energy.

Business: Luxury brands often use black to express sophistication, strength, and quality. Think Prada, Gucci, Chanel, Nike, and Apple.

Because black is achromatic, it works with any colour and produces a dramatic effect. Harley-Davidson uses orange and black to create an impression of rebellious fun. Netflix's bold red lettering on a black background represents drama and technology as a leading streaming service.

Examples of black: Ebony, graphite, onyx, shadow, coal, carbon, midnight, jet, raven, obsidian, ink, pitch, nightfall, velvet, soot, liquorice, Vantablack.

Colour characteristics:[52]

As an achromatic colour, variances in black are not as dramatic as chromatic colours.

Positive characteristics: Sophisticated, elegant, glamorous, authoritative, serious

Negative characteristics: Rebellious, unapproachable, oppressive, threatening, withdrawn

White

Nature's palette and psychological effects: White often conjures up serene and pleasant images, such as endless expanses of crisp snow, fluffy clouds, and delicate flowers. It's a colour found in valued elements of nature, including marble and salt. Animals like polar bears and Arctic foxes use white as camouflage to blend into their icy environments. White animals can evoke sentiments of softness and gentleness as well, as in soft white wool on gentle sheep or the white rabbit. In the wild, white rabbits are rare, and to see one historically signified good luck.

Research shows that the brightness of white leads people to associate it with positive qualities and emotions such as purity, peace, and cleanliness.[53] Fresh snow, for example, is pure, untouched, and clean.

White is achromatic because it reflects all visible light, the opposite of black, which absorbs all light. This reflective quality makes white appear bright and clean and evokes a sense of openness and calmness. People embrace these traits in modern interior design as they seek mental escape from the stimulation of today's world.

The positive attributes of white can have a negative effect if overused. Too much white can shift from calming to cold and sterile, creating an uncomfortable or unwelcoming environment.

Historical and cultural influence: Throughout history and across cultures, people have linked white to sunlight and considered it a symbol of new beginnings, hope, and purity. European white wedding dresses, particularly among royal families, reflected these symbols throughout history. White is now a staple wedding dress colour in the West.

In mythology and folklore, these sentiments extended to white animals in nature, along with the notion of wisdom. The white owl, dove and mythical unicorn reflect these qualities, many of which persist in cultural symbolism today. Egyptians and Romans are believed to have domesticated white doves signalling peace, love, and loyalty. Symbolism that still stands today. Fun fact: the Scottish coat of arms features the unicorn. The idea of wisdom also stems from people with white hair, who are typically older and have accumulated knowledge through lived experiences.

White has also been a symbol of peaceful protest. It was used in the early twentieth-century women's suffragette movement, but this did eventually become militant. The 2002 'Women in White' protests in Liberia played a crucial role in ending the civil war.[54] For centuries and in many cultures, a white flag has also represented truce or surrender during conflict, often seen as a precursor to peace.

Minimalist architects have used white to create simple, uncluttered backdrops that highlight architectural features and promote a calming atmosphere. In fashion, white can convey either a relaxed or sophisticated presence, depending on the materials and styles used, such as white linen in summer or a tailored white suit at an event.

While white's associations with light often elicit positive emotional responses of calm and sophistication, it can also evoke negative feelings. Some cultures associate it with the dominance or invasion of white people. In clinical settings, white can feel sterile and cold. An all-white lounge in the home may appear stylish and be designed to create a calming atmosphere, but depending on someone's sensory profile and current needs, it may feel stark, hindering relaxation or numbing emotions rather than soothing them. Wearing all-white clothing can also convey aloofness or coldness, similar to black. Once again, context and placement are key.

Spirituality: White at funerals reflects purity and is a sign of respect for the deceased. This is common in Southeast Asian countries. In Hinduism, people also wear white as a colour of mourning to represent purity and detachment from worldly goods. Westerners usually wear black to funerals but receive white flowers to acknowledge bereavement.

Christians use the symbolism of white to portray the resurrection of Christ in artwork. There is also the biblical symbolism of the dove, which reflects purity and peace as well as the Holy Spirit.

With similar symbolism, nuns in Thailand wear white robes to signify purity, humility, equality, and the pursuit of enlightenment.

Business: White cannot stand out alone. Combining white with other colours is necessary to create an impression. For example, people use it in health care to represent cleanliness and purity. This is why pills, medicine containers, or pharmacy-related products are predominantly white. Soap, skincare products, and shampoos are also typically coloured white for the same reasons. People often combine white with black to convey luxury, elegance, or sophistication. Bold colours used with white can make a dramatic statement, such as Tesla's bright red with a white symbol and wording.

Examples of white: Pure white, snow, ivory, cream, pearl, eggshell, linen, alabaster, milk, bone, antique white, birch, cotton, ivory, magnolia, vanilla, pristine white.

Colour characteristics:[55]
As an achromatic colour, variances in white are not as dramatic as chromatic colours.
Positive characteristics: Sophisticated, elegant, pure, radiant, healthy, efficient, clean, smart
Negative characteristics: Aloof, emotionless, sterile, solitary

✳ Grey ✳

Nature's palette and psychological effects: In nature, rocks and mountains often display the colour grey. Cloudy skies signify unfavourable weather conditions. We associate this colour with animals like elephants, birds, and rabbits. Grey terrain provides them with camouflage, allowing them to blend into the surroundings.

Research has shown that medium grey is one of the most passive colours. As we move further from grey on the colour spectrum, we tend to feel more energised.[56] Grey does not stimulate us; instead, it can subdue or even drain our energy. Imagine being in a grey room or surrounded by grey furniture: it can feel like a gloomy prison, discouraging action and motivation. Grey weather affects us similarly. People don't enthusiastically say, 'It's such a grey day, let's go outside!' Typically, it makes us want to engage in more low-key activities, like watching a movie or reading a book. To our ancestors, grey may have represented cold, difficulty foraging, or food destruction due to bad weather. It would have made sense to conserve resources and energy.

Consistent grey weather can block UV light, reducing cortisol, serotonin, endorphin, and vitamin D production. This alone can affect our energy, mood, and cognitive abilities.

Urban environments, with their overwhelming grey buildings and streets devoid of trees or parks, can foster a gloomy and lethargic atmosphere. This psychological impact is better understood today, leading city planners to incorporate more colour and natural elements into urban designs to improve mood and energy levels.

Grey is the third achromatic colour, created by combining the polar colours of black and white. Unlike the definitive nature of black or white, grey is neither here nor there. This makes it more passive, noncommittal, and unclear. Hence the metaphor of a 'grey area' to describe a situation that isn't clear.

It's not all bad news for grey, though. The passive and neutral aspect of grey makes it ideal for some artists' walls, allowing them to focus on their projects without distraction. It can work well in galleries, encouraging quiet reflection and allowing each piece of art to be appreciated without colour interference.

Generally, the potential for grey weather to inhibit alertness and positivity makes it challenging to associate grey with lots of positive emotions. This makes it unappealing as an overall wall colour for offices or homes, but it has its place. When used appropriately, grey can introduce a sense of tranquillity. I have seen it used very effectively on house exteriors, where a light grey facade is paired with white and grey tiles on the walkway and green gardens. It makes for a calm and inviting entrance. In clothing, it can help quiet an overexcited mind. Its neutrality can promote objective thinking. Grey can also symbolise wisdom, as seen in older people and the beloved elephant. So, it's not all doom and gloom for grey.

Historical and cultural influence: In medieval Europe, grey was associated with humility and modesty, and often worn by monks and the poor, who needed practical colours and preferred not to stand out in society. The clothing of Japanese monks also reflects these qualities, and minimalist Zen gardens often incorporate grey in their colour schemes.

Throughout history, grey has featured in art and literature to evoke melancholy, which we still relate to.

Today, while the emotional symbolism still holds true, grey does feature in fashion to represent an understated elegance and neutrality that can complement other colours. These qualities are also leveraged in design and architecture. Grey as a fashion statement has evolved through advances in colour chemistry, allowing for the creation of more dramatic variations.

Spirituality: In Hinduism and Buddhism, grey represents detachment, neutrality, and transcendence. It is sometimes associated with letting go of worldly desires.

In Sufi mysticism, grey reflects humility, modesty, and spiritual enlightenment. It's associated with the idea of blending into the background and letting go of the ego.

Business: Technology-driven industries will often use grey. It marries well with metallics to create a luxe look. Car manufacturers use darker greys to reflect sophistication. Many drivers prefer to be incognito, which is another reason grey cars are relatively common. Grey is also the reliable sturdy rock, an important quality in technology and car industries.

Examples of grey: Pearl, dove, platinum, moonstone, ash, concrete, mouse, silver, pewter graphite, smoke, charcoal, slate, steel, shadow, cement, meteorite, storm, lunar.

Colour characteristics: [57]

As a blended achromatic colour, grey has more variance than black or white.

Positive characteristics: Sophisticated, reliable, modern, understated, neutral, calm, strong, balanced, wise

Negative characteristics: Withdrawn, passive, lacklustre, noncommittal

✸ Colour harmony ✸

While understanding how a colour resonates with you is important, it's essential to understand how to combine colours effectively to ensure you create the atmosphere or impression you want.

People commonly use several colours in their environments, whether in clothing or home decor. Harmonious colour combinations are not just pleasing to the eye; they influence our emotions and behaviours. Most of the principles used by designers today come from researchers' observations throughout history. The colour wheel serves as an effective tool to demonstrate these combinations. For example:

Chapter 12. Embrace a Colourful Life

- Monochromatic colours (variations of the same colour, e.g. darker to lighter blues) are usually relaxing and may appeal to a colour Avoider.
- Complementary colours (e.g. red and green) create bold, energetic pairings.
- Analogous colours (e.g. blue and green) feel harmonious and soothing.
- Triadic combinations (e.g. red, yellow, and blue) offer balance and vibrancy.

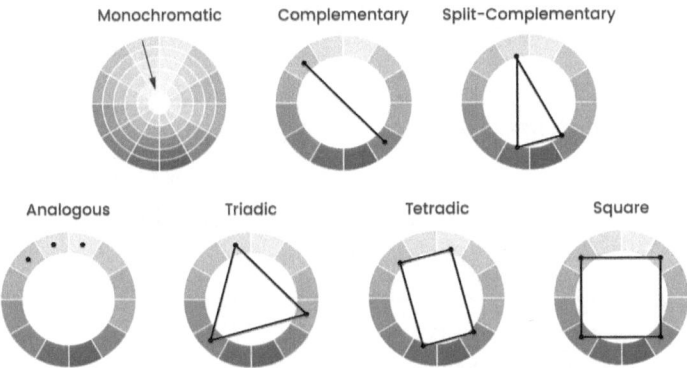

Figure 12.1. Harmonious colour combinations using the colour wheel

Western research concludes that colours with similar brightness and saturation levels are the most harmonious, and this aligns with tried-and-tested colour-harmony principles.[58] However, your personal sensory preferences and cultural influences will also play a role.[59]

✻ How the features of colour affect emotion ✻

Here is an overview of how variations in the colour (hue), saturation (chroma), and brightness (value) can affect emotional effect.

- Pure/intense colours are stimulating, energetic, and convey action and strength.
- Darker colours project a more serious and sophisticated emotion. They can also feel protective and comforting.
- Muted colours (adding another colour) can project calm and sophistication, but may not carry the same level of authority as their darker counterparts.
- Lighter colours are associated with feelings of calm, caring, relaxation, and a lighter mood. They can project purity and innocence.
- Metallic colours project a sense of luxury.

* Behaviour colour guide *

While the majority of examples are for colour in spaces, the emotional sentiments also apply to colour in clothing. Use the guide outlined in Figure 12.2 as a starting point, then personalise it by considering your sensory profile and individual needs.

Behaviour	Description	Colour examples
Invigorating and uplifting	Bright and light colours invigorate the senses. They evoke freshness and vitality, which can uplift your spirits. The greater the saturation, the more energising it is To feel positive in a calm way, opt for lighter variations. You can be bolder in small spaces, particularly if you don't spend a lot of time there, e.g. bathroom or breakfast area	Turquoise, emerald, mint green, canary, jade, rose quartz, seafoam

Focus and clarity	Whites provide a clean, non-distracting background and create a sense of openness. Light grey can be used as an accent to enhance a sense of calm and objectiveness Blues and greens create calm to support focus. Darker blues can aid deep concentration Colours with high brightness and high saturation can be distracting and agitating If you prefer warmer colours, opt for muted or tinted versions, e.g. burgundy, not fire engine red	Ivory, cream, pearl, sky blue, steel blue, navy blue, sage green, olive
Communication	Light and warm colours foster a welcoming atmosphere for open dialogue Energetic colours stimulate lively discussion Darker, richer colours promote more intellectual and intimate conversation	Baby blue, pale daffodil, fern green, persimmon, mauve, sapphire blue, plum
Creativity	Deep, rich colours can stimulate contemplative creative focus, such as writing and design Light and bold colours help with brainstorming and innovation Light achromatics may suit artists by removing stimulation that interferes with their creativity and colour palette Those who are easily distracted may prefer white or very soft colour settings	Mustard, crimson, royal purple, sky blue, tangerine, cerulean, off-whites, pale sky blue
Resilience and confidence	Saturated colours portray strength and radiate a positive, energetic tone Darker colours project a measured confidence In clothing, while light pastel colours will nurture you, their gentleness may not embolden you or project confidence	Saturated reds, regal purple, magenta, raspberry, burgundy, copper, emerald green, racing green, charcoal grey, black, strong whites

Relaxation and sleep	Soft, warm, and muted colours work best to create a soothing and nurturing atmosphere Cooler, lighter colours work well for sleep Light to dark blues are generally calming, as are many greens Avoid stimulating and saturated colours as they can energise you. If you want an energetic colour, desaturate it with a tint, shade, or tone variation. Bright whites may be too stimulating as well Black and grey can drain you and promote rumination, not relaxation	Powder blue, lilac, blush pink, dusty pink, pistachio, pumpkin, warm beige

Figure 12.2. Behaviour colour match guide

WHAT MAKES SENSE TO YOU?

You now have information to select colours that support your moods and behaviours. It's time to evaluate whether your current colours are as effective as they could be.

Before delving into colour considerations, review your responses on your Room Review pages in your Total Sensory Wellbeing notes. You may want to adjust or add comments alongside your existing notes in relation to:

- **Activities:** What is each room used for?
- **Mood and energy:** What feelings and behaviours do you need to support these actions?

Create a colour-specific section, list the colours in your space. You can mark these on your original room sketch, create a dedicated sketch of these in your Room Review section, or alternatively, use the free Shaping Your Sensory Experiences template available under Total Sensory Wellbeing Resources on the Nriched Living website. Tick which ones work well to support your needs and place a question mark or a cross next to ones that might or definitely don't work for you.

Roughly estimate what percentage of the space each of these colours takes up. Here's a standard guide for you to compare to:

- **Walls:** 50–60 per cent
- **Ceilings:** 10–15 per cent
- **Flooring:** 20–25 per cent
- **Furniture:** 10–20 per cent
- **Ornaments/accessories:** 5–10 per cent

Based on what you have read, under the heading 'Colour Potential Improvements', make a note of colours that could support the activities and mood you want in the space. This can include the chroma and brightness descriptions, too. You're not making any commitments here, so challenge yourself and write down a couple of colours you're unsure about but technically should work.

Come to Your Senses

> Try to be an objective observer and consider how you could use these colours in different elements such as flooring, walls, furniture, or decorative objects.
>
> Designers consider colour harmony not just in terms of which colours go together, but also how much of each colour should appear. Typically, a primary colour makes up around 60 per cent of the palette, a secondary colour about 30 per cent, and an accent colour the remaining 10 per cent. The accent colour is often the 'braver' colour choice.
>
> Explore sites like Pinterest to see how colours are used in interiors, and look more consciously at shops, cafes, and hotel lobbies for inspiration. Nothing online will give you the same experience; in the real world, colour interacts with textures, lighting, and space to create an effect. That calming green on the screen could look dull in real life if the lighting isn't right or there's too much of it. Also, look closely at nature when you are outside—believe me, it's not just 'green'. These perspectives will help you refine your feelings to shortlist possible colours and combinations.

After you've read Chapter 17, you can integrate your sensory insights to decide what's best for you.

If that plan sounds good, let's explore how Acoustics influences your day.

CHAPTER 13.
A SOUND MIND

How to create good vibes

In this chapter you'll learn how to harness sound to benefit your everyday life. While research in this area is still evolving, findings show the potential effects sound has on our wellbeing, even if we don't have all the answers yet.

Let's start with something that most people are familiar with: the ancient, universal language of music.

* The magic of music *

While music is a universal language, its forms and what we like varies across cultures. Yet regardless of where we grew up or the genre we most enjoy, music influences our physiology in the same ways. It can make our heart beat faster or slower, or encourage our brains to enter relaxed or focused states.

Many aspects of music can play on our emotional heartstrings too. Melody, the sequence of notes, can create a positive or sad vibe. In Western culture you typically hear major chords used in upbeat or hopeful songs, such as 'Happy' by Pharrell Williams, while minor chords evoke sorrow, like Adele's 'Someone Like You'. Simple, repetitive melodies are soothing because they require less cognitive effort.

Cultural differences also shape our reactions. Studies comparing Western listeners to those in Papua New Guinea[1] and Pakistan[2] reveal that Westerners often found major chords uplifting, while listeners from non-Western cultures preferred minor chords because that is what they were used to. This demonstrates how memory and familiarity, registered in the limbic system, play a key role in shaping our response to music.

* How music moves us *

There are many other ways music can affect us. Here are some aspects that should resonate with you, whether you're musical or not.

Timbre: This is the quality of the sound produced by different instruments and voices. Compare the soothing warmth of an acoustic guitar to the bright, energising tone of an electric guitar.

Dynamics: This is the change in volume within a piece. For example, classical and contemporary instrumental music often use subtle changes to evoke emotions. Explore Debussy's 'Clair de Lune' or Nils Frahm's 'All Melody' for relaxing options.

Harmony: Harmony refers to the blending of different notes to create a sound. Harmonious combinations tend to relax us, while dissonant harmonies can create tension and energise us. For example, 'Seven Nation Army' by The White Stripes uses dissonant harmonies and driving rhythm to evoke intensity and excitement.

Tempo: Music's pace, often measured in beats per minute (BPM), is a key driver of mood and behaviour. For example, slower music (60–90 BPM) aligns with the resting heart rate, promoting relaxation which can reduce stress-related cortisol.[3]

Brainwaves are also affected by music. If we like the music, alpha waves, which are associated with relaxation and focus, can be stimulated. If the music is faster, this stimulates beta waves, which are associated with higher cognitive thinking such as problem-solving.[4] Choosing music you find pleasing is important if you want to achieve positive emotional and cognitive effects.

Music that speaks to us

Music can take us on an emotional rollercoaster. Let's use the Iso Principle discussed in Chapter 6 to see how music can help us transition through a moment of anxiety, irritability, or mental overload. Let's use the example of agitation:

Phase one: Choose music that matches your mood. Listen to fast-tempo tracks that reflect your agitation, featuring punchy rhythms, distorted harmonies, and minor keys, such as 'Smells Like Teen Spirit' by Nirvana or 'Bad Guy' by Billie Eilish.

Phase two: Shift to balance. Transition to a moderate tempo (around 90 BPM), blending minor and major chords, softer dynamics, and warm timbres, such as 'Wonderwall' by Oasis or 'Shivers' by Ed Sheeran. This step lowers your heart rate and bridges intensity with calm.

Phase three: End with calm. Slow the tempo (around 60 BPM) to simple melodic harmonies and mainly major chords, like 'Gymnopédie No. 1' by Erik Satie or 'Motion' by Khalid. This creates mental space for relaxation.

Lyrics can deepen your connection, while instrumentals allow for reflection. Take as long as you need with each phase to let the music work its magic.

A moving performance

Because music affects our physiology and psychology, you can understand why athletes listen to music before an event. Synchronising music with your heartbeat can also be helpful with rhythmic exercises such as running because it motivates you to move along with it. A key influencing factor in exercise is the sense of 'controlling' the beat as you move in sync with the music.[5]

For mental tasks, music may aid memory and focus. A small study found that both slow and fast music improved cognitive task performance compared to silence.[6] While beta waves naturally increase when we try and solve problems, the results showed that they were stimulated more when music was played compared to completing tasks in silence, and that faster music stimulated higher levels of beta waves. It was noted that an element of familiarity and preference for the music also mattered. It must be stressed this study was small, and as you will read, many variables will influence whether music will help or hinder your cognitive ability.

Research aside, throughout history we have had an innate understanding that harnessing music and sounds can influence our wellbeing, whether that was tribal bonding or simply facing the day like Sigrid in Chapter 6, but as with other sensory experiences, there are no absolutes. For example, I would call myself a sound Sensor. This means I may benefit from music *before* I engage in a task, but it would distract me *during* a task. I have attended countless workshops where background music played while we were meant to do individual exercises. I found it incredibly distracting—and don't get me started on facilitators who offer 'handy hints' throughout the session. It made it impossible for me to focus.

Make some noise

Kudos if you play an instrument, another form of Action. Not only do you get a Happy DOSE just by listening to music, especially live music, but you also earn an extra hit of dopamine and endorphins as a reward for the effort and coordination it takes to play, along with a host of cognitive benefits. There is plenty of evidence that shows learning to play a musical instrument and making music can give someone a lifelong advantage in areas such as mathematics, speech processing, and memory compared to not learning an instrument.[7] This may give some parents a reason to pause before discouraging their child from joining a band.

Live music, singing, and playing an instrument with others are great examples of leveraging the interplay of the senses. I guess this also makes choirs cool!

Chapter 13. A Sound Mind

Hum a few bars

As discussed in Chapter 6, singing, chanting, and humming are simple ways to activate the vagus nerve because one of the 'off-ramps' of the 'vagus highway' reaches our vocal cords. This can activate the parasympathetic nervous system supporting a state of calm. Vocal practices can therefore affect several parts of our physiology, helping to lower cortisol while also boosting dopamine, serotonin, and endorphins, which enhance mood and wellbeing.

An international survey-based study with 464 regular chanters examined the psychological effects of chanting, such as focus, mindfulness, mystical experiences, and mind wandering. It found that more frequent and intentional chanting significantly enhanced a state of flow and reduced distracting thoughts. These experiences were strongly linked to higher overall wellbeing and quality of life.[8]

With these types of effects, it is no surprise that chanting has been practiced for centuries and can be found across a variety of countries such as Ethiopia, India, and Finland, to name just a few.[9] In the West, Gregorian chants, dating back to 600 AD, were used in the Roman Catholic Church and are still practiced today.[10]

I explored chanting by participating in a university trial. Initially it felt unnatural, but over time, I noticed increased breath awareness and relaxation. Chanting isn't a habit I have established, but I still benefit from the breathing awareness.

Healing frequencies

Solfeggio frequencies are specific tones that proponents believe can promote healing and wellbeing. These frequencies are supposedly derived from ancient Gregorian scales and are often associated with spiritual practices.[11]

The use of these frequencies as healing frequencies only came about in the 1970s. For example, 528 Hz is known as the 'miracle tone' and is said to promote transformation and DNA repair. However, scientific evidence supporting the healing effects of solfeggio frequencies is lacking.[12] I asked the lead researcher of the chanting trial I participated in about this. She said she wasn't aware of robust evidence that specific frequencies impact specific emotional states.

Following my curiosity, I attended a solfeggio vocalisation session, where the instructor said any effect comes from vocalising with the frequency, not just listening to it. This implies the benefit may come from activating the vagus nerve.

I believe the effect of listening to these frequencies is more likely related to personal belief and the calming effect of any slow, repetitive sound, especially if you vocalise along with it.

Soothing sounds

Binaural beats

Binaural beats use slightly different frequencies in each ear to create a perceived 'third frequency' in the brain. The goal is to stimulate specific brainwave activity. For example, a tone of 300 Hz in one ear and 310 Hz in the other creates a 10 Hz difference, which aligns with alpha brainwaves associated with relaxation and calm, clear thinking.[13] The goal is to directly target specific brainwaves, which we cannot do through normal hearing for a number of reasons. First, we can't physically hear the frequency that most of the brainwaves respond to because they are too low; second, we interpret general sounds through our limbic system, which means our brainwaves are indirectly influenced. Binaural beats seek to bypass these factors and work on the idea that your brain directly 'calculates' the frequency to minimise possible variables.[14] However, evidence for their effectiveness is mixed. A review of fourteen studies found that while some showed benefits, others did not confirm significant effects.[15] In short, the jury is still out.

I understand why people are exploring this; who wouldn't want an easy way to relax or boost productivity? If you want to try binaural beats, always use headphones to ensure the tones are delivered accurately. Without them, you are simply experiencing sound as you normally would, not the intended direct brainwave stimulation.

Figure 13.1 outlines how brainwaves can affect your thinking and behaviour. All brainwave types are active to some degree at any given time, though their dominance shifts depending on your mental, emotional, and physical state.

Brainwave	Frequency hertz (Hz)	Description
Delta	1–4	Associated with deep sleep
Theta	4–8	Drowsiness, low-level alertness. Aspects of theta are seen in meditation, analysis, and creativity
Alpha	8–13	Relaxed awake state, including relaxed concentration
Beta	13–30	Active thinking and concentration. Very high levels associated with stress, tension, and high emotions
Gamma	30–40	High-level cognitive function and information processing

Figure 13.1. How brainwaves affect your thinking and behaviour.
Vilnius University Press.[16]

A rainbow of sounds

Colour labels are often used for sounds that are designed to block out unwanted noise when trying to sleep, work, or relax. However, there is limited and inconclusive research on their ability to alleviate stress or anxiety.

White, pink, brown, and green noise refer to sounds that differ in intensity. White noise is even across all frequencies, sounding like static or a fan. Pink noise reduces in intensity at higher frequencies, resembling the sound of a waterfall, while brown noise further reduces in intensity at higher frequencies, creating a deeper tone like rainfall. Green noise amplifies the frequencies in the middle range and sound similar to ocean waves or a stream. It's not an official scientific category like white or pink noise, but it's often used to describe sounds that feel natural, balanced, and calming. Overall, while research is inconclusive on specific benefits, these steady sounds may mask disruptive noises and promote focus or sleep.[17] The key is finding a sound that resonates with you.

Human experience and science confirm sounds can be a very useful aid to our wellbeing and enjoyment of life, but don't expect miracles. It's easy to get hopeful with so many advocates selling sound as the ultimate de-stressing solution. Luckily, there are plenty of free options online, so explore and see what works for you.

Autonomous sensory meridian response (ASMR)

I'm watching a recipe video on Instagram. Crunch goes the cabbage as the leaves are torn from the base; chop, chop goes the knife through the carrot, while the oil sizzles loudly in the pan. This video amplifies the sounds to grab your attention, making it similar to an ASMR video. ASMR describes the experience of tingling sensations in the crown of the head in response to a range of audiovisual triggers such as whispering, tapping, and hand movements. The focus is often on relaxation and sleep.[18]

With millions of ASMR videos viewed online, it's clear that many people like them. For others, though, they may seem odd or even unsettling. Themes vary, from acknowledging stress to offering virtual treatments like haircuts or acupuncture. The common thread is the attention given to the viewer, which may also appeal to those who are feeling lonely.

In a CNN interview, Giulia Poerio, a lecturer in psychology at the University of Essex, notes that ASMR can feel trance-like and hypnotic to those who enjoy it, potentially creating a meditative state. Her research found that people who experience ASMR showed reductions in heart rate similar to the effects of mindfulness and music-based stress relief. However, she also mentions that research in this area is still in its infancy.[19] If you're curious, search for ASMR videos on platforms like YouTube, focusing on themes that interest you.

✶ Sound business ✶

Just like light and colour, businesses understand how music and sounds can influence consumer mood and behaviour. From hotel lobbies to supermarkets, the right soundscape can create a welcoming atmosphere, boost spending, and even shape how we perceive the quality of a product. Think of advertisements or movies: soundtracks are always carefully selected to evoke specific emotions.

Research shows that slower instrumental music in supermarkets (less than 72 BPM) can encourage shoppers to linger and spend more money compared to upbeat tracks (over 94 BPM). The relaxed tempo creates a sense of ease, making people feel comfortable enough to browse longer and fill their trolleys.[20]

In contrast, a gym or fitness centre might use fast-paced music (120 BPM or more) to energise members, motivating them to move and push through workouts.

Even the characteristics of wine can be influenced by sound. Various studies have found that participants can transfer the attributes of a piece of music to the wine they are drinking. For example, in one study, participants had a choice of words to describe a wine. When music was 'powerful and heavy' the majority of participants marked the wine with the same description, even if it was a white wine.[21] Hosting friends for dinner? Why not pair your wine with some refined melodies. There's every chance it could elevate their perception of the wine and the whole evening.

But not all environments get it right. Loud, energetic music in stores targeting younger customers might seem trendy, but it often drives shoppers to hurry, which can reduce overall spending. I've found that sometimes the volume of supermarket music means I really notice the track, distracting me from shopping as I engage with the upbeat music, not my shopping list.

The key to optimising sound effectively is tailoring it to the purpose of the space. The table in Figure 13.2 provides guidance on sound characteristics across various environments.

Environment	BPM range	Volume (dB)	Sound characteristics
Hotel lobby	50–70 BPM	50–60 dB	Soft instrumental music, no vocals, harmonious tones for a calm and inviting ambience
Supermarket	60–90 BPM	50–70 dB	Positive melodic music, instrumental preferred to avoid distraction or a sense of haste
Fitness centre	120–140 BPM	70–85 dB	High-energy tracks with consistent rhythms encourage movement
Restaurant (fine dining)	60–80 BPM	50–60 dB	Slow, soothing melodies promote conversation and a sense of sophistication
Retail store	80–100 BPM	60–75 dB	Upbeat music to energise but not overwhelm shoppers, while avoiding distracting vocals

Figure 13.2. Sounds to enhance specific spaces

Outside a business environment, the lessons we can apply to our personal soundscapes are:
- Use slower BPMs to relax during dinner or unwind in the evening.
- Choose faster BPMs to energise yourself during workouts or chores.
- Experiment with classical or instrumental music to elevate the atmosphere during special occasions.

These examples highlight how sound, like the other senses, doesn't work in isolation. For example, soft lighting paired with calming music can make a hotel lobby feel more welcoming, relaxing, and luxurious. Likewise, upbeat colours combined with energising music can invigorate gym-goers. The goal is to curate experiences that feel harmonious and intentional. This doesn't mean each sense should always have the same level of intensity. We'll delve further into this in Chapter 17.

✳ They sound smart ✳

Have you heard that listening to classical music can make children smarter? This idea, known as the 'Mozart effect', captivated parents in the 1990s. The concept came from a 1993 study suggesting that listening to a specific piece by Mozart temporarily boosted spatial reasoning skills, such as solving puzzles or navigating mazes. However, the findings were misunderstood, amplified in the media, and used to market products like Mozart CDs. In reality, any improvements were short-lived.[22]

It's now understood that it is the enjoyment of any music or engaging auditory experience can provide short-term cognitive benefits by enhancing mood and focus. For children, this could mean better learning conditions, not necessarily higher intelligence.[23]

So while the hype was overblown, the lesson is clear: whether it's listening to Beethoven, a bedtime story, or an upbeat song, the key is connection through sound.

✷ Black noise ✷

One colour of noise I haven't mentioned refers to the most elusive sound of all—silence. While the term 'black noise' is rarely used, it typically signifies the absence of sound, or near silence, which can feel foreign in a world filled with constant auditory input. Imagine the stereotyped movie scene: city dwellers escaping for a weekend getaway. They arrive at a beautiful countryside homestead. Sally steps out of the car, breathes in the fresh air, and exclaims, 'Oh, it's so quiet, you can't hear a thing!' But if she listened closely, she would realise that the silence isn't completely silent; there is the rustle of leaves, birdsong, or perhaps distant water sounds. These natural sounds act as auditory rest, allowing the brain to relax and recharge. This helps to reduce stress while providing many benefits such as boosting creativity, focus, and problem-solving.[24]

Sadly, today many people feel compelled to fill every moment with a noise such as podcasts, music, or endless scrolling on social media. It's as if silence has become synonymous with wasted time. The constant dopamine hits from screens, emails, and social media can make a lack of information and sound input feel boring. But keep in mind our daily cognitive capacity is limited, even mindless scrolling will deplete your energy.

I struggle to sit in silence. My solution? Walks without headphones. These become moments to tune into what I call 'the podcast of my mind'. With no agenda, I let my thoughts wander freely; ideas flourish, arguments are 'had', and problems are solved. It was during these silent walks that the principles of Total Sensory Wellbeing began to take shape. Walk by walk, thought by thought, the logic of looking after ourselves through our senses became so obvious. As my brain relaxed more and more, I also began noticing the birds in my neighbourhood. They had always been there, but my stress drowned out their presence. I call this experience 'the day I heard the birds'. It was a turning point. If you haven't heard this podcast yet, I urge you to tune in. Subscription is free.

Even if silence feels uncomfortable at first, especially if it amplifies negative thoughts, starting with short, intentional quiet moments can help. Over time, these can become opportunities for clarity, renewal, and creativity. Silence is not a waste of time; it grants freedom for independent thought and fortitude to dream and make decisions.

Silence isn't black; it's golden.

✣ Sleep soundly ✣

In an ideal world, we'd all sleep in soundproof rooms, but for most of us, that's not realistic. Quality sleep is essential for maintaining a healthy circadian rhythm, which underpins sensory wellbeing. Noise disturbances, whether from traffic, household sounds, or even low-level humming from appliances, can impact sleep quality, leaving us irritable and unfocused.[25]

This is when fighting noise with a curated sound may be beneficial. You can experiment with the background sounds discussed, like white noise, nature tracks, or slow, melodic music, to mask disruptions. Keep volumes as low as you can to create a relaxing environment for sleep. You don't want the background sound to be intrusive. Apps and smart devices make these options easily accessible, and there are plenty of options to try.

Physical changes can also make a difference. Soundproof curtains, rugs, or thicker glazing of windows can help reduce external noise, while hallway runners dampen household echoes. Even small acts, like agreeing on quieter night-time routines with family, can improve your sleep environment.

Test different approaches, whether it's calming soundscapes or physical adjustments, because quality rest isn't a luxury, it's essential. After all, wouldn't you and others appreciate a more rested, recharged version of you?

* Sound behaviour guides *

The guidelines in Figure 13.3 are examples of how you can use music and sound to influence your thoughts and behaviour. Consider how you might use them prior to or during an event, such as before a presentation or while exercising. Please don't forget the power of silence to produce states of relaxation, clarity, focus, and creativity.

Mental state	Examples of music/sounds	Description	BPM guide range
Rejuvenated	Upbeat pop or dance music	Energetic beats and positive lyrics with music that builds and falls gently can increase motivation and energy levels	90–140 BPM
	Rhythmic drumming or percussion	Repetitive, lively rhythms stimulate physical energy and mental alertness	100–130 BPM
	Nature sounds (birdsong, waterfalls)	Sounds from nature can refresh the mind and body, promoting a sense of renewal	N/A (natural rhythm)
Focused	Classical and general music with structured harmonies and repetitive instrumental music	Removes distractions to enhance concentration and cognitive function. BPMs closer to 60 can entrain the heart rate for deeper calm focus	60–90 BPM
	Classical and general music with repetitive, melodic patterns that evolve subtly. No or minimal lyrics	Light work or routine, repetitive tasks where the sound acts as a stimulator to boost alertness and make tasks more enjoyable	100–120 BPM

	White or pink noise	Neutral sounds mask distractions and improve sustained attention	N/A
	Binaural beats (alpha waves 8–12 Hz)	Frequencies associated with relaxed but focused mental states	N/A (wave frequencies)
	Binaural beats (beta waves 14–20 Hz, gamma waves around 40 Hz)	Beta waves for analysis, decision-making, and problem-solving. Gamma waves for deeper problem-solving, integration of ideas, learning, and insight. Be careful of overstimulation	N/A (wave frequencies)
Creative	Ambient electronic	Rich, ambient layers stimulate creative thinking without overwhelming the mind	70–90 BPM
	Jazz without vocals	Instrumental jazz provides light improvisational elements to inspire creativity	90–120 BPM
	High-energy sounds	Fast-paced instrumentals boost alertness for problem-solving and creative input	120–140 BPM
	Nature sounds (rain, ocean waves)	Gentle, repetitive sounds reduce cognitive overload, creating space for new ideas	N/A (wave frequencies)
Creative and relaxed	Binaural beats (theta waves 4–8 Hz)	Frequencies that promote deep relaxation, creative and meditative states	N/A (wave frequencies)
Relaxed	Classical music	Slow, melodic compositions calm the mind and reduce stress	50–70 BPM

	Ambient music (soft synthesiser, low tones)	Soothing ambient music lowers heart rate and encourages relaxation	40–60 BPM
	Nature sounds (forest, gentle wind)	The calming effects of nature sounds can induce a relaxed, peaceful state	N/A (natural rhythm)
Uplifted	Upbeat pop or rock music	Positive, high-energy music with motivating lyrics lifts mood and boosts confidence	120–150 BPM
	Latin or reggae rhythms	Rhythmic, upbeat music promotes happiness and movement	80–110 BPM
	Classical music	Light, fast-paced classical compositions can create feelings of joy and optimism	100–120 BPM
	Gospel or choir music	Harmonious, uplifting music enhances a sense of joy and spiritual elevation	70–90 BPM
	Binaural beats -variable	Calm alertness and flow: Alpha waves 8–13 Hz. Uplifted mood, alertness: Beta waves 13-30 Hz. Elevated cognition and joy: Gamma waves 3-40 Hz	N/A (wave frequencies)
Sleep	Ambient music, soft, low tempo	Gentle ambient music helps slow brain activity and prepares the body for sleep	40–60 BPM
	Nature sounds (rain, crickets, ocean waves)	Consistent, rhythmic nature sounds signal relaxation to the brain, aiding sleep onset	N/A (natural rhythm)

	White or pink noise	Neutral, constant noise blocks out sudden environmental sounds, improving sleep quality	N/A
	Binaural beats (delta waves 1–4 Hz)	Frequencies that promote deep sleep by guiding the brain into a restful state	N/A (wave frequencies)
Any state	Black noise	A sense of silence frees the brain to relax or focus on what's important in the moment	N/A

Figure 13.3. Sound behaviour guide

Controlling background noise

If you want to use background sounds either to block noise or to improve focus, there are some guidelines to follow, otherwise you run the risk of disrupting your attention.

Besides blocking unwanted noise, some people prefer sounds in the background to distract them from their own thoughts, which can improve their concentration. Others may want to promote a state of flow or purposefully trigger certain brainwaves or emotions.

To be effective, background sounds or music should be played at low volume without spoken words. This minimises the chance of breaking your train of thought.[26] If you select music that really moves you, it can also distract as you become emotionally engaged in it. For example, if you get caught up in the words and start singing along in your mind, this is a signal that you are not fully engaged in what you're doing in the moment. Remember, it can take up to twenty-five minutes to be truly focused again. Figure 13.4 provides a guide on how to use background sound effectively.

Background sound	Recommendations
Sound levels	Under 40 dB for intense focus, 40–50 dB for light tasks
Characteristics	• Steady rhythm, not emotionally stirring • Instrumental music • Rhythmic nature sounds (e.g. gentle rain, ocean waves) • White, pink, brown noise • Targeted brainwave sounds
No background sound	Noise-cancelling headphones

Figure 13.4. Background sound guide

WHAT MAKES SENSE TO YOU?

In your Total Sensory Wellbeing notes, create a dedicated Acoustics section and observe the sounds you hear during the day and night and which space they occur in.

Note which sounds bother you the most. Consider downloading a free decibel app to gauge the true intrusiveness of these sounds. While we can't eliminate all unwanted noise, remember, a noise as low as 45 dB can be disruptive. Even if you think you're used to it, it's still sapping brain energy, contributing to mental fatigue.

Focusing on the room you are reviewing, under 'Acoustics Potential Improvements', what are some physical ways you could reduce intrusive noises? This is a brainstorming phase, not a financial commitment. Consider thicker curtains, rugs, or even changing the flooring. Would you benefit from improved window or wall insulation, or even a dividing wall? Stylish acoustic panels can also add to an interior's aesthetic. Be open to ideas, even if they seem unrealistic, as they can guide practical decisions later. Browse platforms like Pinterest for ideas.

If you work or study in noisy environments, try noise-cancelling headphones to create silence or listen to instrumental music at a low volume to stay focused.

For better sleep, address disruptive noises with physical changes like rugs, floor-runners, or soundproofing. Use apps or smart devices that play calming sounds, such as nature or coloured noise. Small actions, like asking family members to minimise noise during certain hours, can also make a big difference.

Curate your own soundscapes

Create personal playlists: Build playlists for specific tasks or moods: energising tracks for workouts, calming tunes for relaxation, or feel-good songs to boost your mood. Use the Iso Principle to guide emotional transitions.

Family playlists: Use the power of music to motivate people with everyday tasks. Create themed tracks like 'take out the rubbish', 'clean your room', or 'we're leaving in five minutes'. Yes, it might feel cheesy, but the humour, combined with the right beat, can genuinely shift moods and boost cooperation, especially if each person chooses their own tracks.

Make your own music: Get a Happy DOSE by learning an instrument or even tapping along to a rhythm. Singing or humming can further boost your mood by stimulating the vagus nerve.

Seek silence: Embrace moments of silence for mental clarity and relaxation. If silence feels awkward, start with a walk, allowing your mind to wander freely. Incorporating this into your morning routine offers the added benefit of natural light, supporting your circadian rhythm.

Build connection through sound

Enjoy some live music with friends and strangers to experience the benefits of a full Happy DOSE and brainwave synchronisation.

Challenge yourself to call someone instead of texting. A simple phone call can foster connection, boosting oxytocin and reducing cortisol for both you and the recipient. Even leaving a voice message can have this effect.

> **Sound advice**
>
> Don't overwhelm yourself by trying everything at once. Pick a few actions and build these habits gradually. For example, you might try singing in the shower, making one intentional phone call per week, and walking once a week without your phone. Set reminders in your calendar to prompt you. As silly as it may feel to have a task reminder for 'sing in the shower', if it's not a habit, it's easy to forget. Adjust and refine as needed, but don't hesitate to explore. If you never try, you'll never know.

With this sound advice on board, it's time to take a deep breath and explore the wonderful world of Aroma.

CHAPTER 14.
SCENTS OF WELLBEING

How to use essential oils

The active compounds in essential oils and the skin-nourishing qualities of the carrier oils used to dilute them mean that essential oils are used in industries such as skincare, aging, and health care. Here the focus is on how essential oils can support mental fortitude, resilience, and various states such as a sense of relaxation, rejuvenation, creativity, and productivity.

You may consider certain aromas your 'go-to' scents because they make you feel good. For me, that's jasmine. I instinctively smile when I walk past a blooming jasmine plant. I equate it to a serotonin boost! Blends are extremely popular too. While scientific research hasn't been carried out to clarify the effectiveness of specific blends, there are people who have dedicated their careers to the research and use of essential oil blends to help people. Their work is based on hundreds of years of documented experience. Today some of the most common conditions people seek support for are stress, anxiety, and sleep.

Regardless of the data, if you personally feel a benefit from using blended essential oils then you should continue to enjoy them, while taking note of the preliminary evidence supporting the use of single scents as well.

When using essential oils, be aware that as your mood and circumstances change, the type of scent you want may change as well. This includes choosing no scent at all. For example, even though I am a qualified aromatherapy practitioner, if I feel refreshed, clear-headed and self-motivated, I often don't even think to use essential oils. However, I will gladly reach for the peppermint or lemon when I feel tired or flat and need to engage my brain.

Here's a comprehensive guide on how you can make the most of essential oils to enhance your sense of wellbeing.

∗ Safety first! ∗

- **Do not ingest essential oils:** They are highly concentrated and can be toxic if swallowed.
- **Inhalation:** Use a diffuser, burner, or other method as directed. Using larger quantities or for longer times than recommended can have negative effects.
- **Topical use:** Always dilute essential oils according to instructions before applying them to skin. Direct skin contact can cause skin damage and adverse reactions.
- **Storage:** Keep essential oils out of reach of children and pets.
- **Odour:** A strange smell or colour means the oil is likely spoiled and should be discarded.
- **Pregnancy and health conditions:** If you're pregnant, nursing, or have a medical condition, consult a health care professional before using essential oils.
- **Use in children:** Essential oil is not generally recommended for children under the age of three, and especially not for babies. Infants and babies have very delicate skin, particularly on the face.

If you create a face or body oil preparation, patch-test the oil first:
- Place one or two drops of the oil in a carrier oil (refer to the 'Diluting carrier oils' section below).
- Apply to a plaster and place on the inner elbow. Leave for forty-eight hours.

- If no itching, swelling, or redness occurs, the diluted oil should be safe to use.

Figure 14.1 lists various conditions that may be adversely affected by essential oils.

Do not use in pregnancy	Skin irritant*	High blood pressure—avoid	Sun sensitivity†	Epilepsy‡
Basil	Basil	Camphor	Lime	Camphor
Camphor	Bergamot	Rosemary	Bergamot	Fennel
Cedarwood Atlas	Camphor	Thyme	Lemon	Hyssop
Clary sage	Cinnamon		Bitter orange	Rosemary
Fennel	Clove			Thyme
Hyssop	Geranium			
Rosemary	Lemon			
Thyme	Peppermint			
	Pine			

Figure 14.1. Some essential oils that can cause adverse reactions

*Any essential oil has the potential to be a skin irritant if used incorrectly.
†Avoid sunlight for twelve hours after use.
‡These oils may trigger seizures.

My professional advice

- Consult a qualified health care professional or certified aromatherapist before using essential oils if you have health concerns, are pregnant, nursing, or are taking medications.
- Essential oils are potent and should be used responsibly. Follow usage guidelines provided by professionals to ensure your safety.
- Remember, just because something is natural doesn't mean

it's safe for everyone. Always read up on any essential oil you plan to use.
- The information I provide is for general insight only and not meant as a prescriptive approach.

Protecting essential oils

Ensure that you store your essential oils away from light, heat, and the air. Keep them in dark-brown bottles to protect against the light. I love the cobalt blue bottles, but, sorry, they still let the light in, which destroys the active compounds you have paid for. To protect essential oils from light and heat, you can store them in the fridge.

Buyer beware

Read labels carefully before buying. You want to make sure the contents are 100 per cent pure essential oil. Watch out for misleading claims like '100 per cent pure fragrant oil'. It should also state the botanical name of the plant and its ordinary name.

* Ways to disperse essential oils *

There are different ways to enjoy the aromas of essential oils, such as oil burners, candles, electric diffusers, and reed diffusers. Always follow the manufacturer's instructions. A lot of electric-based diffusers have timers to help with safe use.

Oil burners

Fill the burner bowl with water, add five to ten drops of up to four essential oils, and light the candle underneath. Never leave a lit candle unattended and ensure the water doesn't run dry.

Heat can alter the chemical structure of essential oils, reducing therapeutic value. Typically, the scent doesn't last as long or disperse as evenly as diffuser devices.

Electric diffusers

Follow the manufacturer's instructions regarding the amount of oil to use. As a guide, if the diffuser uses water, consider six to ten drops of essential oil for 100 ml to 200 ml of water. Small spaces and strong essentials would require fewer drops.

Exposure to essential oils

Some of the sleep trials reviewed used aromatherapy for two hours before bed. In the daytime, start with thirty to sixty minutes on and thirty to sixty minutes off. You can repeat this two to three times a day. This way, you can reinvigorate yourself without overdoing it. You don't want to get a headache or feel unwell. The oils' potency, along with room size and ventilation, will influence this.

Research shows that you don't have to consciously notice a scent for it to influence your mood and behaviour. This means running a diffuser all day won't necessarily provide greater benefits, but it will cost you more.

* Diluting essential oils *

Essential oils are diluted in a carrier oil for safe use on the body and face. Carrier oils don't have active compounds, but they can have skin-nourishing qualities. This creates a bonus effect—you can glow on the inside and the outside!

Examples of carrier oils		
Sweet almond oil	Avocado oil	Rosehip oil
Apricot kernel oil	Evening primrose oil	Macadamia oil
Jojoba oil	Grapeseed oil	Argan oil

Figure 14.2. Common carrier oils

The outlined dilutions are a guide. If you are unsure about your specific situation, consult with a trained professional.

Measuring up

While the actual volume of 'a drop' may vary, Figure 14.3 outlines approximately how many drops of essential oil make up a given volume.

Volume	Conversion	Drops of essential oil
30 ml	1 oz	600
5 ml	1 teaspoon	100
15 ml	1 tablespoon	300
1 ml	0.03 oz	20

Figure 14.3. Volume conversion guide

Dilutions for the body

Essential oil percentage	Essential oil drops	Carrier oil teaspoons	Millilitres (ml)	Ounces (oz)
0.50%	1	2	10	0.3
	2	3	15	0.5
	10	20	100	3.4
1%	2	2	10	0.3
	3	3	15	0.5
	20	20	100	3.4

2%	4	2	10	0.3
	6	3	15	0.5
	40	20	100	3.4
3%	6	2	10	0.3
	9	3	15	0.5
	60	20	100	3.4

Figure 14.4. Essential oil body dilution guide

If you want to explore other body dilutions, please seek professional advice. As a guide, for adults the massage dilution of ten drops of essential oil in 20 ml of carrier oil is as high as many spas are comfortable using. This is approximately a 2.5 per cent dilution.

Age	Body dilution	Comments
0–3 years	Not recommended	Oils high in menthol or 1,8-cineole, such as peppermint and eucalyptus, can cause respiratory issues and central nervous system issues in children under 30 months.
3–6 years	0.5%–1.5%	Lavender, citrus, and ginger are considered safe
6–15 years	1.5%–2.5%	Lower concentrations are the safest. Test for sensitivity
Over 15 years	2.0%–3.0%	10 drops of essential oil in 20 ml of carrier oil ~ 2.5% dilution

Figure 14.5. Essential oil body dilution by age guide

Dilutions beyond these ranges should only be considered for specific ailments under certified aromatherapy guidance.

Face dilutions

These typically range from 0.5 per cent to 1 per cent of essential oil in carrier oil. The skin on the face is delicate, so using a higher concentration than recommended increases the chance of experiencing a reaction. Do not use essential oils on the faces of babies and infants. Figure 14.6 outlines standard face dilutions.

Total carrier oil volume	Desired dilution	Essential oil needed
10 ml	0.5%	1 drop (0.05 ml)
10 ml	1%	2 drops (0.1 ml)

Figure 14.6. Essential oil face dilution guide

Out and about

To enjoy essential oil benefits while on the go, use a small brown-glass rollerball bottle. You can inhale lightly from the bottle or apply the oils to the inside of your wrist. If the purpose is to help combat headaches, you can apply it to your temples.

You can also invigorate or calm yourself for the day while driving; two or three drops of your chosen oil on a tissue placed near you is a quick, cost-effective way to achieve this effect.

There is an array of aromatherapy jewellery that allows you to 'wear' the oil. It typically comes in necklace and bracelet forms.

Among other devices are mini pulsed spray diffusers, which are a few centimetres in height. This could be suitable for holidays, work trips, or some office environments.

✳ Essential oils in the home ✳

Bedroom

It is safest to use essential oils before going to sleep. Diffusers and candles should never be left on or burning. Remember, you don't get any extra benefit by taking this risk. An alternative is to sprinkle a couple of drops of essential oil on a tissue and place it near or under your pillow. Be mindful of potential oil stains. Sometimes I use the oils highlighted in the trials outlined in Chapter 7. One night when I used peppermint, I put too much on the tissue. It was so overpowering that my nostrils were on fire and I had to throw it on the floor! Despite that, I slept well. In contrast, another night I used the delicate aroma of jasmine and barely noticed it, but I still enjoyed a restful sleep.

Bathroom

Bath bombs, shower steamers, and sprays can invigorate or relax you. When using products in the shower, create steam to help the oils vaporise. You can achieve the same effect by adding a few drops of a pre-made blend or a single scent to a face washer placed on a shower shelf or taps, or around your neck.

Laundry

Feel invigorated by adding a few drops of an essential oil to your linen and towels. You can achieve this by adding two to three drops to the rinse cycle of a wash. Alternatively, add one or two drops of relatively skin-safe pure essential oil directly to a towel. Lavender and tea tree oil are both good options.

General home use

Besides using diffusers in the home, porous lava rocks and reed diffusers also release scent into the air and are ideal in small spaces. You will need to assess the ratio of rocks or reeds to oil to effectively scent a room.

Having pleasant and uplifting fragrances in your home is a lovely experience and they are often most appreciated when they provide comfort and calm. Consider how you can leverage the interplay of the senses by combining scents with soothing coloured fabrics, soft textures, and warm lighting to create a more relaxing experience.

* Essential oil aroma characteristics *

Some essential oils can display a variety of characteristics, such as cardamom, which has both fruity and spicy notes. These aromas drive the aesthetic appeal of essential oils. Figure 14.7 outlines the aromatic effect of several essential oils.

Fruity	Floral	Herbs	Spicy	Woody/earthy
Lemon	Rose	Rosemary	Cinnamon	Pine
Orange	Lavender	Basil	Clove	Cedarwood
Grapefruit	Jasmine	Marjoram	Nutmeg	Frankincense
Lime	Neroli	Clary sage	Black pepper	Cypress
Mandarin	Ylang-ylang	Peppermint	Cardamom	Sandalwood
Vanilla	Chamomile	Geranium	Coriander	Rosewood

Figure 14.7. Aromatic characteristics of essential oils

Essential oils for mood and mind

Just as an oil can have different characteristics, it can also have different effects. For example, during the day an oil can make you calm, while at night it can make you sleepy. The difference may depend on the intensity of the oil preparation, your energy and mood at the time, and its interaction with other oils in a blend.

Figure 14.8 provides a sample of essential oils that can support you to achieve various states of wellbeing.

Invigorating and uplifting	Focus and clarity	Creativity	Resilience and confidence	Relaxation and sleep
Bergamot	Lemon	Bergamot	Cedarwood	Orange
Basil	Basil	Lemon	Cypress	Jasmine
Black pepper	Lemongrass	Frankincense	Cardamom	Clary sage
Cardamom	Orange	Geranium	Sweet fennel	Lemongrass
Grapefruit	Cedarwood	Neroli	Ginger	Lavender
Cinnamon	Bergamot	Jasmine	Bergamot	Ylang-ylang
Juniper	Eucalyptus radiata	Bay	Grapefruit	Sandalwood
Eucalyptus	Rosemary	Clove	Jasmine	Geranium
Peppermint	Cedarwood	Sandalwood	Pine	Petitgrain
Rosemary	Cardamom	Cypress	Orange	Mandarin

Figure 14.8. Essential oils that influence various states of mind

It's advisable to rotate your use of essential oils so that you don't end up disliking a scent because you either became bored with it or associate it with a difficult time in your life.

Let's look at some ways you can blend these oils creatively for pleasure and purpose.

✻ A positive note ✻

Aromatherapy blends can be created using the same principles as perfume. This approach classifies scents into 'notes'.

Top notes

These are the fresh and light scents you notice first. They are the most volatile and evaporate the fastest. Think floral and citrus aromas.

Middle notes

These form the body of the fragrance and evaporate more slowly than top notes. They usually comprise herb and spice essential oils.

Base notes

The least volatile, they evaporate the slowest and tend to be more relaxing, with rich and heady aromas. They typically include essential oils made from wood or resin.

Some essential oils can be classified as more than one note. For example, cinnamon can be used as a middle or a base note. Tea tree can be used as a top or a middle note. Figure 14.9 outlines how some essential oils are classified into notes.

Top note essential oils	Middle note essential oils	Base note essential oils
Lemon	Lavender	Sandalwood
Orange	Coriander	Vanilla
Bergamot	Geranium	Cedarwood
Grapefruit	Juniper berry	Frankincense
Peppermint	Clary sage	Patchouli
Eucalyptus	Chamomile	Myrrh
Lime	Cinnamon	Vetiver
Tangerine	Black pepper	Agarwood (oud)
Spearmint	Tea tree	Benzoin
Basil	Thyme	Jasmine

Cardamom	Oregano	Clove
Mandarin	Cypress	Peru balsam
Neroli	Fennel	Amyris
Pine	Nutmeg	Ylang-ylang
Petitgrain	Marjoram	Jasmine

Figure 14.9. Essential oils categorised by perfume notes

Blending principles

Feel free to mix essential oils as desired, but always follow dilution recommendations. If you are a beginner, start with traditional blending approaches and identify what appeals to you.

Commercial perfumes often use the 'standard note blend' outlined in Figure 14.10. The amount of each note can vary in this blend, but the middle note will always dominate, followed by the top note then the base note.

Blend combinations	Top note	Middle note	Base note
All one note	1 drop of each top note	1 drop of each middle note	3 drops of each base note
Standard note blend	3 drops	5 drops	2 drops
Basic 1, 2, 3	3 drops	2 drops	1 drop
Base note variation	4 drops	3 drops	2 drops

Figure 14.10. Blending guide: top, middle, and base notes

Start with a maximum of three essential oils to avoid overcomplicating the process and diluting the benefit of the oils. It can also become very expensive if you buy without purpose.

Undiluted blends should not be used directly on the skin. They can be used in pure form in diffusers and oil burners. For safe use, refer to 'Body Dilutions' or 'Face Dilutions'.

Pure blend examples

Have fun experimenting with blend recipes as outlined in Figure 14.11. Some of these examples are a variation on the basic blending guidelines and are based on years of aromatherapy expert experience.

Notes	Rejuvenating	Focus	Day relax	Confidence
Top	Orange, sweet 5 drops	Peppermint 4 drops	Chamomile, roman 3 drops	Cardamom 1 drop
Middle	Jasmine 3 drops	Basil 3 drops	Marjoram 5 drops	Coriander 2 drops
Base	Sandalwood 2 drops	Frankincense 2 drops	Cedarwood 2 drops	Ginger 3 drops

Notes (continues)	Creativity	Deep calm	Sleep
Top	Bergamot 2 drops	Mandarin 3 drops	Lemon 1 drop
Middle	Lavender 2 drops	Petitgrain 2 drops	Clary sage 1 drop
Base	Rosemary 1 drop	Ylang-ylang 1 drop	Vetiver 1 drop

Figure 14.11. Blending recipes: top, middle, and base notes

✶ Essential oil candles ✶

A scented candle can be very alluring, thanks to the interplay of the senses; it has a wonderful fragrance and the gentle flame helps create a warm and relaxing Atmosphere. However, many commercial aromatherapy candles do not use 100 per cent pure essential oils because the scent evaporates faster than synthetically fragranced candles. The volatility of the active compounds in essential oils also makes the production process unstable. Compared to artificially fragranced oils, essential oils have a lack of scent 'throw', or room coverage, and essential oils are more expensive. All these factors place risk and uncertainty on someone producing 100 per cent pure essential oil candles on a commercial level. While artificially fragranced candles can add to the Atmosphere of a room, as you read in Chapter 7, artificial scents just don't have the same impact on our wellbeing as pure essential oils do. This brings us to the point of how to manage and tailor all the scents in your home, the unwanted as well as the desirable.

WHAT MAKES SENSE TO YOU?

In your Room Review notes, revisit what you want to do and how you want to feel. List which basic blends or single scents could benefit you in this space. What are the most practical oil-dispensing options for you?

Have your oils and device on hand ready to use. This is especially useful when you're low on energy and need them the most.

In your Total Sensory Wellbeing notes, create an Aroma section. Consciously assess the smells in your home. Note down the location of odours that could be causing you discomfort or harm, like mould, dampness, and dust. Regular deep cleans can uncover and remove unwanted irritants that you may not have realised were present.

If you experience persistent or invasive problems such as mould, you may want to look at more involved solutions, such as improving window and door seals and installing ventilation systems. You might even consider an inspection from a building biologist to assess the 'health' of your home. These can be listed under 'Aroma Potential Improvements'.

To reduce pollutant fumes in your home, consider homemade cleaning solutions that incorporate essential oils that not only clean your home and keep bugs away, but also positively affect your sense of wellbeing.

Bring the power of plants into your life. Air purifying plants could

> make a positive difference in your home as well as introduce a calming element of nature.
>
> Perhaps you live with someone who pays little attention to their personal space and seems to welcome a messy room with the curtains drawn and the smell of dirty laundry wafting in the air. From what you have read, you can see how all three sensory experiences can create a negative headspace. Aroma could be one subtle way to try and shift the balance.
>
> Finally, consider how you might uplift occasions such as visits from family and friends or parties. There is a plethora of essential oils and possible blends available. Source them from reputable providers who sell 100 per cent pure essential oils. They typically offer advice as well.
>
> Essential oils can be such a delight. Experiment and have fun with them. If you live with others, get them involved. Together you could create a signature scent for each person, including a family blend. They make great gifts too.

Aroma is such a pleasing way to help manage stress, combat fatigue, and enhance your focus, but true resilience comes from the interplay of all the senses. Aroma and Appetite are an example of one type of interplay. Without aroma, there is no flavour. Their combination helps shape our memories, emotions, and taste experiences, making food an evocative part of life. Whether you're enjoying a meal or recalling moments with loved ones, thanks to aroma, the experience of food stirs something deeper. Let's chew on this in the next chapter.

CHAPTER 15.
FOOD FOR THOUGHT

Eat for mood and cognition

I cannot overstate the significance of diet for both physical and mental health. Our sedentary lifestyles, coupled with easy access to nutritionally poor food, predispose us to metabolic health issues. To clarify, metabolism refers to the chemical processes in our cells that manage energy, essential for our survival.[1] Metabolic diseases include obesity, cardiovascular issues, and diabetes. When metabolic issues arise, they exacerbate stress and fatigue, throwing our energy balance out of sync and making it harder to manage daily life.[2]

✳ The gut–brain axis: It's a two-way street ✳

As outlined in Chapter 8, the relationship between diet and mental health is bidirectional. This means what we eat influences our mental state, and our mental state can affect what, how much, and how often we choose to eat. Scientists call this dynamic connection the 'gut–brain axis'.[3]

Dr Christopher M Palmer from Harvard Medical School explains in his book *Brain Energy* how some of these mechanisms work. Diet influences mitochondria, the 'powerhouses' of our cells. Mitochondria exist throughout the body and play a crucial role in producing energy for body, brain, and hormone function. For instance, mitochondria in the gut regulate the energy supply needed for serotonin synthesis, influencing its quality and availability. While the 10 per cent of serotonin produced in the brain regulates emotions, gut-derived serotonin plays a vital role in digestion, metabolism, and sleep, which in turn indirectly influences brain health. Supporting mitochondrial health through diet helps sustain these essential processes and significantly affects our overall wellbeing.[4]

Food beyond fuel

Food is fundamental to how we function, as well as being central to our social interactions and emotional experiences. When we taste we also smell, and those aromas interact with the limbic system, our emotion and memory centre. This is why meals often carry emotional significance; they remind us of who we were with, how we felt, and where we were. It's one of the reasons food is so enjoyable.

As you have read, food triggers our reward centre to release dopamine when we consume calorie-rich foods such as fats and sugars. Our brain is saying 'job well done for finding high-energy foods'. Certain food combinations that include tryptophan can also support the release of another element of the Happy DOSE, serotonin. Unfortunately, this includes foods high in sugar.

With such powerful gut–brain sensory triggers at play, it's no wonder many people struggle to eat well for long-term health. This doesn't mean it's not possible. The more you understand the benefits of brain-healthy eating, as well as the consequences of poor eating patterns, the more motivated you might be to adjust your behaviour to boost brain health one bite at a time. So let's explore what the brain 'likes' to 'eat'.

∗ What the brain eats ∗

The brain relies on three key nutrients: fats, glucose, and protein. Each plays a unique role in supporting energy needs, brain health, mental clarity, and emotional resilience. Let's explore how these nutrients impact your brain, and practical ways to improve your diet.

Fats: Function and framework

Healthy unsaturated fats are essential for brain function, providing critical support for cell membranes, neurotransmission, and inflammation control. Monounsaturated fatty acids (MUFAs) and polyunsaturated fatty acids (PUFAs) also contribute to heart health, improve cholesterol, and decrease inflammation.[5] Our body can make some MUFAs, but we can't make PUFAs, they must come from our diet.[6] If you're wondering, the terms 'monounsaturated' and 'polyunsaturated' refer to the chemical structure of the fat.[7]

Two PUFAs, omega-3 and omega-6, are particularly vital for brain health.

Omega-3 fatty acids:[8]
- maintain brain cell integrity
- support serotonin and dopamine flow, improving mood and focus
- regulate the stress response and reduce inflammation linked to cognitive decline.

Seafood, especially salmon and mackerel, is the best source of omega-3, providing eicosapentaenoic acid (EPA) and docosahexaenoic acid (DHA), two forms of omega-3 essential for brain health. While plant-based omega-3s (like flaxseed, also known as linseed) are beneficial, the body can only absorb about 3 per cent after extensive processing.[9]

Omega-6 fatty acids[10] play a complementary role by:
- supporting immune function with a pro-inflammatory response that helps fight infections
- working alongside omega-3s to balance the body's inflammatory response
- facilitating brain repair and cell communication.

The balance between omega-6 and omega-3 is crucial. A thirteen-year study involving 85,000 UK adults found that those with the highest omega-6 to omega-3 blood ratios had a significantly greater risk of dying from all causes, including cancer and heart disease. In contrast, higher levels of omega-3 were strongly protective, regardless of omega-6 levels.[11] This means omega-3 intake alone plays a critical role in long-term health outcomes. Other studies have also shown that imbalances in these fatty acid ratios can be found in mood disorders.[12]

There are variances in health care recommendations as to what the ideal ratio of omega-6 to omega-3 should be. Commonly quoted ratios are 4:1, 2:1, or even 1:1, which is supposedly closer to what our ancestors would have experienced.[13] Modern diets, heavy in processed foods that use a lot of omega-6 oils, combined with less seafood, skew this balance significantly, with some ratios reaching 20:1.[14] This is a growing trend in countries that have adopted fast-food and convenience-food dietary habits. Many people now take omega-3 supplements to help compensate for these dietary shifts.[15]

In the pursuit of a practical approach, I spoke with nutritionist and health scientist Amelia Phillips, a highly experienced professional who runs wellbeing programmes and shares expert advice with media outlets. Amelia advises prioritising fruit-based oils like olive and avocado over seed oils high in omega-6. She also recommends preparing meals at home to better control oil quality and nutrient balance, following an 80:20 rule: 80 per cent of meals made at home, 20 per cent bought outside the home. This might be your lunch each day. Sometimes even healthy lunches will contain hidden omega-6 and sugar. Reducing consumption of processed foods and meals prepared outside the home is a step-by-step process when convenience means so much to people. It's about finding ways that work for your lifestyle. Besides the health benefit, there's likely to be a financial one too! At the very least, focus on your omega-3 intake.

A comprehensive list of fats and foods that contain other dietary components can be found at the end of this chapter.

Proteins: Repairing and sustaining

Proteins are the building blocks of brain cells and are essential for:[16]
- repair and maintenance of brain tissues
- learning, memory, and cognitive function
- producing Happy DOSE chemicals
- regulating blood glucose and stabilising energy and mood.[17]

Proteins are made up of amino acids. The body can produce eleven amino acids, but nine must come from food, these are called essential amino acids. Animal proteins contain all nine essential amino acids, making them 'complete' proteins. Plant proteins, while rich in amino acids, often lack one or more essential components, requiring a varied diet to ensure all nine are consumed (for example, pairing rice with beans).[18]

Soy, however, contains all nine essential amino acids. While its protein levels are lower than those of animal proteins, it remains an excellent source, particularly for vegetarians and vegans. Despite its benefits, soy has been the subject of controversy, with concerns about its potential links to hormonal imbalance and breast cancer. However, leading health authorities, including Harvard Medical School, confirm there is insufficient evidence to support these claims for the general population.[19] The message that soy neither causes nor protects against breast cancer is also reinforced by breastcancer.org.[20]

For healthy adults, both in Australia[21] and the United States,[22] guidelines recommend consuming approximately 0.8 grams of protein for every kilo of body weight. This quantity is now commonly considered too low. Amelia Philips, as well as other nutrition experts, recommend 1–1.5 grams per kilo of body weight, especially if you exercise regularly.

While vegans need to focus on eating a variety of plant foods to get all nine amino acids, meat-eaters need to watch the level of saturated fat they consume. Processed foods, including cured meats and takeaway fried chicken, are not a healthy source of protein!

Years of research conclude that the healthiest protein sources are plant-based, mainly because they eliminate the risk associated with saturated fats. For example, a forty-year study of over 40,000 nurses found those who ate plant proteins aged with better memory recall and superior physical health than those who consumed animal proteins.[23] The study accounted for lifestyle habits like smoking, drinking, and exercise. This strengthens the case that plant protein itself supports healthier aging.

Glucose: Fuel for thought

Glucose, derived from carbohydrates, is the brain's primary energy source. Here's how it works:

- **Simple carbohydrates** (like fruit and honey) provide quick energy.
- **Complex carbohydrates** (like wholegrains and vegetables) release energy more gradually, sustaining brain function over time.

The natural diets we evolved to eat contained significantly more complex carbohydrates. But over the last few hundred years our consumption of simple carbohydrates has increased, with a dramatic acceleration in Western diets. Frequent glucose spikes from sugary foods can lead to energy crashes, fatigue, and stress. High sugar intake also contributes to inflammation and long-term mood disorders.[24] For instance, one study of more than 10,000 participants linked regular high sugar consumption to increased rates of depression.[25] We can sometimes turn to sugar (both simple and complex) when we are down because it stimulates dopamine, serotonin, and opioids.[26] But, the research is clear: high sugar consumption can cause poor mood, so eating sugary foods is not just a symptom of pre-existing stress or anxiety disorders.[27]

The benefits of artificial sweeteners are often debated. They're unlikely to affect mood directly, but may alter taste preferences, making natural foods less appealing.[28] Research into artificial sweeteners is ongoing, with their impact on the gut microbiome being one area of interest.

Occasionally adding some sugar is fine.[29] If you can cut sugar from your diet altogether, then power to you! But if your mood is balanced and your energy is good, don't criticise yourself for enjoying an occasional treat. The Australian Government health guidelines quote the World Health Organization (WHO) recommendation that 10 per cent or less of your daily energy intake should come from sugar. This includes sugar in foods as well as sugar you add. This is about 50 grams, or twelve teaspoons, for an adult. However, they go on to say that 50 per cent of that would be better, and the less sugar you eat, the more health benefits you will have.[30] Amelia Phillips suggests checking labels and choosing products with less than 10 grams of sugar per 100 grams. With so many hidden sugars even in savoury foods, this is sensible advice.

Small, consistent changes can make a significant difference to how your brain and body perform. Nourish your brain with intention and it will repay you with clarity, resilience, and a sense of wellbeing.

✳ Vitamins and minerals for the mind ✳

The brain thrives on a delicate balance of vitamins and minerals, each playing a unique role in supporting mood, cognition, and overall mental resilience. Here's a closer look at some important nutrients for brain health, and how to incorporate them into your diet.

Vitamin A

Vitamin A supports cognitive function, mood regulation, and sleep. For example, it supports the production of dopamine and serotonin, essential for mood and focus. Serotonin, in turn, is converted into melatonin which, as discussed, regulates the sleep–wake cycle.

Vitamin A is commonly referred to as an antioxidant that protects the brain against oxidative stress that can degrade brain cells. However, research states that vitamin A doesn't have these qualities; this effect comes from compounds found in food known as provitamin A alpha and beta carotenoids. They have antioxidant properties *before* they covert to vitamin A in the body. I'm elaborating on this in case people seek supplements.[31] Ideally, people don't need vitamin A supplements as all forms of it can be included in a diet, as follows.

Active vitamin A (retinol/retinyl esters): Animal products, especially liver and fish liver oils. These forms are ready to be used by the body without conversion and therefore don't have antioxidant properties.

Plant-based foods: Carrots, sweet potatoes, spinach, kale, and mangoes provide provitamin A carotenoids. These carotenoids are precursors to vitamin A which do have antioxidant properties, and are converted into active vitamin A (retinol) by the body.

B vitamins

There are multiple B vitamins that play a role in brain health. Vitamins B1, B6 and B12 are particularly important for supporting brain energy and producing dopamine, serotonin, noradrenaline, and melatonin. Combined, this makes B vitamins essential for alertness, memory formation, cognitive function, mood regulation, and sleep quality.[32]

The richest source of B vitamins comes from animal foods such as meat, seafood, eggs, and dairy. Plant-based foods can also be a source of B vitamins, except for B12. This can only be found in animal products. Vegans should seek fortified foods or supplements to meet their needs. Sourcing the many B vitamins is another great reason to eat a varied diet.

Vitamin C

One of the first signs of vitamin C deficiency is fatigue and weakness.[33] Vitamin C acts as an antioxidant, reducing oxidative stress and enhancing energy and cognitive function. It also aids iron absorption, which is critical for energy. Citrus fruits, berries, and capsicum are excellent sources.

Vitamin D

Vitamin D goes beyond bone health. The brain has vitamin D receptors that support mood regulation, memory, learning, and decision-making.[34] Low levels of vitamin D have been linked to conditions like seasonal affective disorder (SAD), which is why sensible sun exposure is important. Vitamin D is also found in foods such as fatty fish and fortified foods like milk and cereals. Vitamin D deficiency is a growing concern in many countries due to indoor lifestyles. Supplementation is often recommended under health care guidance.[35] In short, we need vitamin D to walk straight and think straight, but do note it is possible to have too much vitamin D.

Vitamin E

Vitamin E, commonly associated with skin health, is another potent antioxidant that helps remove cellular waste. This supports vitality and clear thinking. Nuts, seeds, and vegetable oils are excellent sources.[36]

Iron

Iron is vital for energy, learning, memory, and mood regulation.[37] Deficiencies can lead to fatigue, and various mood disorders.[38] Plant-based iron sources, like spinach, become more bioavailable when paired with vitamin C-rich foods, such as lemon juice. Did you know parsley has twice the iron content of spinach? Incorporating it into stews, salads, or smoothies is a practical way to boost iron intake.

Zinc

Zinc supports neuron connections, protects against oxidative stress, and helps regulate inflammation.[39] Low levels of zinc have been linked to anxiety and depression.[40] We consume zinc in meat, shellfish, legumes, and seeds. Deficiency is rare in Western diets.[41]

Selenium

Selenium, as an antioxidant, can play a role in reducing anxiety and depressive disorders, particularly in individuals with thyroid issues. Found in Brazil nuts, seafood, and wholegrains, selenium is also essential for cognitive function.[42]

Magnesium

Magnesium plays a role in serotonin production and regulates blood sugar, inflammation, and sleep. Nearly half of Americans don't consume enough magnesium, but adverse effects may not occur immediately. Foods like dark leafy greens, nuts, seeds, and wholegrains are great sources. Though magnesium supplements are popular for promoting relaxation and sleep, research on their efficacy remains mixed. Magnesium also comes in many forms, so if you think you would benefit from supplements, consult a health care provider to determine what's best for you.[43]

Potassium

Potassium is vital for brain health, ensuring neurons communicate effectively. This helps to prevent moods swings and allows for greater control of stress and anxiety. It's also essential for cognitive function and sleep. Foods that contain potassium include bananas, potatoes, and beans.[44]

Calcium

Like vitamin D, calcium is more than a bone builder, it is vital for brain health too. It plays a crucial role in chemical messenger signalling between brain cells, which supports neuronal plasticity, essential for learning, memory, and mood regulation. A deficiency in calcium can lead to disruptions in these processes, potentially affecting focus and emotional balance. People often associate dairy products with calcium, but don't ignore non-dairy sources such as nuts, seeds, beans, leafy greens, and fish.[45]

Are supplements worth it?

If you're considering dietary supplements, ensure they address your actual health needs. A comprehensive biomarker review, beyond standard blood tests, can provide valuable insights and identify any deficiencies. A health care professional can interpret these results and recommend targeted supplements if necessary. This approach can save you money and avoid potential harm from unnecessary supplementation.

Remember, the best way to nourish your brain is through a balanced diet rich in wholefoods. Supplements should only complement, not replace, a nutrient-dense diet.

✻ Adaptogens: Nature's stress managers ✻

Adaptogens are plant-based supplements believed to help the body manage stress and restore balance (homeostasis). With roots in traditional Chinese and Ayurvedic medicine, they have been used for centuries to combat fatigue, improve energy, and support better sleep.[46]

While anecdotal evidence and some preliminary studies suggest benefits, conventional medicine stresses the need for standardised trials to confirm their effectiveness. Additionally, adaptogen supplements vary in quality due to limited regulation, so sourcing them from reputable providers is crucial.[47] For all these reasons, adaptogens are classified as complementary, not conventional, medicines. It is advisable to inform your health care provider and complementary medicine practitioner about any supplements you take to avoid potential interactions with medications or treatments.

Even when armed with insights about how food can bolster mood, fortitude, and resilience, we won't all suddenly adopt a 100 per cent healthy diet. Time pressures, convenience, and sheer temptation can foil such a noble goal—life is wabi-sabi. Nevertheless, having this knowledge and a desire to feel your best can guide you in the right direction and reduce the risk of developing conditions that impair brain function.

∗ Inflammation and oxidation: A double-edged sword ∗

Inflammation and oxidation are frequently discussed in terms of dietary health. They are usually considered negative, but they're part of everyday life. Both processes play crucial roles, yet when left unchecked, they can lead to significant health challenges, including brain health issues.

Inflammation: The body's silent alarm system

Inflammation is part of your body's natural defence mechanism. It springs into action, releasing a cascade of chemicals to heal a cut, fight an infection, or repair a sprained wrist. In the short term, it's essential. But chronic inflammation is a different story. When inflammation persists, as with long-term stress, poor diet, or illness, it can drain the body's energy and disrupt critical processes like mood regulation.[48]

Imagine your body as a hospital emergency room. When the system is overwhelmed, resources must be diverted to urgent cases, leaving less capacity for routine care. In terms of our body, this means less energy for functions that are not vital, such as feeling happy or mentally alert. This is one reason chronic inflammation is linked to anxiety, depression, and other mood disorders. Feeling good is a 'luxury' when your body has battles to fight.

Certain foods, especially refined carbohydrates, sugar, and

unhealthy fats, are known to provoke inflammation, exacerbating low mood and energy.[49]

Oxidation: damage at the cellular level

Oxidation is a natural chemical process in the body where oxygen is used to metabolise nutrients (like glucose or fat) to produce energy. Free radicals are natural by-products of this process. However, when free radicals accumulate unchecked, they can damage cells, including cellular DNA. This is commonly referred to as oxidative stress, which can be caused by a number of factors, such as air pollution, smoking, and yes, our food.[50]

Oxidation is like rust on metal. Over time, it weakens the structure. In our bodies, oxidative damage can accelerate aging and has been linked to conditions like dementia and Parkinson's disease. This is because oxidation affects mitochondrial function and reduces the efficiency of brain cell regeneration and overall performance. Unfortunately, oxidative stress doesn't work alone. It can also trigger inflammation, creating a vicious cycle that affects both physical and mental health.

What you can do to combat inflammation and oxidation

- **Adopt an anti-inflammatory diet (often anti-oxidative):** Prioritise fruits, vegetables, wholegrains, lean proteins, and healthy fats like those found in nuts, seeds, and oily fish. These foods are rich in antioxidants that neutralise free radicals.
- **Cook with care:** Use gentle methods like steaming or baking to preserve nutrients and avoid creating harmful compounds often produced by high-heat frying or grilling.
- **Limit processed foods and sugar:** These are common causes of both inflammation and oxidative stress.
- **Moderate alcohol consumption:** Excessive drinking can exacerbate oxidative damage.

- **Manage stress:** Chronic stress is a major contributor to inflammation. Practices like mindfulness, yoga, or simply getting enough sleep can help regulate your body's response.

By addressing inflammation and oxidation through dietary and lifestyle changes, you can protect your body and brain from unnecessary strain, improving both your short-term mood and long-term brain and physical health.[51,52]

Heavy on my mind

As we've explored, diet and eating habits significantly impact short and long-term wellbeing. The quality of the mitochondria that fuel the health of the body and brain can be severely compromised with a poor diet, leaving us feeling subpar. Excess weight, particularly abdominal fat, can heighten these risks through oxidative stress, inflammation, insulin dysfunction, and disturbances in the gut microbiome.[53]

Research on premenopausal women has shown that those with more abdominal fat exhibited higher cortisol levels under stress than those with less abdominal fat, even if their overall weight was normal. These women also experienced prolonged stress responses when exposed to repeated stress triggers, unlike their leaner counterparts.[54] This is another example of the two-way relationship between the body and the mind. Chronic stress can lead to increased belly fat, and belly fat can amplify stress responses.[55]

Not everyone carrying extra weight will experience these issues, but the risk is elevated. Chronic stress associated with high cortisol levels can perpetuate poor eating habits, creating a cycle that must be broken for better mental and physical health.

This is a daunting topic for many, especially as we must contend with factors that may not be in our control. Something we can't change is the fact that we age, which slows our metabolism and changes our hormones, making maintaining a healthy weight more challenging. This applies to men as much as to women. The good news is that with focus we can improve our metabolism and the health of our mitochondria through diet (and exercise).

A second challenge for many is access to healthy food. Most people travel to buy fruit and vegetables, whereas there may be a takeaway outlet much closer to home. In fact, there is a significant link between individuals' health outcomes and their residential locations. Areas with limited availability of healthy food shops, often referred to as 'food deserts', and those saturated with unhealthy food outlets, known as 'food swamps', are associated with higher rates of obesity and related health issues.[56] This isn't about people being 'lazy' or 'greedy' either; hyper-palatable foods are designed to be moreish and trigger feel-good chemicals which, unfortunately, can make healthy food seem boring. With the rapid rise of home delivery services, there is a very real danger that we are creating virtual 'food swamps' everywhere.

Whether it's stress, age, or convenience, I know all these food challenges well. Over the years my weight has fluctuated dramatically, from a bit overweight to obese and back again. I've wondered, *Did stress lead to poor eating, or did poor eating lead to stress?* Even on a 'good' day, as a food Seeker I can easily eat too much and enjoy unhealthy food. Ultimately, understanding the relationship between food and my sense of wellbeing motivated me to experiment and make sustainable changes over time. These changes have improved my mental and physical energy, clarity, and overall sense of wellbeing. Don't get me wrong, I still love my food, such as eating too much of my husband's excellent cakes. But I balance this with healthier choices, focusing on the long-term benefits rather than momentary guilt.

We're all different; the important thing is to make informed and sustainable dietary choices that work for you, not just for your physical health, but for your emotional resilience and mental clarity too. Remember, it's a two-way street: the better your brain feels, the better your food choices will be and vice-versa.

✱ What's on the menu? ✱

With an understanding of how dietary choices can significantly influence mental fortitude and resilience, let's examine some popular diets.

Plant-based versus animal-based diets

Each dietary camp has its supporters and scientific literature to back its benefits. However, research consistently highlights that a diet rich in diverse, natural plant-based foods is key to brain and physical health.

Plant-based diets: While overall healthy, vegans must create food combinations that provide all nine essential amino acids. Additionally, they need to actively source vitamin B12, vitamin D, and omega-3. Iron, too, poses challenges, as plant-based sources are less bioavailable than those found in animal products. This is where strategies like pairing spinach with vitamin C-rich lemon juice can improve iron absorption.

Meat-based diets: Meat-eaters should focus on reducing processed meats and limiting red meat intake to avoid harmful saturated fats.

Both groups benefit from minimising ultra-processed foods. Most of us should prioritise omega-3, vitamin D, and magnesium-rich options, as they are generally lacking in diets today.

The Mediterranean diet

Widely regarded as the gold standard for overall health and mental wellbeing, the Mediterranean diet has been endorsed by health professionals worldwide. Its principles stem from decades of research and studies, such as those that identified the world's Blue Zones, regions associated with longevity.

Core principles:
- **Every meal:** vegetables, fruits, wholegrains, olive oil.
- **At least three times a week:** seafood, nuts, legumes.
- **Maximum one serve a day:** poultry, dairy, eggs.

- **Maximum one serve a week:** red meat, sweets.
- **Occasional/optional:** Red wine, white bread, white rice, and white pasta.

The Mediterranean diet's focus on minimally processed, nutrient-dense foods contributed to its reputation as a foundation for both physical health and brain health.[57]

The MIND diet

Developed in 2015 by Dr Martha Morris, the MIND diet merges the Mediterranean diet and heart health principles with the goal of promoting brain health. Originally designed to reduce neurodegenerative diseases like dementia, it emphasises cognitive-supporting foods while eliminating items linked to cognitive decline.
- **Key foods:** Leafy greens, berries, nuts, legumes, olive oil, wholegrains, fish, and poultry.
- **Exclusions:** Red meat, butter, cheese, pastries, fried foods, and ultra-processed items.

The MIND diet certainly supports mental fortitude and resilience, though its strict guidelines around fats and sugars may feel too restrictive for some.[58]

Ketogenic diets

Ketogenic diets are highly restrictive in terms of food choice as they focus on high-fat, low-carbohydrate diets to shift the body's metabolism to use fat instead of glucose as an energy source. The limited range of food can lead to nutrient imbalances and long-term health risks.

People may have heard of ketogenic diets for weight loss, but the high level of food exclusion means it isn't a healthy weight-loss option. It's been used in medicine for conditions such as epilepsy and there is also ongoing research into ketogenic diets for mental wellbeing.

For individuals with clinically diagnosed mental health conditions, a medically supervised ketogenic diet may help rejuvenate brain cells by stimulating mitochondrial function.[59] However, for the general population, the potential benefits can be outweighed by the diet's lack of fibre, vitamins, and minerals, as well as its reliance on saturated fats.

Brain energy foods

If you're feeling mentally sluggish, consider these nutrient-dense options to boost energy and focus:

- **Staples:** Fatty fish, leafy greens, citrus fruits, wholegrains, eggs, and dairy.
- **Quick snacks:** Nuts (especially walnuts for their PUFA content[60]), seeds, berries, dark chocolate, colourful vegetables (such as capsicum and carrots), and bananas.
- **Hydration:** Drink plenty of water, tea, and moderate amounts of coffee. Caffeine can help stimulate cognitive thinking earlier in the day but can disrupt your ability to relax and sleep at night, so it's better to drink coffee before midday.

The spice of life

Herbs and spices not only elevate flavour but also contribute antioxidants and anti-inflammatory properties to your meals. Dried versions are affordable, and a few indoor herbs in pots can enhance your diet and give you the satisfaction of growing and harvesting your own food.

May I recommend?

When it comes to food, keep it real, varied, and tasty. A healthy diet is unsustainable if you don't enjoy it, and the benefits to your sense of well-being are too great to find reasons why you can't stick to healthy food most of the time.

- Prioritise minimally processed, natural foods to support energy and brain health.
- Try to consume most of your calories earlier in the day, ideally your last meal would be two to three hours before bed.
- Limit ultra-processed items like takeaways or sugary snacks to once a week.
- Move towards eating at least two home-cooked meals a day.
- Aim for dietary patterns like the Mediterranean diet, which are more sustainable and nutritionally balanced.
- For sustained energy and mental clarity, aim to consume a variety of twenty to thirty plant-based foods weekly. Herbs and spices count too!
- Consider omega-3 supplements if you don't consume oily fish regularly.
- If you're vegan, combine plant-based foods to meet your amino acid needs, and consider supplements for nutrients only found in animals or seafood.
- Meat-eaters should try to limit red meat to once a week and review the types of animal fats they consume.
- Balance refined and complex carbohydrates to stabilise blood glucose.
- Stay hydrated to optimise your alertness during the day.

These measures will help reduce corrosive insulin spikes, inflammation and oxidation, and altered metabolism, all of which contribute to mental fatigue, poor sleep, exacerbated stress, dysregulated moods, and a sense of overwhelm. That is a long list of negatives that you can help mitigate just through your diet. Perhaps what's more exciting is that your diet doesn't only have the ability to limit these unwanted feelings and behaviours, it can also enhance your brain health so that you feel more engaged, calm, focused, and capable. We all want our brains to be fertile gardens, so what will you feed yours to make it flourish?

WHAT MAKES SENSE TO YOU?

Start by assessing what your normal diet looks like in terms of brain-friendly food. It's easy to forget what we've eaten in a day, let alone week, therefore it's better to write this information down.

Log the foods you eat for one week. Make this as simple as possible. For example, record this in your phone or a small notebook. If you have easy access to your Total Sensory Wellbeing notes, even better. This is not about judgement; it's simply a fact-collecting exercise to identify patterns.

Within reason, capture the ingredients, quantity, and the time you ate. For example, 'Ate oats for breakfast early', isn't as insightful as 'Half a cup of oats, one banana, one cup of milk, two teaspoons of sugar, and a cup of tea at 8 am'.

At the end of the week, evaluate each day by creating two columns: one for brain-positive foods, the other for brain-negative foods. Place a mark in the column corresponding to the nature of the food. Using the breakfast example, oats, banana, and milk are all brain-positive, meaning you would have three marks in the brain-positive column, while sugar would score one mark in the brain-negative column. Alternatively, you can make a visual assessment; 80 per cent of the breakfast was brain-positive.

Use this objective assessment to identify opportunities to improve your eating plan. For example, you identify that you often snack at night, could you try eating earlier and improving the quality of those snacks to limit glucose spikes? Is there a time you can prepare food at home and make double portions to reduce your reliance on cafe or takeaway meals?

If you already do eat a natural and varied diet but regularly feel low on energy, you may want to consult a health care provider for a comprehensive biomarker review. This can help identify any specific nutrient deficiencies that may be affecting your energy levels. Beyond dietary solutions, they may recommend supplements, even in the short term. At least you will know that the supplements are warranted.

I know there is a lot of information to digest here, so I encourage you to take a thoughtful approach and review the Appetite chapters (Chapter 8 and this one) again to help you consider aspects you would like to focus on. This includes the tables below.

Remember, it's not about perfection, it's about progress, especially with such an emotive sense as Appetite. Experiment and have fun creating meals that nourish both your body and mind. It's a delicious way to boost your mood, cognition, and resilience!

* Brain food reference tables *

The following tables provide examples of brain-boosting foods. These are listed according to the major benefits they provide. Of course, foods aren't just limited to the nutrients highlighted. For example, while olive oil is known as a rich source of omega-3, it also contains low amounts of omega-6. Sunflower oil, which is high in omega-6, is also a good source of vitamin E. How much of something you consume and how it is prepared will determine whether it is healthy or not.

I hope this information inspires you to become creative and 'clever' in the kitchen.

Fats

Unsaturated fats (Healthy)	Saturated fats (Unhealthy)	Trans fats (Unhealthy)
Plant and seafood fats, liquid at room temperature. Most reduce cholesterol	Fats from animal sources, solid at room temperature. Raise LDL cholesterol, increasing risk of heart disease	Industrially created fats linked with health issues. Also found in meat and dairy from ruminant animals

Monounsaturated: Olive oil, avocado, almonds Poly-unsaturated: Sunflower oil, flaxseeds, salmon	Butter, lard, red meat fat	Margarine, packaged baked goods, fried foods, meat and dairy from cows, sheep, and goats

Figure 15.1. Classifications of fats

Monounsaturated fats (MUFA): healthy	Saturated fats: reduce in favour of unsaturated fats	Food with trans fatty acids*
Olive oil	Processed deli-style meats	Manufactured baked goods: e.g. biscuits, cakes, and pies
Avocados and avocado oil	Fat on meat	Deep-fried foods
Pistachios	Skin on poultry	Butter
Cashews and cashew butter	Butter	Takeaways: e.g. hamburgers, pizza, and hot chips
Hazelnuts and hazelnut butter	Coconut oil	Hard margarines made with hydrogenated oil
Almonds and almond butter	Palm oil	Frozen dinners
Olives and olive oil	Cream and ice cream	Instant noodles
Peanuts and peanut butter	Lard	Aerosol and frozen whipped toppings
Sesame oil	Ghee	Shortening

Figure 15.2. Examples of fats

*Trans-fatty acids (TFAs) are banned in the USA and Canada. WHO recommends a maximum of 1 per cent of daily calories from TFAs. On packaging these are often referred to as 'partially hydrogenated oils'.

Omega-3 (PUFA)	Omega-6 (PUFA)
Mackerel	Safflower oil 75%
Salmon	Sunflower oil 66%
Sardines	Corn oil
Anchovies	Soybean oil
Herring	Walnuts
Trout	Sesame seeds

Tuna	Pumpkin seeds
Cod liver oil	Canola oil
Chia seeds	Flaxseed
Walnuts	Olive oil (10%)

Figure 15.3. Examples of omega-3 and omega-6 fats

Proteins with all nine amino acids

Proteins with all nine amino acids
Animal meat
Fish
Turkey and chicken
Eggs
Dairy
Soybean products, e.g. tofu and tempeh (fermented tofu)
Quinoa
Buckwheat
Hemp seeds
Spirulina
Nutritional yeast

Figure 15.4. Proteins will all essential amino acids

Vegan combination proteins with all nine essential amino acids

Legumes and grains	Nuts/seeds and legumes	Grains and seeds/nuts
Beans and rice	Legume-based salad sprinkled with nuts or seeds e.g. chickpeas and quinoa	Oats with chia and almonds

Legume-based curry with rice	Hummus and wholewheat pita	Quinoa salad pumpkin seeds and walnuts
Legume-based soup with bread	Chickpeas and sesame seeds	Peanut butter and wholegrain bread
Tofu and rice	Lentils and almonds	Buckwheat salad with sunflower seeds and hazelnuts

Figure 15.5. Examples of vegan food combinations with all essential amino acids

Vitamins and minerals

Vitamin A (antioxidant)	Vitamin B	Vitamin C (antioxidant)	Vitamin D	Vitamin E (antioxidant)
Sweet potatoes (kumara)	Liver (beef and chicken)	Kakadu plums (Australian native fruit)	Cod liver oil	Wheatgerm oil
Carrots	Salmon	Acerola cherries (Barbados cherries)	Salmon	Sunflower seeds
Spinach	Eggs	Rosehips, including rosehip tea	Trout	Almonds
Kale	Leafy greens e.g. spinach	Guavas	Sardines	Hazelnuts
Butternut pumpkin (squash)	Legumes	Yellow capsicums (sweet yellow peppers)	Liver	Sunflower oil
Red capsicum (red bell peppers)	Nutritional yeast	Blackcurrants	Fortified plant milks	Avocados
Mangoes	Milk	Thyme	Fortified cereals	Spinach
Rockmelon (cantaloupe)	Chicken	Parsley	Eggs	Peanut butter
Liver (beef and chicken)	Sunflower seeds	Kiwifruit	Cheese (minimal)	Olive oil
Eggs	Mushrooms	Broccoli	Mushrooms (negligible)	Red capsicum (red bell peppers)

Figure 15.6. Examples of brain-healthy vitamins

Chapter 15. Food for Thought

Iron	Zinc	Selenium	Magnesium	Potassium	Calcium
Red meat	Oysters	Brazil nuts	Avocados	Bananas	Milk
Liver and other organ meats	Beef	Halibut	Nuts	Sweet potatoes (Kumara)	Cheese
Shellfish	Pumpkin seeds	Sardines	Legumes	Spinach	Yoghurt
Spinach	Lamb	Shrimp	Tofu	Avocados	Sardines
Legumes	Chickpeas	Chicken breast	Seeds	White beans	Tofu
Pumpkin seeds	Cashews	Eggs	Wholegrains	Tomatoes	Almonds
Quinoa	Lentils	Brown rice	Some oily fish: salmon, mackerel, halibut	Beetroot leaves	Kale
Turkey	Quinoa	Sunflower seeds	Dark chocolate	Yoghurt	Broccoli
Tofu	Turkey	Turkey	Bananas	Salmon	Fortified plant milks
Fortified Cereals	Yoghurt	Oats	Leafy greens	Oranges	Fortified cereals

Figure 15.7. Examples of brain-healthy minerals

Fibre

Insoluble fibre (aids motility)	Soluble fibre (slows digestion)	Prebiotic fibre (feeds bacteria)
Lentils	Oats	Chicory root
Chia seeds	Apples	Jerusalem artichoke
Flaxseeds	Pears	Garlic
Broccoli	Barley	Onions
Oats	Psyllium husk	Leeks
Apples	Beans (e.g., black, kidney)	Asparagus
Pears	Sweet potatoes	Bananas

Avocados	Carrots	Oats
Brussel sprouts	Turnips	Apples
Beans (e.g., black and kidney)	Lentils	Barley

Figure 15.8. Examples of fibre

Probiotics

Probiotics (populate bacteria)
Yoghurt
Kefir
Sauerkraut
Kimchi
Miso
Tempeh
Kombucha
Fermented pickles
Natto
Traditional buttermilk

Figure 15.9. Examples of foods with probiotics that contribute healthy bacteria to the gut

Flavonoids

Antioxidants	Anti-inflammatory foods
Blueberries	Turmeric
Dark chocolate	Green tea
Pecan nuts	Blueberries
Strawberries	Broccoli
Artichokes	Salmon

Goji berries	Olive oil
Raspberries	Ginger
Kale	Spinach
Red cabbage	Tomatoes
Spinach	Nuts

Figure 15.10. Examples of foods that protect against cellular damage

Sleep

What and when you eat can impact your sleep. Figure 15.11 highlights foods that either contain tryptophan, a key precursor to serotonin and melatonin, or support melatonin production, helping to promote relaxation, mood balance, and sleep quality.

High in tryptophan	Melatonin triggers
Turkey	Tart Cherries
Chicken	Goji Berries
Soybeans	Grapes
Cheese	Tomatoes (low)
Salmon	Walnuts
Eggs	Milk plus tryptophan
Nuts and seeds—almonds, sunflower, and pumpkin seeds	Bananas plus tryptophan
Lamb	Oats plus tryptophan
Legumes	Barley
Oats	Rice

Figure 15.11. Examples of foods that support rest

CHAPTER 16.
GAUGE THE TEMPERATURE

Use temperature to influence thoughts and behaviour

A third action that influences our sense of wellbeing through the somatosensory system is temperature. Unlike touch and movement, which we often consciously engage in, temperature influences us all the time whether we're focused on it or not. From a cool breeze that sharpens your focus to a heatwave that drains your energy, temperature is just as influential to your mental fortitude and resilience as any other sensory experiences.

Shifts in temperature don't have to be extreme to influence how you feel and behave. For example, you may have been in a meeting and felt irritable and tired. While the meeting topic, length, and attendees can influence these responses, so too can subtle changes in the thermostat.

When it's too hot or too cold, your body prioritises core survival. This means mental clarity and emotional balance can quietly slip as your system redirects energy to stabilise internal temperature, all without you realising.[1]

∗ The cold effect: From alertness to conservation ∗

Short bursts of exposure to cold activate our alert responses through the fight-or-flight pathways, which sharpens our focus and energises the body.[2] It is likely this response relates to our evolutionary instincts, where cold environments demanded heightened awareness for survival.

Controlled cold exposure, like splashing cold water on the face, stepping outside in brisk air, or taking short cold showers, can improve focus, lift mood, and provide a mental reset. The boost to our alert responses and the associated release of endorphins can enhance motivation and reduce feelings of fatigue.[3]

However, prolonged exposure to cold can overwhelm the body. When the body prioritises conserving warmth, mental energy depletes, leaving us feeling tired or withdrawn.[4] To benefit from energising bursts of cold, we must balance it with warmth.

∗ The heat effect: When overheating drains resilience ∗

Heat affects the brain differently. Excessive heat reduces serotonin, the neurotransmitter that stabilises mood. Like cold temperatures, heat diverts energy from cognitive processes to cool the body. Prolonged exposure to high temperatures can lead to irritability, cognitive fog, and impulsive behaviours. Research has also shown that extreme heat correlates with increased aggression and is even linked to higher crime rates.[5]

In countries where people can afford cooling systems, it's easier to avoid extreme temperatures. However, many cannot afford such systems and face challenges, especially during prolonged heatwaves, which can disrupt sleep and exacerbate stress and anxiety.[6] With global warming intensifying, this issue is becoming an increasing concern for households and nations worldwide.

However, moderate warmth, such as outdoor temperatures that range from 22°C to 26°C (71.6°F to 78.8°F), or winter warmth from a heated blanket or a warm drink, can promote comfort and relaxation, helping to reduce stress and enhance emotional connection.

Extreme weather events aside, many people in developed countries spend most of their time indoors, where they can consciously adjust the temperature to invigorate or calm their senses.

✳ How to regulate temperature for wellbeing ✳

We can harness temperature to support our goals, whether it's focus, relaxation, or emotional connection. Consider these strategies:

Work and focus: Keep workspaces slightly cool at 21°C to 22°C (70°F to 72°F). This temperature range enhances alertness, reduces mental fatigue, and promotes productivity.[7]

Social bonding and comfort: Increase warmth in social settings with temperatures around 22°C to 24°C (72°F to 75°F) to encourage relaxation and connection. This is particularly beneficial in conversations or team settings.[8]

Energising the mind: A splash of cold water, exposure to brisk weather, or short cold showers can activate your alert response, making it an excellent tool for breaking mental slumps.

Sleep support: Warming up then cooling down before bed can trigger the body's natural cooling mechanism, preparing you for restful sleep. For example, have a warm shower then enter a cooler room to sleep. The optimal temperature for restful sleep will vary between individuals and may be age associated, with studies showing younger adults respond to cooler environments, typically between 15.6°C and 20°C (60°F and 68°F),[9] while older adults may achieve optimal sleep quality with warmer temperatures, ranging from 20°C to 25°C (68°F to 77°F).[10]

Hydration and layering: Always stay hydrated and dress in layers to manage body temperature effectively.

As you can see, the change in temperature to create a different mood or cognitive effect does not need to be very big at all. So, the next time you feel agitated or lethargic, gauge the temperature in the room—literally.

✻ Lessons from global practices ✻

Across the world, cultures have long used temperature to support health and wellbeing. These practices combine ancient wisdom with modern science, offering valuable lessons on how we can use more extreme temperatures intentionally.

Saunas

The Scandinavian sauna tradition exposes the body to high heat. Regular use of a traditional sauna has been shown to lower blood pressure, reduce stress, and even improve heart health. This is because the body is mimicking the alert response that exercise would induce as it works to maintain a steady core temperature. This means we also release endorphins, creating a sense of relaxation and rejuvenation.[11]

Cold water immersion

So why do those hardy Scandinavians plunge into icy water after a sauna? The benefit is two-fold: it activates both alertness and relaxation responses. Cold exposure triggers the release of endorphins and noradrenalin, boosting energy and mood. Simultaneously, it stimulates the vagus nerve, enhancing parasympathetic activity, reducing cortisol levels, and promoting a sense of calm. A cold shower can offer similar, though milder effects, providing a refreshing start to the day without extreme cold exposure.[12]

The practice of appreciating the benefits of hot and cold environments can be found in many countries, such as Japan, India, Russia, and Türkiye, with evidence that the sensory benefits have been enjoyed throughout history, as recorded in ancient Greece, Rome, and the Ottoman Empire. It's yet another example of how ancient, innate, and universal our sensory appreciation truly is.

Red light and infrared therapy

Light wave-based saunas (covered in Chapter 4) use lower heat than traditional types, making them easier to tolerate for longer sessions. Their skin-penetrating wavelengths continue to be studied for potential therapeutic effects like muscle recovery and arthritis relief. This includes far infrared waves (around 3100 nanometres).[13] It's important to remember that spa settings use much gentler intensities than clinical models, however their growing popularity suggests they're both enjoyable and potentially beneficial.[14]

Harnessing temperature for wellbeing

Temperature is a powerful yet often overlooked tool for improving our mental and physical resilience. By understanding its effects and learning from cultural practices like saunas, cold plunges, and infrared therapy, we can incorporate temperature regulation into our daily lives. Whether it's a brisk walk to refocus, a warm bath to relax, or managing your environment to suit your needs, temperature can be a key ally in achieving balance, focus, and connection.

> **WHAT MAKES SENSE TO YOU?**
>
> Let's bring together the practical Action insights outlined here and in Chapter 9 to enrich your everyday life.

The comfort of touch

In your Total Sensory Wellbeing notes, start an 'Action' section. Refer to your Room Review page and under the heading 'Touch Potential Improvements', write down which textures and types of items would benefit you. Can you also identify any current items and textures that are inhibiting you from optimising your experience in the space?

Identify your comfort zones: In general, what textures, fabrics, or sensations make you feel calm and grounded? Consider introducing soft throws, comfortable clothing, or tactile objects like stress balls into your environment. Remember from Chapter 9 how effective even hugging a pillow can be to reduce stress. These items act as anchors in moments of stress, providing a tangible sense of comfort.

Create a restorative space: Address small irritants like scratchy bedding or an uncomfortable chair. These may seem minor, but these discomforts can amplify stress and irritation, whether you're aware of them or not. This is especially important in bed, where feeling physically comfortable and emotionally secure creates the ideal conditions for quality sleep, a cornerstone of your circadian rhythm. In short, prioritise comfort in the spaces you use most to support relaxation and wellbeing.

Prioritise physical connection: Whether it's a warm hug, a hand massage, or stroking a pet, human and animal contact releases oxytocin, promoting relaxation and trust. If close connections aren't possible, make an effort to engage in other Actions, like professional massage therapy, a trip to the hairdresser, or group activities like dancing. You could also take up a tactile-based hobby, such as a woodwork, or a cooking course.

The power of movement

Move for mental clarity: Incorporate regular physical activity into your day. Aerobic exercise boosts alertness, resistance training builds resilience, and practices like yoga or tai chi support focus and calmness. Collectively they help reduce stress and improve your sense of wellbeing.

Harness the rhythm of repetition: Activities with repetitive movements, like walking or dancing, stimulate bilateral brain activity, helping to reset and calm the mind. A morning walk can also boost cortisol serotonin, endorphins, and vitamin D, setting a positive tone for the day.

Break the sedentary cycle: Schedule regular movement breaks to reduce tension and maintain focus. Think laterally here: remember that even hobbies, cooking, or just stretching can be powerful recharge and rest Actions for your brain. Make it something you enjoy doing. A few minutes of Action a few times a day will help you to be productive and positive.

Mind–body connection: Write, draw, and use visuals to enhance your personal or professional learning and problem-solving skills.

The influence of temperature

Optimise your environment: Maintain comfortable room temperatures for different activities. Keep workspaces slightly cool (20°C to 22°C or 68°F to 72°F) to encourage focus. Make social areas warmer. Consider 22°C to 25°C (72°F to 77°F) to encourage connection.

Embrace temperature shifts: Short bursts of cold exposure, like splashing your face with cold water or stepping outside in brisk air, can invigorate the mind and enhance focus. In contrast, warm showers or baths in the evening signal relaxation and prepare the body for sleep.

Restorative sleep: Ensure your bedroom is set to an ideal sleep temperature. Combine this with calming Action rituals like light stretching, reading, or writing to ease into restful slumber.

When we feel stressed, upset, or unfocused, we are usually quick to pinpoint a person or a task as the cause of these feelings. While this may be the case, don't underestimate how Actions can contribute to this. Pause and assess:

- Are you physically comfortable?
- Have you moved your body today or in the last two hours?
- Have you engaged in Actions that allow your brain to 'breathe'?

Remember, building mental fortitude is a journey, not a destination. Each small adjustment proactively cultivates a deeper sense of wellbeing. With this in mind, let's explore how to integrate various sensory experiences to optimise the Atmosphere of your home and how the interplay of the senses can enhance your mood and behaviour.

CHAPTER 17.
SCOPE YOUR SENSORY SANCTUARY

Create environments for work, rest and play

In Chapter 10 we explored how the natural world helped to shape our sensory processes and how it still influences our wellbeing. From landscapes to textures and materials, we examined how elements of nature can be translated into interior spaces to enhance our sense of comfort and calm.

Let's now delve further into how nature-led interior design styles, such as biophilic design, incorporate the restorative benefits of nature into interiors. We will also look at some elements of design that focus on improving our sense of wellbeing in a space.

* Applying nature-led design principles *

Light

As you know from the Aurora chapters (4, 11), natural light plays a crucial role in supporting the circadian rhythm. You also learned about leveraging artificial light to create environments for specific purposes such as rest, cooking, or working from home. Make sure to revisit the detailed guides to help you select lights for specific purposes.

To harness light to your advantage, first observe how natural light moves through your space at different times of day and try to leverage this in your home, like positioning a work desk near a window that catches the morning or midday sun, or using mirrors to amplify light and a sense of space, especially in small or dark areas. Positioning a large mirror on a wall opposite a window is a great way to achieve this effect.

Artificial light is essential for us to live comfortably indoors, such as brighter lights in a study and soft, friendly light in a dining space. Each room should have more than one light source, with variations in colour warmth to aid functionality. Consider how you could utilise the main types of lighting to benefit you.

For example, in our living room, we don't need the light on when it's sunny. On grey days, we use the overhead light with a cool-kelvin effect. At night, though, this light feels harsh, like stepping into an interrogation room, so I switch on a warm-kelvin lamp instead.

Lamps are a great way to demonstrate the interplay of the senses. With a relatively inexpensive and portable item, you can introduce light, colour, and shapes to enhance how you feel. They are extremely useful to help create zoning, improve lighting for tasks, accentuate decor, and change the mood in an instant. Functional and fabulous!

Layering different lighting effects adds depth and options to your space, improving your experience. Consider how you can adjust the colour and brightness of lights through dimmers, bulbs and shades. Just remember, if different lights are on at the same time in the same area, it's best if their colour temperatures match.

Visiting a lighting store offers the opportunity to see how different lights truly impact a space. Take fabric samples or photos of your home interiors, and consult with knowledgeable staff for feedback on your ideas. Make your lighting selection a fun, creative process through real-world sensory engagement. You just can't achieve that online. Nor can you be sure that an online image will meet your expectations.

Light works on a continuum, so there's no absolute rule for every space. Your choices will depend on variables such as the natural light, purpose of each room, size of the room, the colours present, light shades, and your sensory profile. Remember to refer to Chapter 11 for general lighting guidance using interior design principles.

Airflow and temperature

Natural airflow and varied temperatures help keep you connected to the outdoors, which can sometimes improve air quality. However, living in city environments means that opening a window may be counterproductive as this could allow in pollution and noise. Running an air-conditioning unit may also be cost prohibitive. There is no easy solution here. A ceiling fan may be one way to emulate airflow and costs less money to run than an air-conditioning unit. Ceiling fans can also add an element of nature through the shape of the blades, which can be designed to look like petals or leaves, and they can be made from natural fibres like rattan. You can revisit Chapter 14 for suggestions on improving air quality, and Chapter 16 for details on temperatures that allow you to focus, socialise, and sleep better.

Indoor vegetation

Traditional biophilic design uses a significant number of plants to truly purify indoor air and create a sense of being immersed in nature. However, too many plants can overwhelm some people, creating a sense of claustrophobia. They can also lead to excessive levels of humidity.

Play with the size, type, and positioning of plants until you find what works for you. Seek advice from plant shops or online about what type of plants would thrive in your space and light conditions.

A great way to incorporate plants is to grow herbs, inside or outside. Besides the benefit of fresh produce, you will get a dopamine hit when you see the fruits, or rather herbs, of your labour and a serotonin boost from having done something good for yourself. Even looking after standard indoor plants can stimulate these feel-good chemicals.

If you don't think this is feasible in your space, do some digging! There are many innovative ways to grow plants, like hydroponic and vertical systems. Start small and seek advice. I'm sure you're going to be amazed at how good the experience feels, and of course you'll also benefit from the restful effect that having greenery in the home can provide.

An experience of nature

Indoor plants and indirect nature experiences are highly beneficial for those without access to gardens, parks, or balconies, especially if there is no green scenery outside the windows. In my study, for example, I stared at a brick wall for years until I understood the importance of Total Sensory Wellbeing. I now watch the progress of a palm as it grows in its pot. I can't believe I waited eleven years to do something that took less than two hours to buy, bring home and pot.[1] Actually, I can. I didn't appreciate the good it would do or the joy it would bring. Thank goodness that's all changed.

Remember that experiences of nature can be reflected in imagery, literal or abstract. As an example, I have a close-up photo of a koru (unfurling fern frond) and another of a leaf. These provide restful images of repeating patterns in nature. The literal fabric of your home can also be used to bring natural elements inside, such as nature-themed wallpaper or curtains.

Materials and textures

In Chapter 10 we looked at different natural materials and some of their possible uses. The other consideration about materials is their textures, such as smooth marble, sleek lacquered or rough natural wood, and soft leather. Practicality must come into play here; a glossy marble floor might be too slippery for a bathroom, and a paper screen door provides light and a sense of privacy, but it won't dampen sound. Natural materials also require extra care and maintenance compared to synthetic ones, such as resealing stone and oiling or painting wood.

Chapter 17. Scope Your Sensory Sanctuary

Many of us default to flat, artificial surfaces because that's what dominates commercial interior showrooms, but this overlooks the sensory benefits that natural elements and varied textures can bring, whether that's instinctively touching the surface of wooden furniture or considering the sensory response to accessories such as cushions and rugs. You will recall from Chapter 9 that materials can offer a sense of calm and relaxation. This includes your bedding fabric. You can even improve the quality of your sleep if you find your bedding soothing.

Natural materials in interiors can be costly, so consider using them in feature areas; a wooden side table or even a statement stone coffee table might work for some, or perhaps hessian covering one wall for a calming, textured look. Smaller pieces like wool rugs, rattan mats, or linen curtains are some more ways to introduce natural elements. Soft, natural fibres such as wool, cotton, and linen can also help to absorb and release humidity in the atmosphere.

Explore ideas on apps like Pinterest. Even a broad search phrase like 'natural wall furnishings' will expose you to a plethora of designs, shapes, and ideas beyond the concept of a wall covering. It's likely to expand your thinking about what's possible and what you might like.

∗ The walls around you ∗

British Prime Minister Winston Churchill once said, 'We shape our buildings; thereafter they shape us'. Research has found truth in this statement. One study showed that people are significantly more creative and positive in spaces with curved architectural features compared to those with sharp angles. Participants in curved spaces also had lower heart rates, indicating a calmer state of mind.[2]

Of course, most buildings and rooms are designed with straight lines because this is practical to live in and relatively easy to construct. We can, however, introduce curved shapes and features into a space to benefit from their relaxing effects. Think arched doorways, curved or round mirrors, curved furniture like a bedhead, round rugs, and organic-shaped lights and ornamental objects.

Many new small builds have straight walls jutting up against a flat ceiling. This can feel very plain and box-like. Adding coving or a cornice (a curved moulding strip), can create a softer angle and a more refined atmosphere.

If the goal is to create a sense of solidity, then different panelling effects can help achieve this. Consider styles such as solid wood panelling or lighter, thinner wood strips painted in calming colours.

* Interior tips to create your atmosphere *

Here you can see how the Kaplan and Kaplan preference matrix we discovered in Chapter 10 plays out in design principles.

Open and intimate spaces

Balancing open and intimate spaces is key to promoting both interest and comfort. Open-plan living in large spaces can benefit from the use of different flooring or ceiling finishes to define zones, such as the kitchen and living areas. In compact homes, a single flooring material can enhance flow, while rugs or mats can define the zones. These are examples of legibility. Consider mobile dividers that double as shelving or storage to separate work and relaxation areas. If you have a work desk in the living area, blend the work furniture style and colour with the living room atmosphere to allow your brain to relax when you're not working. This approach adds to a sense of coherence.

Complexity and order

This is an area where individual sensory profiles within a household often battle. Try to balance organisation and variety to suit sensory needs. The goal is to create engagement without overwhelm in shared spaces. For example, a Seeker who loves bright colours and multiple patterns may live with a Sensor who is distracted by such environments, and yet the Seeker would feel flat and disengaged in a room they perceived as boring. An example of compromise could be that the Seeker has 'their' chair that has some colour and patterns they appreciate, but which don't dominate and overwhelm the whole space because they are coherent with the overall colour scheme. The Sensor might, in turn, appreciate and accept bolder artwork in one area of the room or a couple of appropriately coloured lamps, while the Seeker agrees to a more 'neutral' treatment of the walls and floors and a restrained use of decorative items. Both may find comfort in introducing textures through simple patterns to add visual and tactile comfort.

The more complex a space, the greater the cognitive load to interpret it. Remember, even if your surroundings don't bother you, your brain still analyses a space no matter how many times you've been in it. Complexity can be tailored, stimulating, legible, and harmonious, but clutter represents the worst type of complexity; it's neither coherent nor functional, and often, not even legible—it's just mentally taxing.

Flow and harmony

Linking similar shapes, materials, and colours achieves flow and harmony (coherence). Movable pieces like furniture and accessories allow for experimentation, letting you adjust the atmosphere as needed for stimulation or relaxation.

The following interior design principles can help enhance the flow, harmony, and overall aesthetic appeal of a space, which, as you now know, is primarily driven by our sense of survival in the natural world.

* Wellbeing design tips *

Boxed in

In small spaces or where ceilings are low, maximise vertical space with tall shelving or cupboards to create the illusion of height while optimising space.

Compact spaces are ideal for focused study or work, as they minimise peripheral distractions. Some people even create this effect on their person by wearing a baseball cap to help them focus forward. This is akin to putting on their 'thinking' cap to create selective attention.

Curtain call

Position curtain rails well above the window line and let the fabric drop to the floor. This is especially beneficial in small spaces to create a sense of height. Consider natural light when selecting curtains; blocking too much daylight affects the biophilic experience. Aesthetic balance is important: how does the width of each side of an open curtain compare to the height and the width of the visible glass in the window?

Don't cross the line

For small spaces, align artwork with higher building features, like door frames, to draw the eye upward. Maintain proportionality by hanging pictures below curtain rails. Use wall lines and angles to naturally divide zones in open-plan living areas, promoting coherence and balance.

I've got you covered

Rugs and mats enhance a sense of legibility by creating zones and instant focal points to arrange furniture around. They are also a great way to bring nature-inspired colours, patterns, textures, and materials into a space. For example, a wool rug with a botanical motif can add warmth to a modern apartment. Ensure you position the furniture so that at least half of it is on the rug to avoid a disconnected, unanchored feel.

Scale

Scale refers to the visual weight of an object in a room. For instance, two couches may occupy the same floor space, but if one has bulkier features it will feel larger. Take a couch with a streamlined design, for example, it has raised legs and lightweight armrests. This is a smaller scale than one with solid armrests and a base that reaches the floor. Matching scale to room size ensures balance; this includes avoiding pairing couches of different scales in the same space. Generally, smaller apartments feel more spacious with furniture that is raised on legs as you can see more of the floor space.

Scale is also a useful way to determine if elements from different design aesthetics can work together.

Grouping items

When we have similar items or more than one of something, we tend to prefer an odd number of them, because with an even number, our brains immediately fixate on symmetry or balance and home in on something that looks wrong. This is why pairs of items are usually spaced apart in a curated manner, like matching bookends or ornaments on a sideboard. In art and design, odd numbers are also said to stimulate the eye and encourage movement. This is why it's typically three ducks flying up a wall, not two or one. It would be difficult to achieve a sense of movement or visual balance with two ducks, and a single duck might appear isolated and evoke a sense of incompleteness.

✣ Other design styles that support wellbeing ✣

Some people may find it challenging and undesirable to achieve a purely biophilic design. We've seen that aesthetics and sensory disposition are important factors to consider when designing an interior. A home should be a sanctuary that feels welcoming, relaxing, and offers respite from the chaos of daily life.

You don't have to slavishly follow interior design styles; it's not about rules, it's about inspiration. Here are some other styles for you to consider that also draw on nature to soothe our senses.

Feng shui

While not typically associated with nature-inspired interiors, the ancient Chinese practice of feng shui aims to promote wellbeing by harmonising spaces to optimise the flow of positive energy, or qi. Translating to 'wind and water', feng shui uses elements of nature to create a sense of balance, prosperity and safety. You will notice many overlaps with innate sensory experiences already discussed. For example:[3]

- **Earth:** Represents stability and support with warm tones like brown and yellow. It's reflected in square shapes and materials like clay and stone. Items are placed in the centre or northeast of a space.
- **Metal:** Symbolises mental clarity with greys, whites, metallics, and circular shapes. Items are placed in the west of a room.
- **Water:** Promotes flow and reflection through dark blue tones, glass, mirrors, and wavy shapes. Items are placed in the north of an area.
- **Wood:** Evokes growth and vitality with greens, browns, and vertical forms. Items are placed in the east of a space.
- **Fire:** Signifies passion and energy with bold reds, oranges, and triangular shapes. Items are placed in the south of a room.

Feng shui focuses a lot on furniture placement, such as positioning beds to face but not align with doors, to support qi flow and avoid the cultural association with the deceased, whose feet traditionally point to the door.[4] This placement also aligns with our instinct to see potential threats while feeling safe.

Scandinavian serenity

Scandinavian design reflects effortless calm. Rooted in functionality and simplicity, this style emerged as a response to the long, dark Nordic winters, creating spaces that feel light, inviting, and rejuvenating.

Examples of key elements:
- **Bright and airy:** Light hardwood floors, sheer curtains, and carefully positioned mirrors maximise natural light.
- **Organic comfort:** Natural materials like wool, jute, and sisal bring warmth and texture.
- **Coherent simplicity:** Monochromatic light palettes such as beige, greys, and whites are typically favoured to maintain a sense of openness, order and calm, while subtle patterns and textures add a touch of complexity and interest.

Scandinavian spaces focus on coherence; everything flows seamlessly, making it easier for your mind to rest and recharge. Objects are thoughtfully chosen. A conscious effort is made to not create too much complexity.

Warm minimalism: Function meets feeling

At its core, minimalism is about reducing visual clutter and focusing on what truly matters. However, traditional minimalism can sometimes feel cold and austere, with a relentless focus on paring back to the essentials required in a space. Hard, flat materials such as glass and metal are frequently used to create a sleek, clean look. Warm minimalism softens this approach by introducing organic materials and inviting textures to make the space feel more comforting. But even the thoughtfully placed items of a Scandinavian interior might feel too much to someone who embraces warm minimalism.

Examples of key elements:
- **Purposeful design:** Every item has a role, whether functional or emotional. If it doesn't serve a purpose or bring you joy, it's out.
- **Natural aesthetic:** Think light timber, clay vases, and soft textiles paired with muted and shaded hues like olive green, muted orange, or warm beige.
- **Quiet complexity:** A wool rug or linen throw introduces subtle textured layers that add depth without overwhelming the space.

This style embraces legibility and coherence, making it clear and easy to navigate while creating a calm, lived-in feel. Plants are a must, thoughtfully placed to enhance both form and function.

Japandi: The best of two worlds

Japandi blends the minimalism of traditional Japan with the functionality of Scandinavian design, offering a balance of warmth and refinement. Japandi, similar to warm minimalism, embraces the 'less is more' philosophy because of its strong sustainability roots and the desire to appreciate what you have. It also embraces wabi-sabi, in this case, the Japanese art of finding beauty in imperfection, through handcrafted, old or even repaired items.

Examples of key elements:
- **Natural beauty:** Wooden slats and furniture, paper screens, and dark floors create a sense of calm and feeling grounded.
- **Understated elegance:** Unique handmade elements and darker colours bring the Japanese aesthetic to a Scandinavian scheme. For example, darker hues like charcoal and forest green create a sense of sophistication, while lightly structured furniture and natural material such as linen and wool add Scandinavian cosiness.

- **Mindful design:** Negative space, or as the Japanese refer to it, 'ma', is as important as the objects in the room, creating a peaceful and uncluttered environment.

This style offers variety through textures, patterns, and shapes while maintaining a balanced, calming aesthetic.

Why these styles work

These designs connect us to the natural world through light, materials, and thoughtful design. They tap into aspects of the preference matrix, leveraging coherence, complexity, legibility, and mystery to create environments that are visually pleasing and emotionally restorative.

These interior styles provide insight into how your home can leverage nature to support your wellbeing. It's best to start small to see what can work in your space and what resonates with you. It could be as fundamental as rearranging furniture to improve the flow or bringing a textured rug or a plant into your space. Over time, these thoughtful choices can transform your home into a place where you feel both nurtured and inspired.

To make a more comprehensive assessment of your spaces, let's move to your Total Sensory Wellbeing notes.

> **WHAT MAKES SENSE TO YOU?**
>
> Creating a supportive and harmonious Atmosphere begins with reflection. In your Total Sensory Wellbeing notes create an 'Atmosphere' section. Use the prompts below to review and consolidate your assessment of the room you have focused on throughout this book. Be specific with your answers. This will help you understand what works, what doesn't, and what changes could enhance your wellbeing.

Room evaluation

Lighting—reflect on your Aurora Light notes

- Do you have at least two light sources in the space? Are they suitable for different moods or tasks?
- Could changing light covers or adjusting the kelvin and lumen better suit your needs? (Refer to chapters 4 and 11 for a deeper understanding of lighting principles.)
- How does natural light move through the space? Would adding mirrors or adjusting furniture placement amplify its effect?
- Could lighting be adjusted to enhance zoning?

Colour and mood—reflect on your Aurora Colour notes

- Which colours in the space support the mood you want to create? Are there colour combinations you haven't considered yet that could enhance this?
- Factor in the colours of all the objects and furniture, not just walls and floors. Do they complement and make the space feel coherent?
- For guidance, revisit chapters 5 and 12 to refresh on how hues, values, and chroma affect emotional and physical responses.

Preference matrix reflection

- **Coherence:** Does the room feel harmonious, or do certain objects, patterns, or colours clash with the overall design? For example, do the furniture pieces have complementary scale and shape?
- **Complexity:** Is the space visually engaging or overwhelming? For example, are there too many patterns, objects or textures? Or not enough to hold your interest?

- **Legibility:** Can you easily navigate and make sense of the space thanks to anchored features like a coffee table or rug? Is the space easy to walk through or are there 'obstacles' that change how you use the space and cause you frustration?
- **Mystery:** Does the space invite curiosity and exploration, or does it feel uninspiring and flat?

Comfort and layout

- Is your furniture comfortable and well-positioned for the space's purpose? For example, is the chair-to-table height in your study ideal for focus?
- Are items you use frequently in easy reach, or is effort required, which makes you resist using them?

Materials and textures

- Do the hard and soft materials in the space feel comfortable and practical? For instance, could a wool rug add warmth, or is it too difficult to maintain with pets or children?
- Could you introduce more natural elements like wood, cotton, woven fabrics, or leather to bring a sense of grounding and calm?
- In a living space, make sure any decorative cushions have comforting textures. Seating should not only be comfortable to sit on, its fabric should be pleasant to touch as this will enhance your relaxation.

Noise and acoustics

- Is noise an issue? Could carpet, thicker curtains, or cork wall panels, for example, help reduce unwanted sound and create a quieter environment?
- Would it help to introduce background sounds or ambient music to help you focus or relax? For ideas, revisit chapters 6 and 13.

Aromas

- Is pollution hindering how you feel in a space? Address possible air and chemical pollutants.
- Try targeted aromatherapy to shift your mood and energy. Consider broader uses such as enhancing time with friends who visit you or use them in home cleaning products. Review Chapter 14 for ideas.

General quick wins and experimentation

If you're unsure where to start, begin with something small that can be changed (back) easily. Some ideas include:

- **Lighting:** Rearrange lamps or adjust bulbs to test different lighting effects. Use mirrors to capture and bounce natural light in a space.
- **Coherence and complexity:** Declutter surfaces, rotate decorative items, or introduce textures like cushions or throws.
- **Furniture layout:** Experiment with furniture placement to improve flow and create clearer zones.
- **Nature-inspired elements:** Add plants and images of nature through photos or paintings. Incorporate small items made from natural materials, such as cotton or silk cushion covers, and use essential oil aromas. When trying to relax, you might try a nature-inspired soundscape as well.
- **Bedding material:** Ensure the fabric, texture, and weight of sheets, pillows, and blankets or duvets enhance comfort and calm.
- **Clothing:** Use your wardrobe to influence yourself and others. Choose fabrics and colours to enhance how you want to feel and consider what you want to communicate silently to others.
- **Ambience:** Keep essential oils in various spaces to support relaxation, focus, or better sleep. Curate music playlists for different purposes so they are on hand when you want them.

Chapter 17. Scope Your Sensory Sanctuary

Designing spaces and routines that enhance your wellbeing is an evolving process, not a race. It is a wabi-sabi world, after all. Rather than striving for a picture-perfect environment, focus on crafting spaces that feel right to you. Each adjustment, no matter how small, contributes to a home that nurtures your needs. You may have reached this point and clearly identified some significant changes that you are now confident to make. That's great too. The main point is that your home should reflect your individuality, offering spaces for you to relax, focus, rejuvenate, and thrive.

Remember, the power of sensory wellbeing lies in the interplay of your senses. To further explore how to layer these elements and create Atmospheres as well as lifestyle adjustments that align with your goals, dive into the Atmosphere Guidelines section. These can complement or inspire your own Total Sensory Wellbeing notes.

Total Sensory Wellbeing extends to every decision you make about how you live, work, and unwind. Start small, be curious, and experiment to find what works best for you, and enjoy your wabi-sabi life!

CHAPTER 18.
MAKING SENSE IN A WABI-SABI WORLD

A perfectly imperfect philosophy

You can't always control your physical surroundings but now, with your heightened awareness of Total Sensory Wellbeing, you know how to leverage the senses to accommodate your needs.

For example, here's how I start my day using Total Sensory Wellbeing principles: I go on a fifteen to thirty-minute walk or jog, which genuinely boosts my motivation and alertness thanks to the flow of cortisol, endorphins, vitamin D, and serotonin. I do this without listening to anything except the 'podcast of my mind'. It's a wonderful opportunity for my brain to just breathe. I then have a savoury, natural breakfast, which must be tasty! My wabi-sabi twist on this is that I don't walk or jog until I've had my coffee. Purists would say that is not ideal, but it works for me. When I don't get outside or eat properly, boy do I notice it! I don't think as creatively or quickly, and nor do I engage with my work as enthusiastically.

Understanding and acting on my sensory experiences has genuinely changed how I function every day. Total Sensory Wellbeing has allowed me to think more clearly, feel rejuvenated, and renew my enthusiasm to follow my curiosity and engage more in life. From jogging for thirty minutes without stopping to now writing a book, I am amazed at what I have been able to achieve—so far. I still wobble from time to time, but that's okay. This has been, and still is, about progress, not perfection. I am an ordinary person with flaws, which is why I genuinely believe that developing mental fortitude and resilience is in most people's grasp in their own wabi-sabi way.

A key factor is to avoid the trap of overhauling everything at once. Your brain's limbic system naturally resists significant change because it perceives change as unfamiliar and therefore potentially dangerous. As you gradually integrate some sensory-based behaviours and environmental adjustments into your daily life, you will experience more and more Happy DOSEs, which will encourage you to keep going. Don't feel down when things don't go as you want; in fact, you should expect this to happen from time to time because life is not a linear road of progress. It's wabi-sabi.

Any adjustments you make should be done with your unique sensory profile in mind rather than trying to fit in a commercialised or social box. Through Total Sensory Wellbeing you can be confident that you are making choices based on sensory stimuli that are right for you. Your increased awareness and self-reflection throughout this book puts you in a great position to tailor your environment and lifestyle to thrive in today's urban landscapes.

Most people don't realise how much better they could feel. They accept tiredness and stress as unavoidable norms. This isn't their fault; they just haven't been made aware of how modern-day stimuli put pressure on our senses at the most basic level.

Remember, we aren't just dealing with sensory overwhelm. Our online lives create both deprivation and overstimulation, resulting in a rollercoaster of Happy DOSE highs and lows that can leave us feeling depleted, anxious, and lonely. The antidote lies in real-world sensory experiences that provide fulfilment, connection, and contentment, aligning with the stimuli our sensory 'software' evolved to process.

Through these pages, you've gained knowledge and tools to build a life that honours your natural instincts. By embracing Total Sensory Wellbeing and the imperfections of everyday life, you're creating your own wonderful wabi-sabi world filled with resilience, balance, and vitality. Now you can say you have truly *Come to Your Senses*. Enjoy your *sensational* life!

Part Four: Atmosphere Guides

✳✳✳

The interplay of the senses

CHAPTER 19.
TOTAL SENSORY WELLBEING

Every sense matters

Consciously influencing multiple senses simultaneously can enhance your feelings and behaviours, but balance is key. Imagine walking into a brainstorming session after an intense aerobics workout and a coffee. You're greeted with highly stimulating 6,000K lighting, a neon-green accent wall, yellow square-shaped metal furniture, multicoloured posters dotted around the walls, and shiny surfaces everywhere. Peppermint essential oil runs non-stop, and fast-paced music fills the air. For a Seeker, this might feel stimulating for a short time, but for many people, it wouldn't take long before the experience became overwhelming. Here, the facilitator ramped up all the sensory stimuli. You don't have to amplify each sense equally to create an effect. For example, bright lights, bright colours, and fast music in a shop would be a lot for our sensory processes to interpret, leaving little cognitive energy to make purchase decisions. Adding an aroma could make it even more complicated.[1]

Failing to consider the interplay of the senses can also dilute or negate the intended effect. For example, burning a lavender candle and listening to soft music at 60 BPM is unlikely to induce calmness if you're sitting in a cluttered room under bright 5,000K lighting. These mismatched sensory elements compete rather than complement, undermining their potential benefits.[2]

The following guides highlight practical examples of how to activate each sense for specific moods and behaviours. Combine recommendations from across the senses that work for your sensory preferences.

You will also find guides for maintaining a healthy circadian rhythm, the keystone of sensory wellbeing, along with guides on how to stimulate your vagus nerve and administer your own Happy DOSE. Whether it's your environment or your lifestyle, your sensory needs are covered.

Total Sensory Wellbeing	General considerations
Aurora—Light	Aim for more than one light source in a space
Aurora—Colour	Consider 1°, 2°, and 3° placement ratios: 60/30/10
Acoustics	Silence is always an option
Aroma	Aroma does not need to be strong to have an effect
Appetite	Natural food is best. Variety is essential
Action	Consider varieties of touch movement and temperature that can support you
Atmosphere	Include nature-inspired design principles

19.1. General sensory considerations

Total Sensory Wellbeing	Invigorating and uplifting
Aurora—Light	Ideally, get at least 20 minutes of morning natural light to suppress melatonin and stimulate cortisol, serotonin, vitamin D, and endorphins. If extremely fatigued and feeling flat, seek guidance on how a light box or glasses may support you. Note, these are used for short times only Use a kelvin light of 4,000 or more to invigorate energy and mood. Long periods of high kelvins at 5,000 or more may cause headaches, fatigue, and stress

Chapter 19. Total Sensory Wellbeing

Aurora—Colour	Mid- to fully saturated colours generate vibrancy. Consider the ratio of highly saturated colours, as they can overwhelm with prolonged exposure. For example, bright lemon may be ideal for a bathroom to energise you in the morning, but could be distressing if used as the primary colour in a study where you work all day Energising and uplifting colour examples: turquoise, cerulean, fuchsia, canary yellow, emerald, mint green, jade, peach, whites, light pinks, lemon, coral
Acoustics	Upbeat music stimulates your heartbeat and brainwaves. If you are starting from a negative place, use the Iso Principle and first listen to music that 'empathises' with your mood, then switch it up. Around 60–80 BPM can induce calming alpha waves. Listening to music around 120–150 BPM may enhance beta waves, improving your alertness
Aroma	Peppermint, rosemary, eucalyptus radiata, petitgrain, pine, cedarwood, cypress, patchouli, clary sage, grapefruit, jasmine, juniper, ylang-ylang, orange, mandarin
Appetite	Examples of immediate energy-boosting nutrients include: • Coffee: caffeine in coffee is a stimulant that increases alertness • Matcha tea: a green tea rich in antioxidants and a form of caffeine known as theophylline. It also contains a calming amino acid called L-theanine. This combination can sustain energy levels without the coffee caffeine crash • Citrus fruits: high in vitamin C, which supports energy production and immunity. Energy also comes from their natural sugars. Whole citrus fruits also hydrate, which helps fight fatigue. Water is an ideal option for energy through hydration
Action	Revitalising temperatures (18–21°C/65–70°F) can keep you energised A cold-water burst of around 13°C (55°F) can enliven you by boosting circulation, increasing your heart rate, making you breathe in more oxygen and produce endorphins to feel good Exercise can create these effects as well. Morning activity can rejuvenate and lift your mood for the day. This includes a walk outside or any time of the day. Consider dancing for joy or embracing a loved one. Soft and smooth materials can provide physical and psychological comfort
Atmosphere	An element of bright reflective surfaces and mirrors will be visually stimulating. Cohesive and moderate complexity, with an element of mystery, can create a positive and engaging environment. Time in nature and views of nature can rejuvenate and uplift

19.2. Examples of sensory stimuli for invigorating and uplifting experiences

Total Sensory Wellbeing	Focus and clarity
Aurora—Light	4,000K neutral white, commonly found in offices and retail.
	4,000–5,000K is usually tolerated for longer periods of time. This represents neutral to white daylight
	If you are light-sensitive, try 3,500–4,000 K
Aurora—Colour	Blue can calm the mind and support focus. Darker blues typically support deeper thinking, while lighter blues aid creativity. Other considerations include medium purples like amethyst, greens, and blue-green blends such as teal or viridian. Light greys and whites can create calm by removing potentially distracting colour features
Acoustics	During work, use background rhythmical instrumental music with simple melodies at low decibels (eg 45 dB). This can minimise cognitive interference. Music with a tempo of 60–80 BPM can support calm and trigger alpha waves for focus. If work is analytical, beta wave activity is more likely stimulated by 130–150 BPM. If music distracts you but you want to block out noise pollution, consider soundscapes such as white, pink, or brown noise options. You can experiment with brainwave-stimulating sounds and hertz frequencies as well. If silence is preferred but elusive, opt for noise-cancelling headphones or a quiet space
Aroma	Thyme, ginger, basil, lemon, clove, petitgrain, cedarwood, bergamot, fennel
Appetite	Fatty fish with omega-3 for cognitive function. Blueberries with antioxidants and vitamin C for improved focus and memory. Leafy greens with folate, vitamin K, and antioxidants that protect the brain and support mental clarity.
	Nuts and seeds for omega-3 and vitamin E to fight oxidative stress and reduce brain fog. Foods rich in magnesium to calm the mind and reduce fatigue
Action	Cool air (16–20°C/60–68°F) can provide a burst of alertness to help combat mental fatigue; 21–22°C is ideal for productivity
	Comfortable seating and regular movement away from a task is a must to be able to retain focus. Let your brain 'breathe'
Atmosphere	An orderly, coherent space with low complexity can reduce visual distractions that deplete energy as your brain makes sense of the space. Nature-inspired motifs and plants can allow the mind to rest when you need to rejuvenate

19.3. Examples of sensory stimuli for focus and clarity

Total Sensory Wellbeing	Communication
Aurora—Light	For casual work, tea rooms, or inviting spaces (e.g. lobby or interview room), use around 3,500K
	For living rooms, dining spaces, and cafes, ambient lighting from 2,700K–3,500K is inviting and friendly
	For focused discussions such as meetings and brainstorming, select 4,000K–5,000K
Aurora—Colour	Nature-inspired colours are frequently, but not exclusively, used to create an atmosphere of positivity, relaxation, focus, and trust, which aids open communication. Examples include blues, sage, mint green, butter yellow, and sunflower yellow
Acoustics	Unwinding with friends invites slower BPMs, while upbeat tracks are usually played as people enter a venue, encouraging energetic engagement. TV shows and background noise should not distract from engaging in communication. During meals they can distract from connecting with others while eating, and can also influence your perception of what you are eating
Aroma	Consider geranium, chamomile German, and bay for relaxed discussion. Oils such as grapefruit, peppermint, and lemon can help foster more lively discussions
Appetite	Wholegrains: Rich in B vitamins, which are vital for brain health, positivity and cognitive processes Foods high in zinc: Shellfish, nuts, and seeds. Zinc is crucial for neural plasticity, memory, and mental clarity
Action	Comfortable room temperature (20–24°C/68–75°F). The best temperature is the one you don't even notice
	Seating must be comfortable to fully focus on what people are saying and actively contribute to discussions. Soothing fabrics, like pillows, can support calmness
	Walking or doing a task with people can be a way to work through problems and brainstorm personal and work matters. The reduced eye contact and lack of stillness can reduce intensity, increasing openness and trust. The rhythmic motion of walking is also relaxing for the brain
Atmosphere	Furniture angled to create curved or semicircle seating can aid engagement and relaxation. Avoid large tables and desks that can create a barrier. When food is involved, frequently clearing plates or awkwardly holding food and drinks requires effort and distracts people from remaining fully engaged with others. Do the shape and materials of your decor encourage relaxed or more reserved discussions?

19.4. **Examples of sensory stimuli to foster communication**

Total Sensory Wellbeing	Creativity
Aurora—Light	Natural daylight is best. LEDs mimic the quality of natural light well. For intellectual creativity such as brainstorming and problem-solving, use around 5,000K for set timeframes. Some people may be innovative in dark spaces free from visual constraints
Aurora—Colour	Energetic orange, imaginative purple through to grounding green, thought-provoking light blue, and 'blank canvas' white have all been linked to creativity. If you want artwork or objects to stand out, then achromatic colours work well
Acoustics	If you create dramatic artwork in bright colours, you may benefit from faster beats to energise you. Regardless of your creative nature or pace, starting with music at 60–80 BPM, which mimics the heart rate and induces alpha waves, can support clarity and calm. This can also entrain theta waves associated with focus, creativity, and innovative thinking. Silence and nature sounds can also induce free thought
Aroma	Creativity can be spurred with a sense of calm, focus, and energy. Try bergamot, frankincense, geranium, grapefruit, neroli, rose, jasmine, bay, clove, sandalwood, cypress, and juniper
Appetite	Salmon and flaxseeds: Omega-3 fatty acids support cognition Beetroot: Nitrates are converted to nitric oxide, which may improve blood flow to the brain and enhance creative thinking Antioxidants for mental clarity, complex carbohydrates for a steady source of glucose to maintain energy and focus, and hydration to prevent fatigue
Action	Airflow and variance of temperature (20–25°C/68–77°F) can invigorate creativity because creativity is about change, variation, and ideation; therefore, as creative flow shifts, the temperature may need to be adjusted. Irritation or blankness may be driven by temperature, lack of movement, or lack of a mental break. Revitalise your brain with some movement, an activity that shifts your thinking, and views of nature (even pictures or indoor plants)
Atmosphere	For a visually creative space, consider the placement of inspirational items. Avoid lots of items as this may cloud your ability to create something new. Coherence and a lack of complexity will remove distractions. Move into different environments to restimulate ideas

19.5. Examples of sensory stimuli to foster creativity

Chapter 19. Total Sensory Wellbeing

Total Sensory Wellbeing	Resilience and confidence
Aurora—Light	Energy boosts confidence and resilience. Daylight rules supreme to support this. Depending on location, 6 am to 11 am holds the most significant amount of blue light to boost your energy and mood. Higher kelvins in the day can keep you feeling upbeat. Try 4,000K–5,000K
Aurora—Colour	Often, rich and deeper colours can enhance your resolve and convey strength. For example, sapphire blue, deep indigo, plum, burgundy, magenta, chocolate, charcoal, jet, and obsidian black
Acoustics	Sounds from 70–90 BPM can create a state of steadiness; 100–130 BPM will feel dynamic; and 130+ is empowering and energising as it triggers alertness and a faster heart rate. This is when songs with lyrics that resonate with you can be empowering and motivating before or during events as well
Aroma	Try bergamot, cardamom, cedarwood, cypress, fennel, ginger, grapefruit, jasmine, ylang-ylang, pine, petitgrain, and orange
Appetite	Eggs: Provide protein and vitamin B12, which are essential for energy and healthy brain function Quinoa and tofu: Offer a complete protein source for brain function Broccoli: Rich in vitamins C and K, provides antioxidants and fibre
Action	Cool air and water can recharge your resolve and energy. Heavier blankets and throws can create a sense of protection to build resilience. Pets can boost a sense of wellbeing through touch and companionship. Regular exercise is a powerful way to build your mental muscle
Atmosphere	Consider blending sturdy furniture that feels solid with organic shapes (e.g. rectangular dining table with curved back chairs). Stronger and more durable materials such as leather, wood, and metals exude confidence. Use objects that bring joy through their shape and memory association

19.6. Examples of sensory stimuli to bolster resilience and confidence

Total Sensory Wellbeing	Relaxation
Aurora—Light	Aim for warm lighting that mimics sunset. It reduces cortisol and allows for the build-up of melatonin. Try 2,000–3,500K. Use blue-light blocking aids with devices—discussed further in the Sleep guide
Aurora—Colour	Soft and tinted colours: pinks, blues, lavenders, rose, vanilla, seafoam, celadon, beige, magnolia. Warm, soothing colours: mauve, sage, caramel, tan
Acoustics	Ambient music with gentle rhythmic melodies at 60–80 BPM can stimulate theta and alpha waves and lower your heart rate. Consider silence, nature, and soundscapes such as white, pink, or brown noise options. Experiment with brainwave-stimulating binaural sounds
Aroma	Try chamomile (Roman and German), clary sage, jasmine, lavender, petitgrain
Appetite	Chamomile tea: contains apigenin, an antioxidant that binds to certain receptors in the brain, which may promote sleepiness and reduce insomnia. Dark chocolate: rich in magnesium to improve relaxation by regulating neurotransmitters involved in the stress response. Bananas: high in potassium to help regulate muscle contractions and nerve signals, which reduces stress and promotes relaxation. They also support the uptake of tryptophan
Action	Meditation, chanting, and singing are ways to stimulate the vagus nerve, as are breathing exercises. Stretching and yoga can also stimulate your rest-and-digest processes. These activities also help distract your mind from ruminating. Soft, plush and breathable fabrics can be comforting. Engaging in an activity you enjoy or writing down your thoughts can be very calming
Atmosphere	Seek coherent layouts without too much complexity. Opt for curved furniture that feels comfortable and luxurious. Select artwork and objects with pleasing curved features. Plants and nature motifs can evoke calm. A real or artificial flame provides a meditative focal point

19.7. Examples of sensory stimuli to enhance relaxation

Chapter 19. Total Sensory Wellbeing

Total Sensory Wellbeing	Sleep
Aurora—Light	Dim lighting to prepare for sleep is best. Look for kelvins in the yellow to orange range as these interfere less with melatonin production. In the bedroom, use a relaxing overhead light and reading lamp between 2,700K and 3,000K. The lamp brightness should be around 400 lumens with a lux between 300 and 500. No light should point to your face. If viewing a screen, use blue-light filter devices such as glasses or screen covers. Ensure they can block blue light in the 400–460 nm or up to 500 nm range. If your device has a 'night mode' function, go as warm as possible while still being comfortable. Reduce brightness to minimise eye strain, but note this doesn't affect blue light. Opt for ebook readers that are designed not to emit blue light. Block all outside light for sleep. Nightlights do not help children's circadian rhythms
Aurora—Colour	Soft, tinted colours: Cornflower blue, lilac, blush, and greens like sage or pistachio, and whites. Black can be oppressive, and grey can sap your energy in the mornings. If you need to feel cocooned, try muted mixed colours such as terracotta. Energetic, saturated colours should be avoided, such as reds, oranges, and yellows, as they do not allow the eye to rest. The key is to feel relaxed
Acoustics	Silence is ideal, but if outside noise keeps you awake or you feel wired, you can try very slow soundscapes and instrumental music around 30–60 BPM to stimulate theta relaxation and delta sleep waves. Slow, rhythmical, and simple instrumental melodies are best. Consider 'colours' of noise: white, pink, brown or green; soothing nature sounds; or engineered sleep music via an app. Keep the volume low, around 35–45 dB
Aroma	Blends are lovely, but studies show that single scents can reduce stress and support quality sleep. Try these essential oils: lavender, mandarin, clary sage, marjoram, citrus, vetiver, sandalwood, chamomile Roman, lemon
Appetite	Eat dinner as early as possible to improve sleep quality. Avoid sugar and processed foods to minimise insulin resistance. Foods with calcium help produce melatonin. Foods with magnesium help regulate melatonin. Consume foods rich in vitamins D and B6, and omega-3 to aid sleep quality and duration
Action	Keep your bedroom around 16–20°C (65–68°F). Ensure bedding is comforting and comfortable. Develop a routine to help trigger relaxation, e.g. A hot bath, shower, or foot bath can relax muscles and alter your inner body temperature, signalling melatonin production as you cool down. Try writing down your thoughts, stretching, or a guided meditation while lying in bed to help you drift off. Exercising during the day and taking breaks that involve no information consumption can also improve your sleep quality

Atmosphere	Where you sleep needs to be as calming and visually pleasing as possible, as well as comfortable. Uncluttered, coherent, and tidy spaces with relaxing shapes are best to relax your mind. Focus on your light source positions. Use objects or images that are biophilic in nature to help soothe the mind. Your bed and bedding are the foundation of a good night's sleep. If they disrupt your sleep, they disrupt your quality of life

19.8. Examples of sensory stimuli to promote sleep

The circadian rhythm

Throughout this book I've emphasised the importance of the circadian rhythm on your mental fortitude and resilience. It oversees the rest-and-digest, sleep–wake, and feed–fast cycles. It is the keystone of your sense of wellbeing. Besides sensory ways to optimise sleep, a cornerstone of your circadian rhythm, Figure 19.9 outlines other sensory practices you can try.

Activity	Timing	How	Benefit
Exposure to (morning) daylight	6 am–11 am	Minimum 20 minutes outside without sunglasses. Depending on the season or where you live, sunscreen may be required	Sunlight boosts serotonin, vitamin D, and endorphins to affect cognition and mood. Melatonin is reduced and normal cortisol levels are triggered to increase alertness and energy for the day. Following a routine to get up and go to bed the same time each day supports a healthy circadian rhythm

Move	Preferably exercise in the morning or afternoon	Combine aerobic, resistance and focused activities such as yoga, Pilates, walking, and meditation. Move regularly and consistently. Do what you enjoy. Aim for 150–300 minutes of moderate aerobic activity a week, or 75–150 minutes of intensive aerobic activity, as well as 2 to 3 days of muscle-strengthening activities a week. Judge your capability to exercise safely	These actions increase energy and brain health to build your mental fortitude and resilience because physical resilience translates to mental resilience. Exercise also improves sleep quality
Food: Timing and quality	Eat most of your food in daylight hours. Eat dinner early	Eat primarily natural foods. Avoid alcohol 2 to 3 hours before bed. Even 1 alcoholic drink for a woman and 2 for a man can disrupt sleep quality by around 24%	Our digestive system functions best during the day. Late-night eating can interfere with sleep, affecting energy, mood, and alertness. Food quality impacts the gut–brain axis and your sense of wellbeing

19.9. Key sensory stimuli for a healthy circadian rhythm

✶ Cruising the vagus highway ✶

The vagus nerve plays a vital role in regulating your nervous system. Stimulating it can enhance relaxation and reduce stress. Here are some methods.

Action	Description	How it stimulates the vagus nerve	Benefits
Deep breathing	Slow, deep diaphragmatic breathing, focusing on long exhales	Activates the parasympathetic nervous system, stimulating vagal tone	Promotes relaxation, reduces stress, and regulates emotions

Cold exposure	Cold showers or splashing cold water on the face and neck	Activates the 'dive reflex' to stimulate the vagus nerve	Reduces inflammation, improves mood, and increases resilience
Exercising vocal cords	Gentle humming, chanting, or singing	Vibrations in the vocal cords stimulate the vagus nerve	Calms the nervous system and promotes a sense of connection
Gargling	Gargling water	Engages throat muscles, activating the vagus nerve	Enhances relaxation and stimulates parasympathetic activity
Meditation and mindfulness	Mindfulness or meditation practices	Lowers heart rate and activates the vagus nerve through relaxation	Improves emotional regulation and reduces anxiety
Yoga and tai chi	Gentle, mindful movements like yoga or tai chi	Stimulates the vagus nerve through stretching and mind–body integration	Reduces stress, improves focus, and enhances sensory wellbeing
Laughter	Genuine laughter, especially with others	Promotes the release of Happy DOSE chemicals and activates the vagus nerve	Boosts mood, strengthens social bonds, and reduces stress
Massage (especially neck)	Neck and shoulder massage or self-massage	Activates pressure receptors in the skin, stimulating the vagus nerve	Promotes relaxation and reduces tension
Exercise (moderate intensity)	Light to moderate aerobic exercise (e.g. walking, swimming)	Activates the vagus nerve by improving cardiovascular function	Enhances mental clarity, reduces stress, and promotes a positive mood
Socialising and positive interaction	Engaging in meaningful conversations or spending time with loved ones	Influences vagal tone and supports the release of oxytocin	Improves emotional bonding, mood, and wellbeing

19.10. Ways to stimulate the vagus nerve

✲ Your Happy DOSE prescription ✲

Dopamine, oxytocin, serotonin, and endorphins (DOSE) are your brain's natural mood-boosting chemicals. Figure 19.11 outlines Actions to self-administer a Happy DOSE.

Dopamine	Oxytocin	Serotonin	Endorphins
Set a goal with rewards: Break a big task into smaller, achievable steps and reward yourself for each completed step, e.g. cleaning, writing, or a work project	**Physical touch:** Give or receive a hug for 10 to 20 seconds. Hold hands with a loved one or cuddle a pet for emotional comfort	**Morning sunlight exposure to the eye:** Spend 20 minutes outdoors first thing in the morning. Limit blue light at night. Serotonin is a precursor to melatonin and is essential for regulating your circadian rhythm	**Aerobic exercise:** On most days, engage in at least 30 minutes of moderate exercise, like running, swimming or dancing, to promote wellbeing and experience a runner's high. Resistance training also promotes endorphin synthesis, as does sunlight on the skin
Aerobic exercise: Engage in aerobic exercise to stimulate and retain positive mood and cognitive function from dopamine	**Get a massage and a haircut:** The physical touch supports relaxation and human bonding	**Regular physical activity:** Engage in activities like brisk walking, cycling, or yoga to maintain mood and balance	**Laugh often:** Watch a funny video, spend time with friends who make you laugh, or try laughter yoga to promote happiness
Dietary boost: Eat foods high in the amino acid tyrosine like almonds, avocados, bananas, eggs, lean meats, dark chocolate. This amino acid helps produce dopamine and norepinephrine, supporting alertness and motivation	**Spend time with loved ones:** Schedule a lunch or coffee with friends or family to foster relationships. Call someone instead of texting them	**Mindfulness or meditation:** Practice mindfulness, meditation, or yoga to regulate your mood	**Hot bath or sauna:** Enjoy a hot bath, shower, or sauna to relax your muscles and reduce stress

Limit social media time: It can cause dopamine crashes. Set time limits to avoid overstimulation and maintain focus	Acts of kindness: Buy someone a coffee, help a neighbour, give someone a compliment, or thank them. This fosters connection and positivity	Eat tryptophan-rich foods: Include turkey, eggs, cheese, salmon, and nuts in your diet to support emotional balance. Dark chocolate too!	Dietary boost: Eat foods rich in antioxidants and tryptophan to indirectly support endorphins. They can also be triggered through spicy food
Start your day with a positive routine: Make your bed, plan your day, and set priorities to create a positive mindset and increase motivation	Watch a live performance with an audience and laugh: The positive group atmosphere enhances connection	Gratitude practice: At the end of the day, write down three things you are appreciative of	Get a massage: Schedule a professional massage or use self-massage techniques to reduce stress and encourage relaxation

19.11. **Ways to administer a Happy DOSE**

Finally, experience moments of nature as much as possible. After all, this is where Total Sensory Wellbeing began.

ACKNOWLEDGEMENTS

Expert Contributors

Thank you to **Amelia Phillips**, Registered Exercise Scientist and Nutritionist (BSc, Postgraduate Certificate in Nutrition, Master of Human Nutrition), who reviewed the *Action* and *Appetite* chapters. Her early input helped shape the content and boosted my confidence at a crucial stage.

Dr Rohima Badri, Audiologist (PhD, Audiology and Hearing Sciences), generously shared her knowledge and passion for hearing health, shaping the *Acoustics* sections. Thanks also to the Hearing Health Foundation for permission to use their charts.

Izabella Risteski, Psychologist (Bachelor of Psychological Science and Bachelor of Socio-Legal Studies), contributed valuable insights into sensory profiles and neurodivergence. Beyond her expertise, I found Izabella's support for the Total Sensory Wellbeing concept highly motivating.

Lynette Arnold, Building Biologist (AdvDip Building Biology), reviewed the *Atmosphere* chapters. Her expertise in healthy buildings and interior design brought valuable depth to several chapters.

Support & Influence

To **Sam**, my steadfast friend. Thank you for your honesty, humour and unwavering support.

To the **Finding My Sanity crew**, you know who you are. Thank you for applying your professional eyes to parts of my work, and for your warm encouragement to pursue a totally new path.

To the **Pilates people**. A rich and diverse group of good souls with varied professional skills, including marketers, medical experts, academics, energy healers, and shamans. Thank you for your interest, honest feedback, and generous engagement from start to finish.

Thanks also to the many kind souls ranging from childhood friends to serendipitous strangers who added perspective and helped shape my thinking.

To my **aunts, Angelika and Gisela**, thank you for always showing interest, even though my work is far removed from your own paths.

To **Anna and David**, my siblings. As different and far apart as we may be, our shared DNA – in name and spirit – always connects us. Thank you for your support and belief in me.

Finally, to **Mathew**, my husband, who never blinked (much) when I decided to leave my job to explore how the senses influence our wellbeing. You helped bolster my confidence to follow my instinct. An exploration that ultimately led to *Total Sensory Wellbeing* and this book.

Thank you all.

ABOUT THE AUTHOR

Ngahina Richards is the founder of Nriched Living and the creator of Total Sensory Wellbeing, a practical, evidence-informed framework designed to help people restore clarity, energy and focus in today's overstimulating world.

With a background in health science and over two decades in pharmaceutical leadership, Ngahina blends research with real-life insight to create solutions that support everyday wellbeing.

Her focus on sensory wellbeing emerged from a period of feeling disconnected and a persistent desire to understand how environments influence mental clarity and energy. After years of feeling 'tired but wired', she undertook practitioner training in aromatherapy and explored clinical and academic research on light, colour, sound, movement and more. She sought insights from experts across psychology, nutrition, audiology, exercise science and environmental design. This informed an approach that weaves together science, history, cultural perspectives and lived experience. It became the foundation of Total Sensory Wellbeing.

At its core, her work highlights how our senses deeply influence our energy, focus and resilience.

Born in Canada to a German mother and New Zealand father, Ngahina has lived and worked across the Pacific, Southeast Asia, Australia, Europe and the UK. These experiences gave her a lasting appreciation for the cultural nuances of sensory environments.

Now based in Sydney, Ngahina enjoys hiking and exploring new pockets of the city. She is carving a path in the emerging field of sensory strategy, working with individuals and businesses to improve how people feel and function. Her work is grounded, intelligent, practical and human-centred. It is crafted to help people calm the chaos and move through life with confidence, focus and ease.

nrichedliving.com

NOTES AND REFERENCES

Introduction

[1] Neubauer, S., Hublin, J. J., & Gunz, P. (2018). The evolution of modern human brain shape. *Science Advances 4*(1). https://doi.org/10.1126/sciadv.aao5961

[2] Boston Consulting Group. (2024, June 11). *Half of workers around the world struggling with burnout.* https://www.bcg.com/press/11june2024-half-of-workers-around-the-world-struggling-with-burnout

[3] Levitin, D. (2015). *The organized mind: thinking straight in the age of information overload.* Penguin General UK, pp. 15–16.

[4] Levitin, *The organized mind*, pp. 15–16.

[5] Travers, M. (2024, April 4). *A psychologist explains the rise of 'popcorn brain'.* Forbes. https://www.forbes.com/sites/traversmark/2024/04/04/a-psychologist-explains-the-rise-of-popcorn-brain/

[6] Shannon, H., Bush, K., Villeneuve, P. J., Hellemans, K. G., & Guimond, S. (2022). Problematic social media use in adolescents and young adults: Systematic review and meta-analysis. *JMIR Mental Health*, 9(4). https://doi.org/10.2196/33450

[7] Levitin, *The organized mind*, pp. 15–16.

[8] Australian Institute of Health and Welfare. (2021). *Sleep problems as a risk factor for chronic conditions.* Australian Government. https://www.aihw.gov.au/reports/risk-factors/sleep-problems-as-a-risk-factor/summary

[9] Mughal, I. (2024). *Saturated facts: A myth-busting guide to diet and nutrition in a world of misinformation.* Penguin Life, pp. 113–114.

[10] Mughal, *Saturated facts*, pp. 110–111.

Chapter 1

[1] Dunn, W. (2009). *Living sensationally: Understanding your senses.* Jessica Kingsley Publishers, pp. 15–16.

[2] Dunn, *Living sensationally*, p. 32.

[3] Dunn, W. (2014). *Sensory Profile™ 2.* Pearson Clinical Assessment.

[4] Dunn, *Living sensationally*, pp. 33–41.

[5] Bridgers, A. & Layton, C. (2022, 1 April). *How changing attitudes to fidgeting are helping neurodiverse children succeed at school*, ABC News. https://www.abc.net.au/news/2022-04-01/adhd-neurodiverse-fidgeting-evidence-helps-focus-attention/100934054

Chapter 2

[1] Our brains and bodies are extremely complex, with interconnected systems and processes that perform multiple functions. Total Sensory Wellbeing focuses solely on lifestyle and environmental factors that influence emotions and behaviour.

[2] Rathmann, J., Korpela, K. M., & Stojakowits, P. (2022). Pleistocene hypothesis—moving savanna perceptual preference hypothesis beyond savanna. *Frontiers in Psychology*, 13, Article 901799. https://doi.org/10.3389/fpsyg.2022.901799

[3] Robbins, J. (2020, January 9). *Ecopsychology: How immersion in nature benefits your health.* Yale

Environment 360. https://e360.yale.edu/features/ecopsychology-how-immersion-in-nature-benefits-your-health

[4] Watson, S. (2024, April 18). *Dopamine: The pathway to pleasure*. Harvard Health Publishing. https://www.health.harvard.edu/mind-and-mood/dopamine-the-pathway-to-pleasure

[5] The Nutrition Source. (2021, October). *Stress and health*. Harvard T.H. Chan School of Public Health. https://nutritionsource.hsph.harvard.edu/stress-and-health/

[6] Cleveland Clinic. (2024, April 6). *Limbic system*. https://my.clevelandclinic.org/health/body/limbic-system

[7] Cleveland Clinic. (2022, December 5). *Frontal lobe*. https://my.clevelandclinic.org/health/body/24501-frontal-lobe

[8] Cleveland Clinic. (2022, March 27). *Norepinephrine (Noradrenaline)*. https://my.clevelandclinic.org/health/articles/22610-norepinephrine-noradrenaline

[9] Cleveland Clinic. (2022, March 27). Norepinephrine. https://my.clevelandclinic.org/health/articles/22610-norepinephrine-noradrenaline

[10] Thau, L., Ghandi, J., & Sandeep, S. (2023). Physiology, cortisol. In *StatPearls*. StatPearls Publishing. https://www.ncbi.nlm.nih.gov/books/NBK538239/

[11] Thau, L., et al, Physiology, cortisol. https://www.ncbi.nlm.nih.gov/books/NBK538239/

[12] Dziurkowska, E., & Wesolowski, M. (2021). Cortisol as a biomarker of mental disorder severity. *Journal of Clinical Medicine*, 10(21), Article 5204. https://doi.org/10.3390/jcm10215204

[13] The Nutrition Source. (2021, October). *Stress and health*. https://nutritionsource.hsph.harvard.edu/stress-and-health/

[14] Psychology Today. (2022). *Vagus nerve*. https://www.psychologytoday.com/au/basics/vagus-nerve

[15] Encyclopedia Britannica. (2025, January 7). *Acetylcholine*. https://www.britannica.com/science/acetylcholine

[16] Psychology Today, *Vagus nerve*. https://www.psychologytoday.com/au/basics/vagus-nerve

[17] Watson, *Dopamine*. https://www.health.harvard.edu/mind-and-mood/dopamine-the-pathway-to-pleasure

[18] Dellwo, A. (2024, November 2). *What does dopamine do for the body? Neurotransmitter linked to attention and movement*. Verywell Health. https://www.verywellhealth.com/dopamine-5086831

[19] Dellwo, *What does dopamine do?* https://www.verywellhealth.com/dopamine-5086831

[20] Watson, S. (2023, June 13). *Oxytocin: The love hormone*. Harvard Health Publishing. https://www.health.harvard.edu/mind-and-mood/oxytocin-the-love-hormone

[21] Cleveland Clinic. (2022, March 27). *Oxytocin*. https://my.clevelandclinic.org/health/articles/22618-oxytocin

[22] Seltzer, L. J., Prososki, A. R., Ziegler, T. E., & Pollak, S. D. (2012). Instant messages vs. speech: Hormones and why we still need to hear each other. *Evolution and Human Behaviour*, 33(1), pp. 42–45. https://doi.org/10.1016/j.evolhumbehav.2011.05.004

[23] Watson, S. (2023, November 20). *Serotonin: The natural mood booster*. Harvard Health Publishing. https://www.health.harvard.edu/mind-and-mood/serotonin-the-natural-mood-booster

[24] Watson, S. (2024, April 18). *Endorphins: The brain's natural pain reliever*. Harvard Health Publishing. https://www.health.harvard.edu/mind-and-mood/endorphins-the-brains-natural-pain-reliever

[25] Watson, *Endorphins*. https://www.health.harvard.edu/mind-and-mood/endorphins-the-brains-natural-pain-reliever

[26] Cleveland Clinic. (2022, May 19). *Endorphins*. https://my.clevelandclinic.org/health/body/23040-endorphins

[27] Palmer, C. M. (2022). *Brain energy: A revolutionary breakthrough in understanding mental health – and improving treatment for anxiety, depression,* OCD, PTSD, and more. BenBella Books, pp. 221–229.

[28] National Institute of General Medical Sciences. (2023, September). *Circadian rhythms.* National Institutes of Health, US Department of Health and Human Services. https://www.nigms.nih.gov/education/fact-sheets/Pages/circadian-rhythms.aspx#what-scientists-know

[29] Mughal, I. (2024). *Saturated facts: A myth-busting guide to diet and nutrition in a world of misinformation.* Penguin Life, p. 103.

[30] Zou H, Zhou H, Yan R, Yao Z, Lu Q. (2022). Chronotype, circadian rhythm, and psychiatric disorders: Recent evidence and potential mechanisms. *Frontiers in Neuroscience,* 16. https://doi.org/10.3389/fnins.2022.811771

Chapter 3

[1] Francis, C. (2020, October 15). *How many senses do we have?* Sensory Trust. https://www.sensorytrust.org.uk/blog/how-many-senses-do-we-have#:~:text=Because%20there%20is%20some%20overlap,sensation%20of%20hunger%20or%20thirst

[2] Markowsky, G. (2025, January 5). *Physiology.* Encyclopedia Britannica. https://www.britannica.com/science/information-theory/Physiology

Chapter 4

[1] Palmer, C. M. (2022). *Brain energy: A revolutionary breakthrough in understanding mental health – and improving treatment for anxiety, depression,* OCD, PTSD, and more. BenBella Books, pp. 221–222.

[2] National Institute of General Medicine Sciences (2023). *Circadian rhythms.* National Institutes of Health, US Department of Health and Human Services. https://www.nigms.nih.gov/education/fact-sheets/Pages/circadian-rhythms.aspx#

[3] Knutson, K.L. & von Schantz, M. (2018). Associations between chronotype, morbidity and mortality in the UK Biobank cohort. *Chronobiology International,* 35(8), pp. 1045–1053. https://doi.org/10.1080/07420528.2018.1454458

[4] The Physics Classroom (2022). *The electromagnetic and visible spectra.* https://www.physicsclassroom.com/Class/light/u12l2a.cfm

[5] Foster, R.G. (2009, April 1). *Do blind people suffer from seasonal depression?* Scientific American. https://www.scientificamerican.com/article/ask-the-brains-do-blind-people/

[6] Liquid LEDs. (2021, March 20). *What is the difference between lumens, kelvins, and watts?* https://liquid-leds.com/en-au/blogs/news/what-is-the-difference-between-lumens-kelvins-and-watts

[7] Liquid LEDs, *What is the difference between lumens, kelvins, and watts?* https://liquid-leds.com/en-au/blogs/news/what-is-the-difference-between-lumens-kelvins-and-watts

[8] Green Business Light UK (2023). *Lux, lumens, and watts: Our guide.* https://greenbusinesslight.com/resources/lighting-lux-lumens-watts/

[9] Cleveland Clinic. (2021, December 1). *Red light therapy.* https://my.clevelandclinic.org/health/articles/22114-red-light-therapy

[10] Huang YY, Chen AC-H, Carroll JD, Hamblin MR. (2009). Biphasic dose response in low level light therapy. *Dose-Response,* 7(4), 358–383. https://doi.org/10.2203/dose-response.09-027.Hamblin

[11] Nairuz, T., Cho, S., & Lee, J.-H. (2024). Photobiomodulation therapy on brain: Pioneering an innovative approach to revolutionise cognitive dynamics. *Cells,* 13(11), 966. https://doi.org/10.3390/cells13110966

Notes and References

Chapter 5

[1] Robinson, M.D., Liu, T., & Bair, J.L. (2015). Affect-related influences on color perception. In *Handbook of color psychology*, Elliot, A.J., Fairchild, M.D., & Franklin, A. (Eds.). Cambridge University Press, p. 664. https://doi.org/10.1017/CBO9781107337930

[2] Fox, J. (2023). The world according to colour: *A cultural history*. Penguin Press, pp. 98, 99

[3] Jonauskaite, D. et al. (2020). Universal patterns in color-emotion associations are further shaped by linguistic and geographic proximity. *Psychological Science*, 31(10), pp. 1245–1260. https://doi.org/10.1177/0956797620948810

[4] Jonauskaite, et al, Universal patterns in color-emotion associations, pp. 1245–1260. https://doi.org/10.1177/0956797620948810

[5] Robinson et al, Affect-related influences on color perception, *Handbook*, pp. 662, 664. https://doi.org/10.1017/CBO9781107337930

[6] Ou, L.C. (2015). Color emotion and color harmony. In *Handbook of color psychology*. Elliot, A.J., Fairchild, M.D., & Franklin, A. (Eds.). Cambridge University Press, pp. 401–405. https://doi.org/10.1017/CBO9781107337930

[7] Robinson et al, Affect-related influences on color perception, *Handbook*, p. 663. https://doi.org/10.1017/CBO9781107337930

[8] Robinson et al, Affect-related influences on color perception, *Handbook*, p. 663. https://doi.org/10.1017/CBO9781107337930

[9] Wikipedia contributors. (2024). *Art Deco*. Wikipedia. https://en.wikipedia.org/wiki/Art_Deco

[10] Palmer, S.E., & Schloss, K.B. (2010). An ecological valence theory of human color preference. Proceedings of the National Academy of Sciences of the United States of America (PNAS), 107(19), pp. 8877–8882. https://doi.org/10.1073/pnas.0906172107

Chapter 6

[1] Bailey, R. (2024, September 23). *Overview of the five senses*. ThoughtCo. https://www.thoughtco.com/five-senses-and-how-they-work-3888470

[2] ScienceDirect. (n.d.). *Startle response*. https://www.sciencedirect.com/topics/neuroscience/startle-response

[3] Stothart, C., Mitchum, A., & Yehnert, C. (2015). The attentional costs of receiving a cell phone notification. *Journal of Experimental Psychology: Human Perception and Performance*, 41(4), pp. 893–897. https://pubmed.ncbi.nlm.nih.gov/26121498/

[4] An, R., Wang, J., Ashrafi, S. A., Yang, Y., & Guan, C. (2018). Chronic noise exposure and adiposity: A systematic review and meta-analysis. *American Journal of Preventive Medicine*, 55(3). https://doi.org/10.1016/j.amepre.2018.04.040

[5] European Environment Agency. (2024, December 12). *The effect of environmental noise on children's learning and development*. https://www.eea.europa.eu/en/analysis/publications/the-effect-of-environmental-noise-on-children

[6] Chen, X., Liu, M., Zuo, L., Wu, X., Chen, M., Li, X., An, T., Chen, L., Xu, W., Peng, S., Chen, H., Liang, X., & Hao, G. (2023). Environmental noise exposure and health outcomes: An umbrella review of systematic reviews and meta-analysis. *European Journal of Public Health*, 33(4), 725–731. https://doi.org/10.1093/eurpub/ckad044

[7] Mucci, N., Traversini, V., Lorini, C., De Sio, S., Galea, R.P., Bonaccorsi, G. & Arcangeli, G. (2020). Urban noise and psychological distress: A systematic review. *International Journal of Environmental Research and Public Health*, 17(18). https://doi.org/10.3390/ijerph17186621

[8] Hahad, O., Prochaska, J.H., Daiber, A., & Muenzel, T. (2019). Environmental noise-induced

effects on stress hormones, oxidative stress, vascular dysfunction: Key factors in the relationship between cerebrocardiovascular and psychological disorders. *Oxidative Medicine and Cellular Longevity*, Article 4623109. https://doi.org/10.1155/2019/4623109

[9] Hahad et al,. Environmental noise-induced effects on stress hormones, oxidative stress, vascular dysfunction: Key factors in the relationship between cerebrocardiovascular and psychological disorders. https://doi.org/10.1155/2019/4623109

[10] Mills, K. (Host). (2022, December). How our brain makes sense of a noisy world, with Nina Kraus, PhD (218). [Audio podcast episode and transcript]. In *Speaking of Psychology*. American Psychological Association. https://www.apa.org/news/podcasts/speaking-of-psychology/noisy-world

[11] Radun, J., Maula, H., Rajala, V., Scheinin, M., & Hongisto, V. (2022). Acute stress effects of impulsive noise during mental work. *Journal of Environmental Psychology*, 79, Article 101751. https://doi.org/10.1016/j.jenvp.2022.101819

[12] University of California. (2023, May 11) *Can't pay attention? You're not alone*. https://www.universityofcalifornia.edu/news/cant-pay-attention-youre-not-alone

[13] Raypole, C. (2023, May 30). *Music and studying: It's complicated*. Healthline. https://www.healthline.com/health/does-music-help-you-study#benefits-of-music-for-studying

[14] Lawrence, B.J., Jayakody, D.M.P., Bennett, R.J., Eikelboom, R.H., Gasson, N., & Friedland, P.L. (2020). Hearing loss and depression in older adults: A systematic review and meta-analysis. *Gerontologist*, 60(3), pp. e137–e154. https://doi.org/10.1093/geront/gnz009

[15] Chia, E.M., Wang, J.J., Rochtchina, E., Cumming, R.R., Newall, P. & Mitchell, P. (2007). Hearing impairment and health-related quality of life: The Blue Mountains Hearing Study. *Ear and Hearing*, 28(2), pp. 187–195. https://doi.org/10.1097/AUD.0b013e31803126b6

[16] Cejas, I., Coto, J., Sanchez, C., Holcomb, M., & Lorenzo, NE. (2021). Prevalence of depression and anxiety in adolescents with hearing loss. *Otology and Neurotology*, 42(4), pp. e470–e475. https://doi.org/10.1097/MAO.0000000000003006

[17] National Institute for Occupational Safety and Health (NIOSH). *Noise and hearing loss: Understand noise exposure*. US Centers for Disease Control and Prevention. https://www.cdc.gov/niosh/noise/prevent/understand.html

[18] Dehankar, S. S. & Gaurkar, S. S. (2022). Impact on hearing due to prolonged use of audio devices: A literature review. *Cureus*, 14(11), Article e31480. https://doi.org/10.7759/cureus.31425

[19] Seltzer, L.J., Prososki, A.R., Ziegler, T.E. & Pollak, S.D. (2012). Instant messages vs speech: Hormones and why we still need to hear each other. *Evolution and Human Behaviour*, 33(1), pp. 42–45. https://www.ncbi.nlm.nih.gov/pmc/articles/PMC3277914/

[20] Scott, S.K, Cai, C.Q., & Billing, A. (2022). Robert Provine: The critical human importance of laughter, connections and contagion. *Philosophical Transactions of the Royal Society Biological Sciences*, 377(1863). https://doi.org/10.1098/rstb.2021.0178

[21] NeuroLeadership Institute. (2020, September 17). *The neuroscience of laughter, and how to inspire more of it at work*. https://neuroleadership.com/your-brain-at-work/neuroscience-laughter-at-work/

[22] Koelsch, S. (2014). Brain correlates of music-evoked emotions. *Nature Reviews Neuroscience*, 15, pp. 170–180. https://doi.org/10.1038/nrn3666

[23] Salimpoor, V., Benovoy, M., Larcher, K. et al. (2011). Anatomically distinct dopamine release during anticipation and experience of peak emotion to music. *Nature Neuroscience*, 14, pp. 257–262. https://doi.org/10.1038/nn.2726

[24] Evers, S. & Suhr, B. (2000). Changes of the neurotransmitter serotonin but not of hormones during short-time music perception. *European Archives of Psychiatry and Clinical Neuroscience*,

250(3), pp. 144-147 https://doi.org/10.1007/s004060070031

[25] Pelletier, C.L. (2004). The effect of music on decreasing arousal due to stress: A meta-analysis. *Journal of Music Therapy*, 41(3), pp. 192-214. https://doi.org/10.1093/jmt/41.3.192

[26] Starcke, K., Mayr, J. & von Georgi, R. (2021). Emotion modulation through music after sadness induction—The Iso principle in a controlled experimental study. *International Journal of Environmental and Public Health*,18(23). https://doi.org/10.3390/ijerph182312486

[27] Neuroscience News. (2018, April 9). *Brain waves synchronise at live music performances*. https://neurosciencenews.com/music-brain-synch-8740/

[28] Fan, L. & Baharum, M.R. (2024). The effect of exposure to natural sounds on stress reduction: A systematic review and meta-analysis. *Stress*, 27(1). https://doi.org/10.1080/10253890.2024.2402519

[29] Pasco. (2024, August 1). *Sound waves*. https://www.pasco.com/products/guides/sound-waves#:~:text=How%20is%20Sound%20Produced%3F,sound%20further%20through%20the%20medium

[30] Razak, A., Izani, M., & Komiya, R. (2003, 21-24 September). *Emotion pitch variation analysis, in Malay and English voice samples* [Conference paper]. The 9th Asia-Pacific Conference on Communications IEEE Xplore. https://www.researchgate.net/figure/Average-pitch-for-each-emotions-English-and-Malay_fig3_4059569

Chapter 7

[1] Spurlock Museum of World Cultures. (2023). *Egyptian mummification*. University of Illinois. https://www.spurlock.illinois.edu/exhibits/online/mummification/materials.html

[2] Battaglia, S. (2003). *The complete guide to aromatherapy* (2nd ed.). The International Centre of Holistic Aromatherapy, pp. 12, 13.

[3] Battaglia, *The complete guide to aromatherapy*, p. 318.

[4] Battaglia, *The complete guide to aromatherapy*, pp. 12, 13.

[5] Battaglia, *The complete guide to aromatherapy*, pp. 12, 13.

[6] Wikipedia contributors. *Smoking ceremony*. (2025). Wikipedia. https://en.wikipedia.org/wiki/Smoking_ceremony

[7] Battaglia, *The complete guide to aromatherapy*, pp. 12, 13.

[8] Juergens, U. R. (2014). Anti-inflammatory properties of the monoterpene 1.8-cineole: current evidence for co-medication in inflammatory airway diseases. *Drug Research (Stuttgart)*, 64(12), pp. 638-646. https://doi.org/10.1055/s-0034-1372609

[9] Sowndhararajan, K., & Kim, S. (2016). Influence of fragrances on human psychophysiological activity: With special reference to human electroencephalographic response. *Scientia Pharmaceutica*, 84(4), pp. 724-751. https://doi.org/10.3390/scipharm84040724

[10] Cleveland Clinic (2023, September 21). *Aromatherapy*. https://my.clevelandclinic.org/health/treatments/aromatherapy

[11] Cheng, H., Lin, L., Wang, S., et al. (2022). Aromatherapy with single essential oils can significantly improve the sleep quality of cancer patients: A meta-analysis. *BMC Complementary Medicine and Therapies*, 22, Article 187. https://doi.org/10.1186/s12906-022-03668-0

[12] Cui, J., Li, M., Wei, Y., et al. (2022). Inhalation aromatherapy via brain-targeted nasal delivery: Natural volatiles or essential oils on mood disorders. *Frontiers in Pharmacology*, 13. https://doi.org/10.3389/fphar.2022.860043

[13] Sowndhararajan, et al. Influence of fragrances on human psychophysiological activity. https://doi.org/10.3390/scipharm84040724

14 Sowndhararajan, et al, Influence of fragrances on human psychophysiological activity. https://doi.org/10.3390/scipharm84040724

15 Woo, C. C., Miranda, B., Sathishkumar, M., et al. (2023). Overnight olfactory enrichment using an odorant diffuser improves memory and modifies the uncinate fasciculus in older adults. *Frontiers in Neuroscience*, 17. https://doi.org/10.3389/fnins.2023.1200448

16 McGlone, F., Osterbauer, R. A., Demattè, L. M., & Spence, C. (2013). The crossmodal influence of odor hedonics on facial attractiveness: behavioural and fMRI measures. *IntechOpen*. https://doi.org/10.5772/56504

17 Marinova, R., & Moss, M. (2014). The smell of success? The impact of perfume-gender congruency on ratings of attraction and the halo effect. *Advances in Chemical Engineering and Science*, 4(4). https://www.scirp.org/journal/paperinformation?paperid=50543

18 Li, W., Moallem, I., Gottfried, J. A., et al. (2007). Subliminal smells can guide social preferences. *Association for Psychological Science*, 18(1). https://doi.org/10.1111/j.1467-9280.2007.02023.x

19 Park, B. J., Tsunetsugu, Y., Kasetani, T., Kagawa, T., & Miyazaki, Y. (2010). The physiological effects of shinrin-yoku (taking in the forest atmosphere or forest bathing): Evidence from field experiments in 24 forests across Japan. *Environmental Health and Preventive Medicine*, 15(1), 18–26. https://doi.org/10.1007/s12199-009-0086-9

20 Battaglia, *The complete guide to aromatherapy*, pp. 157–252.

21 Stromberg, J. (2013, April 2). *What makes rain smell so good?* Smithsonian Magazine. https://www.smithsonianmag.com/science-nature/what-makes-rain-smell-so-good-13806085/

22 Department of Climate Change, Energy, the Environment and Water. (2021, October 10). *Indoor air*. Australian Government. https://www.dcceew.gov.au/environment/protection/air-quality/indoor-air

23 United States Environmental Protection Agency. (2024, December 31). *Indoor air quality (IAQ)*. United States Government. https://www.epa.gov/indoor-air-quality-iaq

24 Building Research Establishment Group. (2023, August 31). *Navigating urbanisation: a focus on better standards for indoor air quality*. https://bregroup.com/insights/urbanisation-indoor-air-quality

25 Jewell, T. (2019, September 11). *The effect of negative ions*. Healthline. https://www.healthline.com/health/negative-ions

26 Nunez, K. (2021, August 29). *How does an air ionizer work?* Healthline. https://www.healthline.com/health/what-does-an-ionizer-do

27 Jewell, *The effect of negative ions*. https://www.healthline.com/health/negative-ions

28 Xiao, S., Wei, T., & Petersen, J. D. et al. (2023). Biological effects of negative ions on human health and integrated multiomics to identify biomarkers: A literature review. *Environmental Science and Pollution Research*, 30, pp. 69824–69836. https://doi.org/10.1007/s11356-023-27133-8

29 Xiao, et al, *Biological effects of negative ions*. https://www.ncbi.nlm.nih.gov/pmc/articles/PMC10175061/

30 Jewell, *The effect of negative ions*. https://www.healthline.com/health/negative-ions

31 Riley, E. (2024, January 3). *Can plants purify the air in your home?* Healthline. https://www.healthline.com/health/air-purifying-plants#benefits-of-plants

32 Aimprosoft Collaborator. (2019, October 28). *Top reasons for why you should scent your casino*. Aroma360. https://www.aroma360.ae/blogs/news/top-reasons-for-why-you-should-scent-your-casino

33 Sanfilippo, M. (2024, January 24). *The smells that make shoppers spend more*. Business News Daily. https://www.businessnewsdaily.com/3469-smells-shoppers-spend-more.html

Chapter 8

[1] The Nutrition Source. (2021, October). *Stress and health*. Harvard T.H. Chan School of Public Health. https://nutritionsource.hsph.harvard.edu/stress-and-health/

[2] Barjamovic, G., Gonzalez, P.J., Graham C.A., Lassen, A.W., Nasrallah, N., & Sörensen, P. M. (2019). The ancient Mesopotamian tablet as cookbook. *Lapham's Quarterly*, 12(2). https://www.laphamsquarterly.org/roundtable/ancient-mesopotamian-tablet-cookbook

[3] Koenig, D. (2022, June 2). *Ancient concepts made new: A timeline of food as medicine*. WebMD. https://www.webmd.com/diet/future-of-food-special-report/20220602/a-timeline-of-food-as-medicine

[4] Prasad, S., & Aggarwal, B. B. (2011). *Turmeric, the golden spice*. In Benzie, I.F.F, & Wachtel-Galor, S., (eds). *Herbal medicine: Biomolecular and clinical aspects* (2nd ed.). CRC Press/Taylor & Francis. https://www.ncbi.nlm.nih.gov/books/NBK92752/

[5] Koenig, *A timeline of food as medicine*. https://www.webmd.com/diet/future-of-food-special-report/20220602/a-timeline-of-food-as-medicine

[6] Wikipedia contributors. (2024). *Doctrine of signatures*. Wikipedia. https://en.wikipedia.org/wiki/Doctrine_of_signatures

[7] Queensland Brain Institute. (2023). *How your brain makes and uses energy*. University of Queensland. https://qbi.uq.edu.au/brain/discovery-science/how-your-brain-makes-and-uses-energy

[8] Mughal, I. (2024). *Saturated facts: A myth-busting guide to diet and nutrition in a world of misinformation*. Penguin Life, pp. 135–137.

[9] Mughal, *Saturated facts*, p. 137.

[10] Ng, Q. X., Peters, C., Ho, C. Y. X., Lim, D. V., & Yeo, W. S. (2018). A meta-analysis of the use of probiotics to alleviate depressive symptoms. *Journal of Affective Disorders 228*, pp. 13–19. https://doi.org/10.1016/j.jad.2017.11.063

[11] Mughal, *Saturated facts*, pp. 144–145.

[12] Palmer, C. M. (2022). *Brain energy*. BenBella Books, pp. 237.

[13] Nicolucci, C., Padovani, M., Rodrigues, F. D. C., Fritsch, L. N., Santos, A. C., et al. (2023). Flavonoids: the use in mental health and related diseases. *Natural Product Research 38*(23). https://doi.org/10.1080/14786419.2023.2275275

[14] Bryan, L., & Singh, A. (2024, May 7). *Alcohol and sleep*. Sleep Foundation. https://www.sleepfoundation.org/nutrition/alcohol-and-sleep

[15] Breadon, P., & Fox, L. (2023). *Sneaky salt*. Grattan Institute. https://grattan.edu.au/wp-content/uploads/2023/10/Sneaky-Salt-Grattan-Institute-Report.pdf

[16] Breadon, et al, *Sneaky salt*. https://grattan.edu.au/wp-content/uploads/2023/10/Sneaky-Salt-Grattan-Institute-Report.pdf

[17] Wolfson, J. A., Tucker, A. C., Leung, C. W., Rebholz, C. M., Garcia-Larsen, V., & Martinez-Steele, E. (2025). Trends in adults' intake of un-processed/minimally processed, and ultra-processed foods at home and away from home in the United States from 2003–2018. *Journal of Nutrition*, 155(1), 280–292. https://doi.org/10.1016/j.tjnut.2024.10.048

[18] Lakhan, S. E., & Vieira, K. F. (2008). Nutritional therapies for mental disorders. *Nutrition Journal BMC 7*, Article 2. https://www.ncbi.nlm.nih.gov/pmc/articles/PMC2248201/

[19] Wurtman, R. J., Hefti, F., & Melamed, E. (1980). Precursor control of neurotransmitter synthesis. *Pharmacol Rev*, 32(4), 315-35. https://pubmed.ncbi.nlm.nih.gov/6115400/

[20] Mughal, *Saturated facts*, pp. 104–105.

[21] Gu, C., Brereton, N., Schweitzer, A., Cotter, M., et al. (2020). Metabolic effects of late dinner in healthy volunteers—A randomized crossover clinical trial. *The Journal of Clinical Endocrinology & Metabolism*, 105(8). https://doi.org/10.1210/clinem/dgaa354

[22] Lopez-Minguez, J., Gomez-Abellan, P., & Garaulet, M. (2019). Timing of breakfast, lunch, and dinner: Effects on obesity and metabolic risk. *Nutrients 11*(11). https://doi.org/10.3390/nu11112624

[23] Mughal, *Saturated facts*, pp. 110–111.

[24] Palmer, C. M. (2022). *Brain energy: A revolutionary breakthrough in understanding mental health – and improving treatment for anxiety, depression, OCD, PTSD, and more.* BenBella Books, p. 96.

[25] Pierone, B. C., Pereira, C. A., Garcez, M. L., & Kaster, M. P. (2020). Stress and signalling pathways regulating autophagy: From behavioral models to psychiatric disorders. *Experimental Neurology*, 334. https://doi.org/10.1016/j.expneurol.2020.113485

Chapter 9

[1] Cleveland Clinic. (2022, June 15). *Somatic nervous system.* https://my.clevelandclinic.org/health/body/23291-somatic-nervous-system

[2] Cascio, C. J., Moore, D., & McGlone, F. (2019). Social touch and human development. *Developmental Cognitive Neuroscience*, 35. https://doi.org/10.1016/j.dcn.2018.04.009

[3] Purves, D., et al. (Eds). (2001). Mechanoreceptors specialized to receive tactile information. In *Neuroscience* (2nd ed.), Sinauer Associates. https://www.ncbi.nlm.nih.gov/books/NBK10895/

[4] Purves, et al. (Eds), Mechanoreceptors, *Neuroscience*. https://www.ncbi.nlm.nih.gov/books/NBK10895/

[5] Pawling, R., et al. (2017). C-tactile afferent stimulating touch carries a positive affective value. *PLOS One*. https://doi.org/10.1371/journal.pone.0173457

[6] Pawling, et al., C-tactile afferent stimulating touch. https://doi.org/10.1371/journal.pone.0173457

[7] Cascio, C., Moore, D., & McGlone, F. Social touch and human development. https://doi.org/10.1016/j.dcn.2018.04.009

[8] Pawling, et al., C-tactile afferent stimulating touch. https://doi.org/10.1371/journal.pone.0173457

[9] Benisek, A. (2023, September 15). *Touch starvation: What to know.* WebMD. https://www.webmd.com/balance/touch-starvation

[10] Tannen, J. N. (2020, April). *Scholar touts the advantages of touch.* University of Miami. https://news.miami.edu/stories/2020/04/scholar-touts-the-advantages-of-touch.html

[11] Alloway, T. P. (2022, January 19). *What 20 seconds of hugging can do for you.* Psychology Today. https://www.psychologytoday.com/au/blog/keep-it-in-mind/202201/what-20-seconds-hugging-can-do-you

[12] McNichols, N. K. (2021, August 3) *The vital importance of human touch.* Psychology Today. https://www.psychologytoday.com/intl/blog/everyone-top/202108/the-vital-importance-human-touch

[13] King, D., & Janiszewski, C. (2011). Affect-gating. *Journal of Consumer Research*, 38(4), pp. 687–711. https://doi.org/10.1086/660811

[14] King, D., & Janiszewski, C. Affect-gating. https://doi.org/10.1086/660811

[15] Fetell, I. (2011, June 20). *Sad times call for soft textures.* Psychology Today. https://www.psychologytoday.com/us/blog/design-and-the-mind/201106/sad-times-call-soft-textures

[16] Dreisoerner, A., Junker, N. M., Schlotz, W., Heimrich, J., Bloemeke, S., Ditzen, B., & van Dick, R. (2021). Self-soothing touch and being hugged reduce cortisol responses to stress: A randomized controlled trial on stress, physical touch, and social identity. *Comprehensive Psychoneuroendocri-*

nology, 8, Article 100091. https://doi.org/10.1016/j.cpnec.2021.100091

[17] Forsell, L. M., & Åström, J. A. (2012). Meanings of hugging: From greeting behavior to touching implications. *Comprehensive Psychology*, 1(13). https://doi.org/10.2466/02.17.21.CP.1.13

[18] Peck, J., & Childers, T. L. (2008). Sensory factors and consumer behavior. In C. P. Haugtvedt, P. M. Herr, & F. R. Kardes (Eds.), In *Handbook of consumer psychology* (pp. 208, 209). Taylor & Francis. https://www.researchgate.net/publication/267819177_Sensory_Factors_and_Consumer_Behavior

[19] Kumar, K. (2024, April 11). *How do hugs make you feel?* MedicineNet. https://www.medicinenet.com/how_do_hugs_make_you_feel/article.htm

[20] Field, T. (2024). Massage therapy research: A narrative review. *Current Research in Psychology and Behavioral Science*, 5(1), Article 10108. https://doi.org/10.54026/CRPBS/10108

[21] Field, T. (1999). American adolescents touch each other less and are more aggressive toward their peers as compared with French adolescents. *Adolescence*, 34(136), 753–758. Retrieved from https://www.thefreelibrary.com/AMERICAN+ADOLESCENTS+TOUCH+EACH+OTHER+LESS+AND+ARE+MORE+AGGRESSIVE...-a059810232

[22] Dozier, M. (2014). Romania's abandoned children: Deprivation, brain development, and the struggle for recovery. *American Journal of Psychiatry*, 171(6). https://doi.org/10.1176/appi.ajp.2014.14030320

[23] Cherry, K. (2025, January 29). *What is attachment theory?* Verywell Mind. https://www.verywellmind.com/what-is-attachment-theory-2795337

[24] Moraska, A., Pollini, R. A., Boulanger, K., Brooks, M. Z., & Teitlebaum, L. (2008). Physiological adjustments to stress measures following massage therapy: A review of the literature. *Evidence-Based Complementary and Alternative Medicine*, 7(4), pp. 409–418. https://doi.org/10.1093/ecam/nen029

[25] Tannen, *Scholar touts the advantages of touch*. https://news.miami.edu/stories/2020/04/scholar-touts-the-advantages-of-touch.html

[26] Maurer, N., Nissel, H., Egerbacher, M., Gornik, E., Schuller, P., & Traxler, H. (2019). Anatomical evidence of acupuncture meridians in the human extracellular matrix: Results from a macroscopic and microscopic interdisciplinary multicentre study on human corpses. *Evidence-Based Complementary and Alternative Medicine*, 2019, Article 6976892. https://doi.org/10.1155/2019/6976892

[27] Cerino, E. (2018, December 4). *Reflexology 101*. Healthline. https://www.healthline.com/health/what-is-reflexology#takeaway

[28] Gaesser, A.H. (2020). Emotional freedom techniques: Stress and anxiety management for students and staff in school. In C. Maykel & M. A. Bray (eds.), *Promoting mind–body health in schools: Interventions for mental health professionals* (pp. 283–297). American Psychological Association. https://doi.org/10.1037/0000157-020

[29] Stapleton, P., Baumann, O., O'Keefe, T., & Bhuta, S. (2022). Neural changes after emotional freedom techniques treatment for chronic pain sufferers. *Complementary Therapies in Clinical Practice*, 49, Article 101653. https://doi.org/10.1016/j.ctcp.2022.101653

[30] Singh, B., Olds, T., Curtis, R., Dumuid, D., Virgara, R., et al. (2023). Effectiveness of physical activity interventions for improving depression, anxiety and distress: An overview of systematic reviews. *British Journal of Sports Medicine*, 57(18), pp. 1203–1209. https://doi.org/10.1136/bjsports-2022-106195

[31] Erickson, K. I., et al. (2011). Exercise training increases size of hippocampus and improves memory. *Proceedings of the National Academy of Sciences*, 108(7), pp. 3017–3022. https://doi.org/10.1073/pnas.1015950108

[32] Oppezzo, M., & Schwartz, D. L. (2014). Give your ideas some legs: The positive effect of walking on creative thinking. *Journal of Experimental Psychology: Learning, Memory, and Cognition* 40(4), pp. 1142–1152. https://doi.org/10.1037/a0036577

[33] Godoy, L. D., Rossignoli, M. T., Delfino-Pereira, P., et al. (2018). A comprehensive overview on stress neurobiology: Basic concepts and clinical implications. *Frontiers in Behavioral Neuroscience, 12*(2018). https://doi.org/10.3389/fnbeh.2018.00127

[34] Hill, E. E., Zack, E., Battaglini, C., et al. (2014). Exercise and circulating cortisol levels: The intensity threshold effect. *Journal of Endocrinological Investigation, 31*, pp. 587–591. https://doi.org/10.1007/BF03345606

[35] Smith, P. J., & Mervin, R. M. (2020). The role of exercise in management of mental health disorders: An integrative review. *Annual Review of Medicine, 72*, pp. 45–62. https://doi.org/10.1146/annurev-med-060619-022943

[36] Harvard Health Publishing. (2020, July 7). *Exercising to relax*. Harvard Medical School. https://www.health.harvard.edu/staying-healthy/exercising-to-relax

[37] Arida, R. M., & Teixeira-Machado, L. (2021). The contribution of physical exercise to brain resilience. *Frontiers in Behavioral Neuroscience, 14*, Article 626769. https://doi.org/10.3389/fnbeh.2020.626769

[38] Streeter, C. C., et al. (2010). Effects of yoga versus walking on mood, anxiety, and brain GABA levels: A randomized controlled MRS study. *Journal of Alternative and Complementary Medicine, 16*(11). https://doi.org/10.1089/acm.2010.0007

[39] Wayne, P. M., Walsh, J. N., Taylor-Piliae, R. E., Wells, R. E., Papp, K. V., Donovan, N. J., & Yeh, G. Y. (2014). Effect of tai chi on cognitive performance in older adults: Systematic review and meta-analysis. *Journal of the American Geriatrics Society, 62*(1), pp. 25–39. https://doi.org/10.1111/jgs.12611

[40] Caldwell, K., et al. (2013). Pilates, mindfulness and somatic education. *Journal of Dance & Somatic Practices, 5*(2), pp. 141–153. https://libres.uncg.edu/ir/asu/f/Caldwell_Karen_2013_Pilates_Mindfulness_.pdf

[41] Singh, et al, Effectiveness of physical activity interventions for improving depression, anxiety and distress, pp. 1203–1209. https://doi.org/10.1136/bjsports-2022-1061

[42] Marano, G., Kotzalidis, G. D., Lisci, F. M., Anesini, M. B., Rossi, S., Barbonetti, S., Cangini, A., Ronsisvalle, A., Artuso, L., Falsini, C., Caso, R., Mandracchia, G., Brisi, C., Traversi, G., Mazza, O., Pola, R., Sani, G., Mercuri, E. M., Gaetani, E., & Mazza, M. (2025). The neuroscience behind writing: Handwriting vs. typing—Who wins the battle? *Life, 15*(3), 345. https://doi.org/10.3390/life15030345

[43] Van der Weel, F. R., & Van der Meer, A. L. H. (2024). Handwriting but not typewriting leads to widespread brain connectivity: A high-density EEG study with implications for the classroom. *Frontiers in Psychology, 14*. https://doi.org/10.3389/fpsyg.2023.1219945

[44] Chowdhury, R. (2019, April 9). *The neuroscience of gratitude and effects on the brain*. Positive Psychology. https://positivepsychology.com/neuroscience-of-gratitude/

[45] Baikie, K. A., & Wilhelm, K. (2005). Emotional and physical health benefits of expressive writing. *Advances in Psychiatric Treatment, 11*(5), pp. 338–346. https://doi.org/10.1192/apt.11.5.338

[46] Fernandes, M. A., Wammes, J. D., & Meade, M. E. (2018). The surprisingly powerful influence of drawing on memory. *Current Directions in Psychological Science, 27*(5), pp. 302–308. https://doi.org/10.1177/0963721418755385

[47] Russo, M. A., Santarelli, D. M., & O'Rourke, D. (2017). The physiological effects of slow breathing in the healthy human. *Breathe, 13*(4), pp. 298–309. https://doi.org/10.1183/20734735.009817

[48] Neuroscience News. (2017, May 24). *Fidgeting: Does it help or hinder focus?* https://neuroscience-

news.com/fidgeting-neuroscience-6763/

[49] Lin, Y., & Gao, W. (2023). The effects of physical exercise on anxiety symptoms of college students: A meta-analysis. *Frontiers in Psychology, 14.* https://doi.org/10.3389/fpsyg.2023.1136900

[50] Arida, et al, The contribution of physical exercise to brain resilience. https://doi.org/10.3389/fnbeh.2020.626769

[51] Singh, et al, Effectiveness of physical activity interventions for improving depression, anxiety and distress, pp. 1203–1209. https://doi.org/10.1136/bjsports-2022-1061

[52] World Health Organization. (2020) *WHO guidelines on physical activity and sedentary behaviour.* World Health Organization. https://iris.who.int/bitstream/handle/10665/337001/9789240014886-eng.pdf

Chapter 10

[1] Rathmann, J., Korpela, K. M., & Stojakowits, P. (2022). Pleistocene hypothesis—moving savanna perceptual preference hypothesis beyond savanna. *Frontiers in Psychology, 13,* Article 901799. https://doi.org/10.3389/fpsyg.2022.901799

[2] Lothian, A. (2008). *Landscape theory.* Scenic Solutions. https://scenicsolutions.world/theory-of-landscape-aesthetics/#kaplan

[3] Lothian, *Landscape theory.* https://scenicsolutions.world/theory-of-landscape-aesthetics/#kaplan

[4] Lothian, *Landscape theory.* https://scenicsolutions.world/theory-of-landscape-aesthetics/#kaplan

[5] Ulrich, R. S., Simons, R. F., Losito, B. D., Fiorito, E., Miles, M. A., & Zelson, M. F. (1991). Stress recovery during exposure to natural and urban environments. *Journal of Environmental Psychology, 11*(3), pp. 201–230. https://doi.org/10.1016/S0272-4944(05)80184-7

[6] Lothian, *Landscape theory.* https://scenicsolutions.world/theory-of-landscape-aesthetics/#kaplan

[7] Weir, K. (2020, April 1). *Nurtured by nature.* American Psychological Association. https://www.apa.org/monitor/2020/04/nurtured-nature

[8] Pinconsult Associates Limited. (2022, June 15). *Biophilic design and its principles.* LinkedIn. https://www.linkedin.com/pulse/biophilic-design-its-principles-pinconsult-associates-limited/

[9] NSW Health. (2024, May 7). *Wood burning heaters and your health.* NSW Government. https://www.health.nsw.gov.au/environment/factsheets/Pages/wood-smoke.aspx

[10] Pinconsult, *Biophilic design and its principles.* https://www.linkedin.com/pulse/biophilic-design-its-principles-pinconsult-associates-limited/

[11] Chuquichambi, E. G., Vartanian, O., Skov, M., Corradi, G. B., Nadal, M., Silvia, P. J., & Munar, E. (2022). How universal is preference for visual curvature? A systematic review and meta-analysis. *Annals of the New York Academy of Sciences, 1518*(1), pp. 151–165. https://doi.org/10.1111/nyas.14919

[12] Ou, L.C. (2015). Color emotion and color harmony. In *Handbook of Color Psychology.* Elliot, A. J. Fairchild, M. D.& Franklin, A. (Eds.). Cambridge University Press, pp. 402–403. https://doi.org/10.1017/CBO9781107337930

[13] Britannica (2025, February 14). *Alhambra.* https://www.britannica.com/topic/Alhambra-fortress-Granada-Spain

[14] Abdelaal, M. S., & Soebarto, V. (2018). History matters: The origins of biophilic design of innovative learning spaces in traditional architecture. *International Journal of Architecture Research, 12*(3), pp. 108–127. http://dx.doi.org/10.26687/archnet-ijar.v12i3.1655

[15] Kauffman, E. (2025, February 12). *International success and acclaim of Frank Lloyd Wright.* Encyclopedia Britannica. https://www.britannica.com/biography/Frank-Lloyd-Wright/International-success-and-acclaim

[16] Abbas, S., Ali, M., Smith, T., & Khan, R. (2024). Neuroarchitecture: How the perception of our surroundings impacts the brain. *Biology, 13*(4), Article 220. https://doi.org/10.3390/biology13040220

[17] El Sayad, Z., Farghaly, T., & Hamada, S. M. (2017). Integrating human-centred design methods in early design stage: Using interactive architecture as a tool. *Journal of Al-Azhar University Engineering Sector, 12*(44), pp. 947–960. https://doi.org/10.21608/auej.2017.19180

[18] Lothian, *Landscape theory*. https://scenicsolutions.world/theory-of-landscape-aesthetics/#kaplan

Chapter 11

[1] Rea, M.S. & Figueiro, M.G. (2018). Non-visual effects of colored light. In *Handbook of color psychology*. Elliot, A.J., Fairchild, M.D. & Franklin, A. (Eds.), Cambridge University Press, p. 628. https://doi.org/10.1017/CBO9781107337930

[2] Cleveland Clinic. (2022, March 18). *Serotonin.* https://my.clevelandclinic.org/health/articles/22572-serotonin

[3] Cleveland Clinic. (2022, August 2). *Vitamin D deficiency.* https://my.clevelandclinic.org/health/diseases/15050-vitamin-d-vitamin-d-deficiency

[4] Dick, M., Pohl, W., Lackner, H. K., Weiss, E. M., & Canazei, M. (2024). Effects of personalized lighting on subjective ratings, cognitive performance, and physiological stress response in a simulated office environment. *LEUKOS – The Journal of the Illuminating Engineering Society, 20*(4), pp. 347–366. https://doi.org/10.1080/15502724.2023.2292960

Chapter 12

[1] Robinson, M.D., Liu, T. & Bair, J.L. (2015). Affect-related influences on color perception. In *Handbook of Color Psychology*. Elliot, A.J., Fairchild, M.D., & Franklin, A. (Eds.). Cambridge University Press, p. 671. https://doi.org/10.1017/CBO9781107337930

[2] Jordan, W. (2015, May 13). *Why is blue the world's favorite color?* YouGov. https://today.yougov.com/international/articles/12335-why-blue-worlds-favorite-color

[3] Ghose, T. (2022, July 25). *What's the most popular color in the world?* LiveScience. https://www.livescience.com/34105-favorite-colors.html

[4] Hurlbert, A. & Owen, A. (2015). Biological, cultural and developmental influences on color preferences. In *Handbook of color psychology*. Elliot, A.J., Fairchild, M.D. & Franklin, A. (Eds.), Cambridge University Press, p. 454. https://doi.org/10.1017/CBO9781107337930

[5] Fox, J. (2023). *The world according to colour: A cultural history.* Penguin Press, p. 114.

[6] Grannan, C. (2022, August 16). *Has pink always been a 'girly' color?* Britannica. https://www.britannica.com/story/has-pink-always-been-a-girly-color

[7] Fox, *The world according to colour*, pp. 124, 125.

[8] Haller, K. (2019). *The little book of colour: How to use the psychology of colour to transform your life*, Penguin Life, p. 155.

[9] Mentzel, S. V., Schücker, L., Hagemann, N., & Strauss, B. (2017). Emotionality of colors: An implicit link between red and dominance. *Frontiers in Psychology*, 8, Article 317. https://doi.org/10.3389/fpsyg.2017.00317

[10] Hill, R. A., & Barton, R. A. (2005). Red enhances human performance in contests. *Nature*, 435(7040), Article 293. https://doi.org/10.1038/435293a

[11] Al-Ayash, A., Kane, R.T., Smith, D. & Green-Armytage, P. (2015). The influence of colour on student emotion, heart rate, and performance in learning environments. *Color Research & Application, 41*(2), pp. 196–205. https://doi.org/10.1002/col.21949.

Notes and References

[12] Haller, *The little book of colour*, p. 154.

[13] Cherry, K. (2024, September 16). *What does the colour purple mean?* Verywell Mind. https://www.verywellmind.com/the-color-psychology-of-purple-2795820

[14] Fox, The world according to colour, pp. 169–171.

[15] Hongrui, L. (2017, December 8). *Ultra violet, an auspicious colour in Chinese culture.* China Daily. https://www.chinadaily.com.cn/a/201712/08/WS5a2a01bda310la51ddf8e32e_2.html

[16] Fox, *The world according to colour*, pp. 188, 189.

[17] Outright International (2023). *Flags of the LGBTQI community.* https://outrightinternational.org/insights/flags-lgbtiq-community

[18] Hongrui, *Ultra violet*, https://www.chinadaily.com.cn/a/201712/08/WS5a2a01bda310la51ddf8e32e_2.html

[19] Haller, *The little book of colour*, p. 156.

[20] Irish, J. (2018, September 28). *The surprisingly dark history of the colour pink.* Fast Company. https://www.fastcompany.com/90243505/the-surprisingly-dark-history-of-the-color-pink.

[21] Irish, *The surprisingly dark history of the colour pink*. https://www.fastcompany.com/90243505/the-surprisingly-dark-history-of-the-color-pink.

[22] Haller, *The little book of colour*, p. 154.

[23] Colour Matters (2022). *Colour and vision matters.* https://www.colormatters.com/color-and-vision/color-and-vision-matters.

[24] Robinson, M.D., Liu, T. & Bair, J.L. (2015). Affect-related influences on color perception. In *Handbook of color psychology*, Elliot, A.J., Fairchild, M.D., & Franklin, A. (Eds.). Cambridge University Press, p. 664. https://doi.org/10.1017/CBO9781107337930

[25] Robinson et al, Affect-related influences on color perception, *Handbook*, p. 664. https://doi.org/10.1017/CBO9781107337930

[26] George Mason University. (2022). *The color yellow.* https://mason.gmu.edu/~mgraha16/507/module3-3.html.

[27] Bendtfelt-Diaz, P. (2023). *Why are marigolds important in the Day of the Dead celebrations?* Growing Up Bilingual. https://growingupbilingual.com/why-are-marigolds-important-in-the-day-of-the-dead-celebrations/.

[28] George Mason University. (2022). *The colour yellow.* https://mason.gmu.edu/~mgraha16/507/module3-3.html.

[29] George Mason University (2022). *The colour yellow.* https://mason.gmu.edu/~mgraha16/507/module3-3.html.

[30] Fox, *The world according to colour*, pp. 98, 99.

[31] Silzer, K. (2020, March 30). *The staying power of the smiley face.* CNN. https://edition.cnn.com/style/article/artsy-smiley-face-origin/index.html

[32] TOI-Online. (2021, February 16). *Saraswati Puja 2021: Why yellow colour is so important?* https://timesofindia.indiatimes.com/religion/festivals/saraswati-puja-2021-why-yellow-colour-is-so-important/articleshow/80967580.cms

[33] Haller, *The little book of colour*, p. 154.

[34] Beyen, M. (2019, April 25). *Orange: A colour that unites and divides.* The Low Countries. https://www.the-low-countries.com/article/orange-a-colour-that-unites-and-divides-2/

[35] Haller, *The little book of colour*, p. 155.

[36] Robinson et al, Affect-related influences on color perception, *Handbook*, p. 664. https://doi.org/10.1017/CBO9781107337930

[37] Palmer, S.E. & Schloss, K.B. (2010). An ecological valence theory of human color preference. *Proceedings of the National Academy of Sciences of the United States of America (PNAS)*, 107(19), pp. 8877–8882. https://doi.org/10.1073/pnas.0906172107

[38] Fox, *The world according to colour*, p. 204.

[39] Fox, *The world according to colour*, p. 94.

[40] The Guardian. (2021, February 15). *Readers reply: Why is envy green? Is it the same in other cultures?* https://www.theguardian.com/lifeandstyle/2021/feb/14/readers-reply-why-is-envy-green-is-it-the-same-in-other-cultures

[41] Haller, *The little book of colour*, p. 156.

[42] NoLimit Creatives. (2024, March 22). *Exploring the deeper meaning behind the color brown.* NoLimit University. https://nlc.com/university/exploring-the-deeper-meaning-behind-the-color-brown/

[43] 1000 Logos. (2024, October 4). *UPS logo.* https://1000logos.net/ups-logo/

[44] Haller, *The little book of colour*; p. 155.

[45] Fox, *The world according to colour*, pp. 26–33.

[46] Fox, *The world according to colour*, pp. 26–33.

[47] Fox, *The world according to colour*, pp. 26–33.

[48] Fox, *The world according to colour*, pp. 26–33.

[49] Preston, J.P. (2013, September 21). *The history of the 'black dog' as a metaphor.* Joshua Panduro Preston. https://jppreston.com/2013/09/21/the-history-of-the-black-dog-as-metaphor/

[50] Robinson et al, Affect-related influences on color perception, *Handbook*, p. 663. https://doi.org/10.1017/CBO9781107337930

[51] Fox, *The World according to colour*, pp. 36, 37.

[52] Haller, *The little book of colour*, p. 157.

[53] Robinson et al, Affect-related influences on color perception, *Handbook*, p. 663. https://doi.org/10.1017/CBO9781107337930

[54] Kuwonu, F. (2018, April–July). Women: Liberia's guardians of peace. *Africa Renewal.* https://www.un.org/africarenewal/magazine/april-2018-july-2018/women-liberia%E2%80%99s-guardians-peace.

[55] Haller, *The little book of colour*, p. 155.

[56] Ou, L.C. (2015). Color emotion and color harmony. In *Handbook of color psychology*, Elliot, A.J., Fairchild, M.D. & Franklin, A. (Eds.). Cambridge University Press, p. 405. https://doi.org/10.1017/CBO9781107337930

[57] Haller, *The little book of colour*, pp. 156.

[58] Ou, Color emotion and color harmony, *Handbook*, pp. 401–405.

[59] Ng, W.L. (2021). The teaching of the concept of color harmony and its ambiguity. *Asia-Pacific Journal of Humanity and Social Sciences, 1*(2), pp. 20–27. https://dr.ntu.edu.sg/handle/10356/152447

Chapter 13

[1] Smit, E. A., Milne, A. J., Sarvasy, H. S., & Dean, R. T. (2022). Emotional responses in Papua New Guinea show negligible evidence for a universal effect of major versus minor music. *PLOS One 17*(6). https://doi.org/10.1371/journal.pone.0269597

[2] Anasopoulos, G. N. (2022, February 3). *Cross-cultural research in music and emotions.* Music & Science @ Durham University. https://musicscience.net/cross-cultural-research-in-music-and-emotions/

Notes and References

[3] Ooishi, Y., Mukai, H., Watanabe, K., Kawato, S., & Kashino, M. (2017). Increase in salivary oxytocin and decrease in salivary cortisol after listening to relaxing slow-tempo and exciting fast-tempo music. *PLOS One, 12*(12). https://doi.org/10.1371/journal.pone.0189075

[4] Hurless, N., Mekic, A., Peña, S., Humphries, E., Gentry, H., & Nichols, D. F. (2013). Music genre preference and tempo alter alpha and beta waves in human non-musicians. *IMPULSE, (10)*1. https://impulse.pubpub.org/pub/idmxseha

[5] Terry, P.C., Karageorghis, C.I., Saha, A.M. & D'Auria, S. (2012). Effects of synchronous music on treadmill running among elite triathletes. *Journal of Science and Medicine in Sport, 15*(1), pp. 52–57. https://pubmed.ncbi.nlm.nih.gov/21803652/

[6] Fekri Azgomi, H., Branco, F., Amin, M.R. & et al. (2023). Regulation of brain cognitive states through auditory, gustatory, and olfactory stimulation with wearable monitoring. *Scientific Reports, 13*, Article 12399. https://doi.org/10.1038/s41598-023-37829-z

[7] Svard, L. (2023). Does music really make you smarter? *In The Musical Brain: What Students, Teachers and Performers Need to Know*. Oxford Academic. https://academic.oup.com/book/45551/chapter-abstract/394681783

[8] Perry, G., Polito, V. & Thompson, W.F. (2021). Rhythmic chanting and mystical states across traditions. *Brain Science, 11*(1). https://doi.org/10.3390/brainsci11010101

[9] Encyclopedia.com. (2025, February 10). *Chanting*. https://www.encyclopedia.com/environment/encyclopedias-almanacs-transcripts-and-maps/chanting

[10] Editors of Encyclopedia Britannica (2025, February 1). *Gregorian chant*. Encyclopedia Britannica. https://www.britannica.com/art/Gregorian-chant

[11] Guided by Elements. (2025). *Solfeggio frequencies: The history and origin of Solfeggio frequencies*. https://guidedbyelements.com/health-wellbeing/body-mind-and-spirit/solfeggio-frequencies/#the-history-and-origin-of-solfeggio-frequencies

[12] RationalWiki contributors. (2024). *Solfeggio frequencies*. RationalWiki. https://rationalwiki.org/wiki/Solfeggio_frequencies

[13] Summer, J. V., & Cotliar, D. (2023, October 25). *Can binaural beats help you fall asleep?* Sleep Foundation. https://www.sleepfoundation.org/noise-and-sleep/binaural-beats

[14] Ingendoh, R.M., Posny, E.S., & Heine, A. (2023). Binaural beats to entrain the brain? A systematic review of the effects of binaural beat stimulation on brain oscillatory activity, and the implications for psychological research and intervention. *PLOS One, 18*(5), Article e286023. https://doi.org/10.1371/journal.pone.0286023

[15] Ingendoh, et al, Binaural beats to entrain the brain? https://www.ncbi.nlm.nih.gov/pmc/articles/PMC10198548/

[16] Kučikienė, D., & Praninskienė, R. (2018). The impact of music on the bioelectrical oscillations of the brain. *Acta Medica Lituanica, 25*(2), pp. 101–106. https://www.journals.vu.lt/AML/article/view/21305

[17] Summer, J. V. & Rehman, A. (2024, May 2). *How noise can affect your sleep: white noise*. Sleep Foundation. https://www.sleepfoundation.org/noise-and-sleep/white-noise

[18] Poerio, G. L., Blakey, E., Hostler, T. J., & Veltri, T. (2018). More than a feeling: Autonomous sensory meridian response (ASMR) is characterized by reliable changes in affect and physiology. *PLOS One, 13*(6), Article e0196645. https://doi.org/10.1371/journal.pone.0196645

[19] CNN Health. (2022, January 31). *ASMR explained: What it is and how to use it* [Video]. CNN. https://edition.cnn.com/videos/health/2022/01/31/what-is-asmr-videos-how-to-lbb-orig.cnn

[20] Milliman, R.E. (1982). Using background music to affect the behaviour of supermarket shoppers. *The Journal of Marketing, 46*(3), pp. 86–91. http://www.jstor.org/stable/1251706

[21] Spence, C. & Wang, Q. (2015). Wine and music (II): Can you taste the music? Modulating the experience of wine through music and sound. *Flavour 4*, Article 33. https://flavourjournal.biomedcentral.com/articles/10.1186/s13411-015-0043-z

[22] Pietschnig, J., Voracek, M., and Formann, A. K. (2010). Mozart effect–Shmozart effect: A meta-analysis, *Intelligence, 38*(3), pp. 314–323. https://doi.org/10.1016/j.intell.2010.03.001

[23] Schellenberg, E. G. (2005). Music and cognitive abilities, *Current Directions in Psychological Science, 14*(6), pp. 317–320. https://doi.org/10.1111/j.0963-7214.2005.00389.x

[24] Garone, S. (2021, September 24). *8 physical and mental health benefits of silence, plus how to get more of it*. Healthline. https://www.healthline.com/health/mind-body/physical-and-mental-health-benefits-of-silence

[25] Smith, M.G., Cordoza, M., & Basner, M. (2022). Environmental noise and effects on sleep: An update to the WHO systematic review and meta-analysis, *Environmental Health Perspectives, 130*(7). https://www.researchgate.net/publication/361923788_Environmental_Noise_and_Effects_on_Sleep_An_Update_to_the_WHO_Systematic_Review_and_Meta-Analysis

[26] Raypole, C. (2023, May 30). *Music and studying: It's complicated*. Healthline. https://www.healthline.com/health/does-music-help-you-study#benefits-of-music-for-studying

Chapter 15

[1] Kornberg, H. (2025, January 31). *Metabolism*. Encyclopedia Britannica. https://www.britannica.com/science/metabolism

[2] Palmer, C.M. (2022). *Brain energy: A revolutionary breakthrough in understanding mental health – and improving treatment for anxiety, depression, OCD, PTSD, and more*. BenBella Books, pp. 63–74.

[3] Palmer, *Brain energy*, pp. 214–216.

[4] Palmer, *Brain energy*, pp. 189, 235–238.

[5] Sanchez-Villegas, A., Verberne, L., De Irala Jokin, D., et al. (2011). Dietary fat intake and the risk of depression: The SUN Project. *PLOS One*. https://doi.org/10.1371/journal.pone.0016268

[6] Moll, J. (2024, May 27). *Polyunsaturated fat vs. monounsaturated fat: What's the difference?* Verywell Health. https://www.verywellhealth.com/monounsaturated-and-polyunsaturated-fats-differences-697740

[7] Sinn, N., Milte, C., & Howe, P. R. C. (2010). Oiling the brain: A review of randomized controlled trials of omega-3 fatty acids in psychopathology across the lifespan. *Nutrients, 2*(2), pp. 128–170. https://doi.org/10.3390/nu2020128

[8] Zhou, L., Xiong, J. Y., Chai, Y. Q., et al. (2022). Possible antidepressant mechanisms of omega-3 polyunsaturated fatty acids acting on the central nervous system. *Frontiers in Psychiatry, 13*. https://doi.org/10.3389/fpsyt.2022.933704

[9] Wang, Q., Zhang, H., Jin, Q., & Wang, G. (2023). Effect of dietary plant-derived low-ratio linoleic acid/alpha-linolenic acid on blood lipid profiles: A systematic review and meta-analysis. *Foods, 12*(16), Article 3005. https://doi.org/10.3390/foods12163005

[10] Innes, J. K., & Calder, P. C. (2018). Omega-6 fatty acids and inflammation. *Prostaglandins, Leukotrienes and Essential Fatty Acids, 132*, pp. 41–48. https://doi.org/10.1016/j.plefa.2018.03.004

[11] Zhang, Y., Sun, Y., Yu, Q., et al. (2024). Higher ratio of plasma omega-6/omega-3 fatty acids is associated with greater risk of all-cause, cancer, and cardiovascular mortality: A population-based cohort study in UK Biobank. *eLife, 12*, Article RP90132. https://doi.org/10.7554/eLife.90132

[12] Berger, M. E., Smensy, S. M., Kim, S. W., et al. (2017). Omega-6 to omega-3 polyunsaturated fatty acid ratio and subsequent mood disorders in young people with at-risk mental states: A 7-year longitudinal study. *Translational Psychiatry, 7*(10), Article e1220. https://doi.org/10.1038/tp.2017.190

[13] Simopoulos, A. P. (2002). Omega-3 fatty acids in wild plants, nuts, and seeds. *Asia Pacific Journal of Clinical Nutrition, 11*(s6). https://doi.org/10.1046/j.1440-6047.11.s.6.5.x

[14] Simopoulos, A. P. (2016). An increase in the omega-6/omega-3 fatty acid ratio increases the risk for obesity. *Nutrients, 8*(3), Article 128. https://doi.org/10.3390/nu8030128

[15] Meyer, B. J. (2016). Australians are not meeting the recommended intakes for omega-3 long chain polyunsaturated fatty acids: Results of an analysis from the 2011–2012 National Nutrition and Physical Activity Survey. *Nutrients, 8*(3), Article 111. https://doi.org/10.3390/nu8030111

[16] National Academies of Sciences, Engineering, and Medicine. (2005). Protein and amino acids. In *Dietary Reference Intakes for Energy, Carbohydrate, Fiber, Fat, Fatty Acids, Cholesterol, Protein, and Amino Acids*. The National Academies Press. https://doi.org/10.17226/10490

[17] Cleveland Clinic. (2021, October 1). *De-stress eating: Foods to help reduce anxiety*. https://health.clevelandclinic.org/eat-these-foods-to-reduce-stress-and-anxiety

[18] Cleveland Clinic. (2021, December 22). *Amino acids*. https://my.clevelandclinic.org/health/articles/22243-amino-acids

[19] The Nutrition Source. (2022, January). *Straight talk about soy*. Harvard T.H. Chan School of Public Health. https://nutritionsource.hsph.harvard.edu/soy/

[20] DePolo, J. (2024, July 19). *Soy and breast cancer*. Breastcancer.org. https://www.breastcancer.org/managing-life/diet-nutrition/breast-cancer-risk-reduction/foods/soy

[21] Dietitians Australia. (2022, March). *Protein*. https://dietitiansaustralia.org.au/health-advice/protein

[22] The Nutrition Source. (2023). *Protein*. Harvard T.H. Chan School of Public Health. https://nutritionsource.hsph.harvard.edu/what-should-you-eat/protein/

[23] Ardisson Korat, A. V., Shea, M. K., Jacques, P. F., et al. (2024). Dietary protein intake in midlife in relation to healthy aging—results from the prospective Nurses' Health Study cohort. *The American Journal of Clinical Nutrition, 119*(2), pp. 271–282. https://doi.org/10.1016/j.ajcnut.2023.11.010

[24] Knuppel, A., Shipley, M., Llewellyn, C. H., & Brunner, E. J. (2017). Sugar intake from sweet food and beverages, common mental disorder, and depression: Prospective findings from the Whitehall II study. *Scientific Reports, 7*(1), Article 6287. https://doi.org/10.1038/s41598-017-05649-7

[25] Knuppel, et al, Sugar intake from sweet food and beverages, common mental disorder, and depression. https://doi.org/10.1038/s41598-017-05649-7

[26] Avena, N. M., Rada, P., & Hoebel, B. G. (2009). Evidence for sugar addiction: Behavioral and neurochemical effects of intermittent, excessive sugar intake. *Neuroscience and Biobehavioral Reviews, 32*(1), pp. 20–39. https://doi.org/10.1016/j.neubiorev.2007.04.019

[27] Mughal, I. (2024) *Saturated facts*, Penguin Life, p. 157.

[28] Mughal, *Saturated Factsfacts*, p. 158.

[29] Mughal, *Saturated facts*, pp. 50–52.

[30] Healthdirect. (2023). *Sugar*. https://www.healthdirect.gov.au/sugar#:~:text=World%20Health%20Organization%20recommendations,per%20day%20for%20an%20adult

[31] Olson, C. R., & Mello, C. V. (2010). Significance of vitamin A to brain function, behavior and learning. *Molecular Nutrition & Food Research, 54*(4), pp. 489–495. https://doi.org/10.1002/mnfr.200900246

[32] Calderón-Ospina, C. A., & Nava-Mesa, M. O. (2019). B Vitamins in the nervous system: Current knowledge of the biochemical modes of action and synergies of thiamine, pyridoxine, and cobalamin. *CNS Neuroscience & Therapeutics, 26*(1), pp. 5–13. https://doi.org/10.1111/cns.13207

[33] Palmer, C. M. (2024, May 27). *Depression, the gut microbiome, and vitamins*. Psychology

Today. https://www.psychologytoday.com/au/blog/advancing-psychiatry/202405/depression-the-gut-microbiome-and-vitamins

[34] Doğan Bulut, S., Bulut, S., Atalan, D. G., Berkol, T., Gürçay, E., Türker, T., & Aydemir, Ç. (2016). The relationship between symptom severity and low vitamin D levels in patients with schizophrenia. *PLOS One, 11*(10), Article e0165284. https://doi.org/10.1371/journal.pone.0165284

[35] Cui, A., Zhang, T., Xiao, P., et al. (2023). Global and regional prevalence of vitamin D deficiency in population-based studies from 2000–2022: A pooled analysis of 7.9 million participants. *Frontiers in Nutrition, 10*. https://doi.org/10.3389/fnut.2023.1070808

[36] Mughal, *Saturated facts*, pp. 176–177.

[37] Kim, J., & Wessling-Resnick, M. (2014). Iron and mechanisms of emotional behavior. *Journal of Nutritional Biochemistry, 25*(10), pp. 1101–1107. https://pubmed.ncbi.nlm.nih.gov/25154570/

[38] Lee, H. S., Chao, H. H., Huang, W. T., et al. (2020). Psychiatric disorders risk in patients with iron deficiency anaemia and association with iron supplementation medications: A nationwide database analysis. *BMC Psychiatry, 20*(216). https://doi.org/10.1186/s12888-020-02621-0

[39] Mohammadi, H., Talebi, S., Ghavami, A., et al. (2021). Effects of zinc supplementation on inflammatory biomarkers and oxidative stress in adults: A systematic review and meta-analysis of randomized controlled trials. *Trace Elements in Medicine and Biology, 68*, Article 126857. https://doi.org/10.1016/j.jtemb.2021.126857

[40] Totten, M. S., Davenport, T. S., Edwards, L. F., & Howell, J. M. (2023). Trace elements and anxiety: A review of zinc, copper, iron, and selenium. *Dietetics, 2*(1), pp. 83–103. https://doi.org/10.3390/dietetics2010008

[41] Healthdirect. (2023, June). *Zinc deficiency*. https://www.healthdirect.gov.au/zinc-deficiency

[42] Totten, et al, Trace elements and anxiety. https://doi.org/10.3390/dietetics2010008

[43] Mayo Clinic. (2024, February 7). *Magnesium glycinate: Is this supplement helpful for you?* https://mcpress.mayoclinic.org/nutrition-fitness/magnesium-glycinate-is-this-supplement-helpful-for-you/

[44] Samard, F. (2024, October 6). *Potassium facts: The impact of potassium on mental health*. Ask The Nutritionist. https://askthenutritionist.net/potassium-facts-the-impact-of-potassium-on-mental-health

[45] Du, C., Hsiao, P. Y., Ludy, M.-J., & Tucker, R. M. (2022). Relationships between dairy and calcium intake and mental health measures of higher education students in the United States: Outcomes from moderation analyses. *Nutrients, 14*(4), Article 775. https://doi.org/10.3390/nu14040775

[46] Lubeck, B. (2024, August 24). *Adaptogens: What are they and should you take them?* Verywell Health. https://www.verywellhealth.com/what-are-adaptogens-4685073

[47] UCLA Health. (2022, February 16). *What are adaptogens and should you be taking them?* https://www.uclahealth.org/news/article/what-are-adaptogens-and-should-you-be-taking-them

[48] Palmer, *Brain energy*, pp. 214–216.

[49] Selhub, E. (2022, September 18). *Nutritional psychiatry: Your brain on food*. Harvard Health Publishing. https://www.health.harvard.edu/blog/nutritional-psychiatry-your-brain-on-food-201511168626

[50] Van Thomme, G. (2024, August 6). *What are free radicals? A dietitian explains.* MD Anderson Cancer Center. https://www.mdanderson.org/cancerwise/what-are-free-radicals-a-dietitian-explains.h00-159699912.html

[51] Selhub, *Nutritional psychiatry: Your brain on food*. https://www.health.harvard.edu/blog/nutritional-psychiatry-your-brain-on-food-201511168626

⁵² Cleveland Clinic. (2024, March 22). *Inflammation.* https://my.clevelandclinic.org/health/symptoms/21660-inflammation

⁵³ Mughal, *Saturated facts,* pp. 63, 67–69.

⁵⁴ Epel, E. S., McEwen, B., Seeman, T., Matthews, K., Castellazzo, G., Brownell, K. D., Bell, J., & Ickovics, J. R. (2000). Stress and body shape: stress-induced cortisol secretion is consistently greater among women with central fat. *Psychosomatic Medicine, 65*(5), pp. 623–632. https://doi.org/10.1097/00006842-200009000-00005

⁵⁵ Shomon, M. (2024, October 23). *Getting rid of cortisol belly fat.* Verywell Health. https://www.verywellhealth.com/the-cortisol-weight-loss-controversy-3233036

⁵⁶ Demeke, S., Rohde, K., Chollet-Hinton, L., Sutton, C., Kong, K. L., & Fazzino, T. L. (2022). Change in hyper-palatable food availability in the US food system over 30 years: 1988–2018. *Public Health Nutrition, 26*(1), pp. 182–189. https://doi.org/10.1017/S1368980022001227

⁵⁷ Cleveland Clinic. (2024, March 7). *Mediterranean diet.* https://my.clevelandclinic.org/health/articles/16037-mediterranean-diet

⁵⁸ The Nutrition Source. (2023, August). *Diet review: MIND diet.* Harvard T.H. Chan School of Public Medicine. https://nutritionsource.hsph.harvard.edu/healthy-weight/diet-reviews/mind-diet/

⁵⁹ Palmer, *Brain energy,* pp. 249–251.

Chapter 16

¹ Rony, M. K. K, & Alamgir, H. M. (2023). High temperatures on mental health: Recognizing the association and the need for proactive strategies—A perspective. *Health Science Reports, 6*(12), Article e1729. https://doi.org/10.1002/hsr2.1729

² Budidha, K., & Kyriacou, P. A. (2019). Photoplethysmography for quantitative assessment of sympathetic nerve activity (SNA) during cold stress. *Frontiers in Physiology, 9,* Article 1863. https://doi.org/10.3389/fphys.2018.01863

³ Shevchuk, N. A. (2008). Adapted cold shower as a potential treatment for depression. *Medical Hypotheses, 70*(5), pp. 995–1001. https://doi.org/10.1016/j.mehy.2007.04.052

⁴ Falla, M., Micarelli, A., Hüfner, K., & Strapazzon, G. (2021). The effect of cold exposure on cognitive performance in healthy adults: A systematic review. *International Journal of Environmental Research and Public Health, 18*(18), Article 9725. https://doi.org/10.3390/ijerph18189725

⁵ Tiihonen, J., Halonen, P., Tiihonen, L., Kautiainen, H., Storvik, M., & Callaway, J. (2017). The association of ambient temperature and violent crime. *Scientific Reports, 7,* Article 6543. https://doi.org/10.1038/s41598-017-06720-z

⁶ Rony, M et al, High temperatures on mental health. https://doi.org/10.1002/hsr2.1729

⁷ Seppänen, O., Fisk, W. J., & Lei, Q. H. (2006). Room temperature and productivity in office work. *Lawrence Berkeley National Laboratory.* https://digital.library.unt.edu/ark:/67531/metadc882029/

⁸ Association for Psychological Science. (2017, August 2). *Turning up the heat on prosocial behavior.* https://www.psychologicalscience.org/news/minds-business/turning-up-the-heat-on-prosocial-behavior.html

⁹ Pacheco, D. (2024, March 7). *Best temperature for sleep.* Sleep Foundation. https://www.sleepfoundation.org/bedroom-environment/best-temperature-for-sleep

¹⁰ Vogel, K. (2023, August 28). *Scientists say this is the best temperature for a good night's sleep.* Healthline. https://www.healthline.com/health-news/scientists-say-this-is-the-best-temperature-for-a-good-nights-sleep

¹¹ Laukkanen, T., Kunutsor, S. K., & Laukkanen, J. A. (2018). Cardiovascular and other health

benefits of sauna bathing: A review of the evidence. *Mayo Clinic Proceedings, 93*(8), pp. 1111–1121. https://doi.org/10.1016/j.mayocp.2018.04.008

[12] Tanner, L. (2023, February 10). *Ice baths are hot on social media. Here's how they affect your body*. PBS NewsHour. https://www.pbs.org/newshour/health/ice-baths-are-hot-on-social-media-heres-how-they-affect-your-body

[13] Vatansever F, Hamblin MR. (2012). Far infrared radiation (FIR): its biological effects and medical applications. *Photonics & Lasers in Medicine*, 4(4), 255–266. https://doi.org/10.1515/plm-2012-0034

[14] Mayo Clinic. (2024, September 13). *Do infrared saunas have any health benefits?* Mayo Clinic. https://www.mayoclinic.org/healthy-lifestyle/consumer-health/expert-answers/infrared-sauna/faq-20057954

Chapter 17

[1] Credit goes to my husband for doing this. I just delegated.

[2] Strachan-Regan, K., & Baumann, O. (2024). The impact of room shape on affective states, heart-rate, and creative output. *Heliyon, 10*(6) Article e28340. https://www.cell.com/heliyon/fulltext/S2405-8440(24)04371-8

[3] Feng Shui Mall. (n.d.). *Feng Shui Color*. https://www.fengshuimall.com/feng-shui-color

[4] Cho, A. (2023, October 20). *Want to use feng shui at home? Start with these top do's & don'ts*. Mind Body Green. https://www.mindbodygreen.com/articles/feng-shui-for-every-room-in-your-home

Part Four

[1] Homburg, C., Imschloß, M., & Kühnl, C. (2012). *Of dollars and senses: Does multisensory marketing pay off?* Institute of Market-Oriented Management, University of Mannheim Business School. https://www.bwl.uni-mannheim.de/media/Einrichtungen/imu/Research_Insights/2012/RI_009.pdf

[2] Spence, C. P. (2021), Sense-hacking: *How to use the power of your senses for happier, healthier living*, Penguin, pp. 163–167.

www.ingramcontent.com/pod-product-compliance
Lightning Source LLC
Chambersburg PA
CBHW020355080526
44584CB00014B/1026